QUESTIONS OF QUALITY
PRIMARY EDUCATION AND DEVELOPMENT

HUGH HAWES AND DAVID STEPHENS

Longman Group UK Limited
Longman House, Burnt Mill, Harlow,
Essex CM20 2JE, England
and Associated Companies throughout the world

First published 1990

Set in 10/11 Times
Produced by Longman Group (F.E.) Ltd
Printed in Malaysia
by The Commercial Press Sdn. Bhd.,
Serdang Raya, Selangor Darul Ehsan

British Library Cataloguing in Publication Data
Hawes, Hugh
    Questions of quality: primary education and development.
    — (Education and development; v. 1).
    1. Developing countries. Primary education
    I. Title   II. Stephens, David   III. Series
    372.91724

ISBN 0-582-05200-9

ACKNOWLEDGEMENTS

The Publishers are grateful to the following for their permission to reproduce
tables:

Institute of Education, University of London for page 10; Ministry of
Education, Malaysia for pages 38 and 39; Swahili Language Consultants and
Publishers, Nairobi for page 51; UNICEF for page 29; and World Bank from
'World Bank Development Report 1989' for page 37.

CONTENTS

TABLES

PREFACE

This book results from collaboration between friends and colleagues in three continents. We, the principal authors, are both now teaching in British universities but we have spent practically all our professional lives associated with schools in Africa and Asia, where we have watched teachers perform the yearly miracle of achieving creditable results on a level of resources which no teacher in Europe or North America would countenance. Both of us have taught in such schools and worked with ministries and university departments of education in many different countries. Some of the research for this book comes from recent working attachments in Kenya, Lesotho and Indonesia but some derives from special visits made during the four years (1986–89) in which this book has been in preparation.

However, much of the data related to the five countries chosen as examples in the study has been supplied by our collaborators, all of whom have been deeply involved in attempts to improve quality at primary level and thus have experience of the hard decisions which need to be made, almost daily, between conflicting priorities in an attempt to deliver better primary education.

Agus Tangyong is head of the primary and pre-school division in the Curriculum Development Centre within the Indonesian Office of Educational and Cultural Research and Development. Together with his colleague **Wahyudi Suseloardjo** he has been associated, from its inception, with the project 'Active Learning Through Professional Support for Teachers' which figures so prominently in this book.

Henry Ayot is currently Dean of the Faculty of Education in Kenyatta University. He has taken the lead in a number of important attempts to involve the University in providing leadership in the improvement of primary school quality in Kenya including the introduction of new degrees for primary teacher-educators, a major innovation in a system where, like so many others, further education seemed designed to remove good manpower from the primary sector rather than strengthen it.

Barnabas Otaala is a professor in the Department of Educational Psychology in the University of Namibia. At the time of writing he was adviser to Lesotho's National Teacher Training College as part of a large project assisted by USAID to improve quality in basic and non-formal education systems. Prior to working in Lesotho he was Professor and Dean of Education in the Universities of Botswana and Kenyatta (Kenya). He has been involved, from its inception, with the Child-to-Child programme frequently referred to in this book.

Siti Hawa Ahmed is an assistant director in Malaysia's Curriculum Development Centre. At the time of the introduction of the New Primary Curriculum, described in this book, she headed its primary division. Later she conducted an important study to evaluate its implementation. She has thus been involved at every stage with what is probably the best planned and best funded programme of national primary curriculum improvement in Asia in recent years.

Beverley Young currently heads the British Council's education department. At the time that work on this book commenced he was chief adviser to the UNICEF-supported Primary Education Project in Nepal. Previously he had been involved in projects in both Indonesia and Nigeria to raise the quality of primary education. He has also been closely associated with Child-to-Child.

In addition to our main collaborators we have sought help and advice from a large number of others in the countries we have visited and, most particularly among colleagues and students at the Universities of Sussex, Kenyatta, and London. In both the latter we have held seminars to discuss the content of individual chapters.

Many others have also helped us greatly: those who have prepared the manuscripts, most particularly, Christine Scotchmer of the London Institute of Education; library staff in both London and Sussex and, of course, Colette and Claire, our wives, who in addition to having to put up with our working hours and our absences abroad, have given so much of their professional expertise in reading, criticising and sometimes even rewriting successive drafts.

We are all too well aware that the book which has emerged from all these efforts provides no instant *answers* to the problem of providing a better quality primary education with fewer resources. Rather, we have concentrated on finding the right *questions* to ask about quality in primary schools. If, in so doing, we have succeeded in raising the level of concern (which is currently too low) and the level of debate (which is currently too restricted), this book must be accounted worthwhile.

Hugh Hawes *University of London, Institute of Education*

David Stephens *University of Sussex, Institute of Professional and Continuing Education*

CONCERN FOR QUALITY

CAUSE FOR CONCERN

Nine out of ten of the world's children attend primary school. For well over half of these this represents all the formal schooling they will receive.

During their time at school we as educators, parents, employers and politicians expect children to learn a long catalogue of things. We wish them to become effectively literate and numerate, to acquire the knowledge and skills they need for a secondary school *and* the knowledge and skills to make a living if they don't get there. We wish them to respect their traditional cultures *and* to become effective citizens in a modern society. We would like them to be obedient citizens *and* to be self-reliant.

Not surprisingly the products of our schools don't always measure up to our expectations. So we publish our intention to improve quality. What it is we wish to improve, how we may best go about it and how realistic our goals were in the first place are rarely analysed as deeply as they should be. This book attempts to illuminate both the decisions to be made and the process of making them.

The children for whose benefit the decisions are being made will grow up into a world changing at a pace faster than at any time in its history. A world closely linked by a revolution in transport and communication and by the realisation of the common problems which beset it, yet deeply divided between rich and poor, city dwellers and country folk. It is with these realities in mind that education must seek positively to influence development, a task which sceptics doubt to be possible but which we as authors believe is not only necessary but eminently possible.

FOCUS ON PRIMARY SCHOOLS IN DEVELOPING COUNTRIES

The book focuses on primary schools in developing countries. However we would in no way suggest that the issues it raises are self-contained. In the first place the whole concept of developing countries is a difficult one to handle and to generalise about them is always dangerous and sometimes patronising.

We shall examine similarities and differences among richer and poorer countries in Asia and Africa, taking five as particular examples. Readers will appreciate that many of the questions and issues raised by this analysis will be equally valid in the so-called industrial countries and outside the two continents we have selected.

Secondly, although we seek to concentrate on primary schools in the formal sense, it is in the full knowledge that this is but one mode and level of education. Indeed we shall stress that it is only through recognising how that level relates *horizontally* with the other less formal education which goes on at the same time, as well as *vertically* with the educational experiences which have happened to the learners before and are planned to happen afterwards, that we shall be able satisfactorily to achieve the raising of quality.

Notwithstanding the limitations of this perspective, the field covered by this book is enormous. Although it takes its examples from five countries, it derives data from and suggests implications for many more. It draws, though at no great depth, from a wide spectrum of educational scholarship: philosophy, psychology, social and political theory, studies on management and innovation as well as those on the design, implementation and evaluation of curriculum. It seeks to relate these to different educational tasks from the building of schools to the writing of syllabuses and textbooks, the training of teachers and the planning of approaches to evaluation, assessment and selection.

A CRISIS IN PRIMARY EDUCATION

When authors use emotive words such as 'crisis' they need to be able to justify the position they take. Today's schools and today's youth are invariably the target of those who were the product of yesterday's system. Unfortunately the present conditions in primary schools in poorer countries cannot be explained away as misunderstandings between generations. For in almost all such countries the expectations of primary schools have become very difficult to reconcile with the resources available to meet them. Enrolments have increased dramatically whereas national budgets available to support schools have remained static.

There are three contributory reasons for this. The first and second are readily apparent. In country after country population increases have outstripped economic growth. Yet at the same time the demand for universal education has caused rises in primary school enrolments which often go far beyond the simple arithmetic of rises in population. With few exceptions attendance at primary school has become a social norm.[1] Gone are the days when a nation or a family could, with dignity, send only a proportion of its children to school. It is now generally appreciated that in a world transformed by a revolution in technology, transport and communications; in a world which preaches equity and democracy, even if it does not always practise them, illiterate children stigmatise both their families and their local and national communities. We consequently witness heroic, sometimes even desperate efforts to send young children to schools of whatever quality.

The result is that in some countries in Asia and Latin America and many in Africa the plight of primary education is stark. In a sombre UNICEF report entitled *Within Human Reach, a Future for Africa's Children*, Manzoor Ahmed writes:

Throughout Africa, educational infrastructure, deficient to begin with, has
deteriorated further in recent years due to lack of such basic items as books,
equipment, vehicles and fuel; inadequate teacher training and supervision;
and inadequate data, planning and management. Teachers in several
countries have gone for months without pay; many classes are held
outdoors or in badly overcrowded, under-equipped classrooms; and the
gaps between wealthy and poor areas have been widening. The education
landscape as in other areas of social services, is littered with incomplete and
rundown institutions and projects, broken equipment and low morale. In
most countries, according to experienced observers, a substantial
proportion of children are unable to read and write even after going to
primary school for four or five years. Dropout rates reach 50 per cent
between enrolment in first grade and completion of the primary cycle. The
pressure to expand the system without the resources to pay for teachers,
facilities and institutional materials has caused this situation.[2]

The situation in the poorer of our five countries is indeed bleak. Nepal,
the poorest in terms of GNP, suffers from a combination of factors
which constrain quality at primary level. Only 28% of children who enrol
complete the primary cycle; a mere 29% of the education budget is
spent on primary education and the meagre per capita expenditure this
allows for is shrinking still further in the face of a population growth of
2.7% per annum. Schools have desperately poor physical amenities. A
survey in 1986 revealed 70% with leaking roofs and only 30% with
toilets for children.[3]

Only in the most prosperous of the five countries, Malaysia, can one
contemplate prospects of improvement in resources provided for
primary education. Indonesia and Kenya, though struggling to maintain
a minimum level of provision, face a daunting task. In 1987 and 1988 the
government of Indonesia cut out virtually all provision for teacher
improvement courses in order to maintain basic salary payments. In
Kenya a survey of primary schools indicates that less than 50% of the
teachers in the sample possessed any white chalk. On average one
textbook was shared between five to ten children and 30% of children
had nothing to write with.[4]

Faced with such a decline there is a natural reaction to seek the
reassurance of the old standards. Unfortunately this solution offers little
hope for raising quality for not only were the old standards by no means
as admirable as we remember them, they are also quite inapplicable to
the world into which our youth will be growing up. Children entering
school in 1990 will become adults in a new century, in a new and
changing world. Naturally they will need to maintain the traditional
values of assimilating knowledge, acquiring skills and developing
attitudes to enable them to fit into the society and the economy in which
they live and will continue to live. At the same time however, they must
be prepared to face the quite unprecedented challenges which all
citizens of the next century must face. These challenges include:

(i) *The need to face radically different economic futures.* These include the imperative of intensifying efficient food production in the face of population growth, a growth which must slow down if the quality of life for individuals is to rise.[5] Equally they imply a whole new perspective on employment as the concept of one job for life becomes increasingly inapplicable.

(ii) *The need to preserve a finite environment and resources from the dangers of exploitation, waste and pollution.* This process is made more difficult yet at the same time more urgent by forces which waste and destroy on a massive scale, and against which individuals are often powerless.

The extract which follows is from an important study called *Global 2000* presented to the President of the United States in 1981. It makes sombre reading, the more so because as the years go by its truth becomes all the more evident.

> The world in 2000 will be different from the world today in important ways. There will be more people . . .
> There will be fewer resources to go around. While on a worldwide average there was about four tenths of a hectare of arable land per person in 1975, there will be only about one quarter hectare per person in 2000 . . .
> The environment will have lost important life-supporting capabilities. By the year 2000, 40 per cent of the forests still remaining in LDCs in 1978 will have been razed. The atmospheric concentration of carbon dioxide will be nearly one-third higher than pre-industrial levels. Soil erosion will have removed, on the average, several inches of soil from the croplands all over the world. Desertification (including salinisation) may have claimed a significant fraction of the world's rangeland and cropland . . .
> The world will be more vulnerable both to natural disaster and to disruptions from human causes . . .[6]

At a more local level the dangers and the challenges are very clear to see: the great erosion gulleys in Lesotho; the denudation of soil from the Himalayan foothills; the destruction of Malaysia's and Indonesia's forests; the desertification of Kenya's northern province; and the uncontrolled pollution of Nairobi's slums. All these not only affect the quality of life now but take resources away from the environment which future generations may find impossible to replace.

(iii) *The need to understand, control and manage a revolution in communication and technology which has the potential for controlling mankind as well as serving it.* This involves not only the mastery of new language, knowledge and skills to be able to control technology, but also the ability to sift, criticise and reason so that the messages and arguments which are so persuasively spread through the media are not accepted uncritically. This challenge is complicated by the unequal access of individuals and communities to both technology and information. For there exists a danger, a very serious danger, that societies will become increasingly divided between those who are information-rich and technologically literate and who are thus able to support or even manage change; and those who are none of these things. Further, that this division will intensify the present rift not only between classes within society but between the 'fast folk' in the cities and the 'slow folk' outside them.

(iv) *The need to control human aggression which, assisted by technology, now possesses means of destruction which can threaten the survival of the species.* It is alarming to note that even if the nuclear threat is discounted, the expenditures on conventional military weapons remain unacceptably high and are growing higher in comparison to national incomes. In Asia as a whole it is almost double the joint expenditures on education and health.[7] Moreover, 'If one combines regular and paramilitary forces, there are still far more people wearing military uniforms than there are teachers.'[8]

A major task of education is, therefore, to spread information about the dangers and costs of conflict, and even more fundamentally to create attitudes which will reduce hatred and aggression towards our fellow men, canalising energies towards other ends: hatred of suffering, of disease, of ugliness, of poverty.

(v) *The need to narrow the gap between the 'haves' and the 'have-nots'; those with power and those without.* To distribute the wealth we have more equitably and to arrest the trend of the concentration of power, resources and opportunities in the hands of a few.

(vi) *The importance of preserving and strengthening moral, cultural and spiritual values which are in danger of being unacceptably weakened and eroded.* Never has it been more important for us to retain our belief in the good or to appreciate the importance of the depth and stability which cultural heritage provides in our lives. Such stability is all the more important because the choices we have to make are much more difficult and confusing. At one time decisions were taken within the security of a relatively stable value system: one social code of ethics, one religion and limited information on which to base judgement. Today the situation is quite different. Society is pluralistic, choices are many, pressures are great. Hence it becomes essential for learners to develop the autonomy to make moral choices based on reason rather than custom.

A NEW VIEW OF LEARNING

All six of these challenges invite us to consider a view of learning in direct opposition to what Paulo Freire has called 'the banking concept' in education.[9] Such new learning must enable us not only to adapt to the changes which others propose for us but also to anticipate them, participate in them and even in some degree to influence them. As one study puts it:

For us learning means an approach, both to knowledge and to life, that emphasises human initiative. It encompasses the acquisition and practice of new methodologies, new skills, new attitudes and new values necessary to live in a world of change. Learning is the process of preparing to deal with new situations. It may occur consciously or often unconsciously, usually from experiencing real life situations, although simulated and imagined situations can also induce learning. Practically every individual in the world, whether schooled or not, experiences the process of learning – and probably none of us at present are learning at the levels, intensities and speeds needed to cope with the complexities of modern life.[10]

QUALITY MATTERS

At this point it may be necessary to examine the argument, in our opinion a fairly ludicrous one, that what we most need is more primary schools rather than better ones.

The World Bank, whose reports and research studies tend to define quality as efficiency in attaining desired school outputs, has a considerable body of research which suggests that investment in primary education and its quality gives a higher rate of return than at any other level in the formal system,[11] also that better schools produce fewer dropouts,[12] contribute to higher achievement levels[13] and enhance future economic productivity.[14] World Bank research has concentrated on the determinants which make up a better school and which most contribute to better achievement. TABLE I[15] briefly summarises the available research data. It makes interesting reading, particularly since in many cases studies confound conventional wisdom. Class size, for instance, does not appear to affect achievement. However results are often contradictory and, as we shall argue later, tell us a good deal less about quality than we should like to know.

It seems to us somewhat unnecessary further to stress that quality in education matters. This book is designed to be read by education workers and we would be strange educationists who denied that the ultimate purpose of our efforts was to help learners to learn better. Yet two aspects of public concern for betterment are disturbing. The first is that there is too little of it about, the second that where it does exist its focus is far too restricted.

LACK OF EMPHASIS ON QUALITY IN PRIMARY EDUCATION

This is apparent in many ways and at many levels. If we examine, for instance, the concern over universal primary education and the literature which surrounds it, it will immediately be clear that the interest in the provision of places in schools far outweighs any concern about what those schools should teach.[16]

Equally striking is an examination of university commitment, or the lack of it, to research and training at this level. Until 1989 among all the educational universities in Indonesia,[17] for instance, there was only one with a department specifically focused on the elementary school,[18] and it is only in the last years and against massive professorial opposition that universities in anglophone Africa have begun to face the crucial task of preparing leadership for this level. When attempts were being made in Kenya to steer the B.Ed. Primary Education, designed for precisely such a purpose, through the university senate, one professor remarked

TABLE I

Summary: School factors and achievement in the Third World

School quality indicator	Expected direction of relationship	Total number of analyses	Number of analyses confirming effect
SCHOOL EXPENDITURES			
1 Expenditures per pupil	+	11	6
2 Total school expenditures	+	5	2
SPECIFIC MATERIAL INPUTS			
3 Class size	−	21	5
4 School size	+	9	4
5 Instructional materials			
Texts and reading materials	+	24	16
Desks	+	3	3
6 Instructional media (radio)	+	3	3
7 School building quality	+	3	2
8 Library size and activity	+	18	15
9 Science laboratories	+	11	4
10 Nutrition and feeding programs	+	6	5
TEACHER QUALITY			
11 Teacher's length of schooling			
Total years of teacher's schooling	+	26	12
Years of tertiary & teacher training	+	31	22
12 In-service teacher training	+	6	5
13 Teacher's length of experience	+	23	10
14 Teacher's verbal proficiency	+	2	2
15 Teacher's salary level	+	14	5
16 Teacher's social class background	+	10	7
17 School's percentage of full-time teachers	+	2	1
18 Teacher's punctuality & (low) absenteeism	+	2	0
TEACHING PRACTICES/CLASSROOM ORGANIZATION			
19 Length of instructional program	+	14	12
20 Homework frequency	+	8	6
21 Active learning by students	+	3	1
22 Teacher's expectations of pupil performance	+	3	3
23 Teacher's time spent on class preparation	+	5	4
SCHOOL MANAGEMENT			
24 Quality of principal	+	7	4
25 Multiple shifts of classes each day	−	3	1
26 Student boarding	+	4	3
27 Student repetition of grade	+	5	1

(handwritten annotation: ✱ Worth noting)

Summary from a review undertaken by Bruce Fuller (1987) for the World Bank.

derisively, 'What do you want to teach them. Two plus two?' 'And where, Professor,' asked the programme's designer, 'do you send your own children to school?' Everyone knew the answer to that – to a high cost school in Nairobi, with a largely graduate staff.

RESEARCH ON QUALITY: TOO LITTLE; TOO NARROW

Of equal concern is the record of research into primary school quality and the narrow scope of the enquiries made.

At national level one is struck by the very low volume of research even into conventional measures of achievement. For example, in most countries, including all five we surveyed, no standardised texts have been devised to measure and compare achievements in reading in the national language. There is a similar dearth of material examining the implications of national goals for primary education, or illuminating the context of primary education or the realities of life in classrooms. Consequently, planners seeking to improve quality and measure achievement work largely in the dark.

International research seems to have been dominated by an input/output paradigm which, though valuable within the narrow limits it sets itself, is impossibly restrictive given the challenges outlined earlier in this chapter.

We need to examine, for instance:

not only   whether school content makes leavers immediately more employable
but also   whether it makes them, in the long term, more adaptable

not only   whether certain approaches in school make children perform better in conventional multiple-choice tests
but also   whether such tests cause learners and their teachers to question what it is that these tests are measuring

not only   whether the existence of trained teachers or textbooks make a difference to achievement
but also   what kind of teachers and what kind of textbooks are desirable given the real needs of learners

not only   whether school knowledge is efficiently transmitted
but also   whether such knowledge remains school knowledge or whether it transfers into the home and community once the pupils walk out of the school compound

REASONS FOR THE NEGLECT OF THE STUDY OF QUALITY AT PRIMARY LEVEL

There appear to be three main reasons for low concern and low investment on qualitative issues at primary level.

The first is that we may lack the expertise and the research traditions to embark on qualitative enquiries which are illuminative and descriptive in character. Moreover we have been conditioned to place less weight on the results of such enquiries because in the main they are not statistical. (The fact that the raw data from which statistical results are obtained is often both subjective and suspect seldom troubles us as much as it should.)

The second reason that policy makers may fight shy of obtaining qualitative data about their primary systems is that they may have a very shrewd suspicion that information uncovered about their schools may be too hot to handle. To discover and publicise the fact that a large proportion of children in primary school cannot read the books which are provided them;[19] that classes of one hundred children exist with no furniture to sit on or no paper to write on;[20] that a brand new syllabus of instruction produced by the government's curriculum development centre is overloaded and, to a considerable degree, inappropriate to learning needs;[21] that only about one in four children who start primary school actually finish it;[22] that the government expenditure per capita on tertiary education may be *one hundred times* greater than that spent on a primary child.[23] Such disclosures are likely to hit the headlines with unfortunate consequences to those responsible for the educational policy (over which they may have only very limited effective control). Indeed when countries have been bold enough to commission an investigation into the condition of their primary schools (as in Jamaica in 1974) they have sometimes found the information too embarrassing to make public.[24]

The final reason for holding back on both the enquiries and the action which they imply is because both the concept of quality and the task of achieving it are exceptionally complex and difficult to unravel. They involve many different aspects and perspectives which change depending on the light in which they are being examined (discussed in this chapter). Involved too are contradictions and conflicts between many interest groups (discussed in Chapter Two).

Yet we must seek to unravel the notion of quality if we are to work together to achieve betterment. (As suggested in Chapter Three and later chapters in this book.)

DEFINING THE ELEMENTS OF QUALITY

In order to discuss how to improve quality in education we need to start by defining the term.

Short definitions of quality in this context are likely to serve no useful purpose. Even if we ask an average teacher what she means by quality, her answer would depend on who was asking the questions:

> To the *parent* she will speak of examination results.
> To the *inspector*, of better general standards of reading or handwriting or mathematics.

TABLE II
CODE FOR TAMIL VERNACULAR SCHOOLS STRAITS SETTLEMENTS (now Malaysia), 1905

SUBJECT	STANDARD I	STANDARD II	STANDARD III	STANDARD IV	STANDARD V
READING	To read correctly two or three lines from any approved book not previously studied, equal in difficulty to the first part of the First Book of Lessons.	a) To read correctly a few lines from any approved book not previously studied, equal in difficulty to the second part of the First Book of Lessons. b) To answer simple questions on the meaning and subject matter of the second part of the First Book of Lessons, giving the equivalents of the commonest words in English or Malay. (One only).	a) To read with ease and correctness a few lines from any approved book, not previously studied, equal in difficulty to the Second Book of Lessons. b) To answer questions on the meaning and subject matter of the lessons comprised in a portion previously prepared of the Second Book of Lessons, giving the equivalents of the commonest words in it in English or Malay. (One only).	a) To read with ease and correctness a few lines from any approved book not previously studied, equal in difficulty to the Third Book of Lessons; and also from any ordinary manuscript. b) To answer questions on the meaning and subject matter of lessons comprised in a portion previously prepared of the Third Book of Lessons. Increased facility in giving English or Malay equivalents. (One only).	To read and answer questions on the subject matter comprised in Book I of the *Panchitantram*, and explain it in English or Malay. (One only).
WRITING	To transcribe in large hand, on slate, a short sentence from the Reading Book in use.	To write from dictation words out of the Reading Book in use.	To write from dictation not more than 4 lines from a book equal in difficulty to the Second Book of Lessons.	To write from dictation a longer passage out of any book equal in difficulty to the Third Book of Lessons.	To write from dictation a passage of increased difficulty.
ARITHMETIC	Numeration, Notation and Addition of numbers of not more than 3 digits. Multiplication Table to 4 times 12.	Notation to 100,000. Addition, Subtraction and Multiplication. Tables extended to 12 times 12.	Notation to nine figures. First four rules, with long-division, applied to abstract numbers or Straits' or Indian currency.	Compound rules applied to British, Indian, or Straits' currency, and Straits' weights and measures.	Simple Rule of Three. Simple Problems. Conversion of Straits into Indian or British currency and vice versa.

(Extract from Board of Education, *Special Reports on Educational Subjects*, 1905)

To the *chairman* of the school board she may emphasise making good use of money.
To the *professor*, good teaching and learning practices.
To the *mayor* or *member of parliament*, effective work-orientation.
To the *clergyman*, character-building.
To the *village elder*, conservation of traditional values.

In each case her answers would be valid for the purpose and audience she was addressing. Consequently we, too, must not shy away from a complex definition of quality.

Quality can imply:

- efficiency in meeting set goals
- relevance to human and environmental needs and conditions
- 'something more' in relation to the pursuit of excellence and human betterment

QUALITY AS EFFICIENCY IN MEETING SET GOALS

When grandfather holds forth, or newspapers write leading articles about falling standards in schools, it is certainly this aspect that they are talking about, though the two words 'efficiency' and 'standard' can be taken in at least three different ways.

1 Quality as efficiency in reaching standards

The word 'standard' has an interesting educational history. It was much in favour in Britain in the late nineteenth century as a measure of assessing progress of classes (and the rate of pay of their teachers) according to a 'revised code'. This code was exported with little amendment to colonial dependencies. The code for the Straits Settlement Tamil Vernacular Schools in 1905 is reproduced in Table II.[25]

The word 'standard' used in Kenya, Lesotho and many other former colonial dependencies stems from this era. In recent years 'standards' in this sense have come back into fashion. Behavioural objectives, mastery learning, codes of accountability and performance-based teacher education are all motivated by the same idea: an attempt to measure exactly where learners have got to.

No one can doubt the importance of such assessment of standards as a measure of quality, but we have to be fully aware that there are a number of different kinds of standards: standards of attainment in knowledge and learning skills; standards of creativity and critical thinking; and finally, standards of behaviour, including involvement in family and community life. The last two categories are just as important as the first in any educational system, but since they are far more difficult to measure there exists a danger that they will be neglected or marginalised.

Standards are also strongly influenced by the motivation of those who set them, hence the real danger that they may be used as a means of social control through using different sets of standards in different orders of schools.

Moreover since standards can be applied individually as well as collectively, it will always be important to balance one against another. A school which neglects its weakest children entirely (and many do) in favour of getting 'good passes' for its better ones can hardly be complimented on its standards, yet schools also have a responsibility to develop the potential of their more gifted and creative pupils.

2 Quality as efficiency in improving standards

The Universities of Oxford and Cambridge have very high standards of output which they achieve at remarkably little effort from the teaching staff because their entry standards are so high. Similarly if a primary school in Kenya, Lesotho or Malaysia only selects children from families who can afford to pay substantial fees or if it imposes a literacy test on entrants, or if it does both these things, it can hardly be complimented on achieving a better output than an impoverished and isolated rural school or an overcrowded treble-shift school in an urban slum.

Perhaps the latter performed far more impressively in *raising the standard* of both groups and individuals in the school from something very modest to something much higher. Perhaps they gave children from these bleak backgrounds the ability and the will to break out from the oppression of their surroundings.

Thus, as Richard Peters reminds us, we must always consider quality of *process* alongside quality of *product*.[26]

3 Quality as standards of efficiency

Efficiency, in industrial language means obtaining maximum output from a given input.

Schools are efficient when they know what they are trying to do and when they function smoothly and happily. In some respects efficiency depends on 'having the right tools for the job'. But even more important is the principle of 'making the most of what you have'.

Certain key aspects of efficiency include:

(i) Maximising the time spent on task (e.g. teachers actually teaching and learners actually learning rather than doing other things, or not doing anything).

(ii) Suiting the demands of teaching and learning to the ability of teachers to teach and learners to learn, because if the curriculum is so wide of the mark that it makes no contact with the clients then it is highly inefficient.

(iii) Providing suitable feedback to both teachers and learners, so that it is possible to build on strengths and remedy weaknesses.

(iv) Making best use of resources available, including what equipment there is as well as the environment and the direct experience of the learners.

There are, of course, more subtle measures of efficiency but many of us who have lived and worked in contexts where few if any of the conditions noted above were met, would be pleased to encounter a school where:

* The teachers were consistently in their classes teaching (or at least in the staff room preparing work).
* The children were regularly engaged in learning (rather than wasting their time).
* Both the teachers and the children understood what the syllabus and textbooks were trying to convey.
* Both the teachers and the pupils had the opportunity of consistently building up from the known to the unknown, and of learning from their mistakes.
* Available learning resources in the school and its natural and human environment were effectively used.

To achieve such efficiency may sound simple. It is far from it. To engender a climate which allows this efficiency to operate may mean raising morale which has sunk to a very low ebb, and building up a spirit of trust and commitment which may at present be frequently wanting in difficult circumstances. Why this is so and what we can do about it will be examined later.

QUALITY AS RELEVANCE

Efficiency cannot be the only measure of quality. It is perfectly possible to have an education which is efficiently orientating learners towards the wrong ends, either because what they are learning is not socially useful or, more sinister, because it is not desirable. The principles of apartheid can be very efficiently taught.

Consequently we need education which is relevant:

* to context
* to needs
* to humanity

RELEVANCE TO CONTEXT

Relevance to *context* is both clear and unambiguous. Education must be rooted in a society and a culture which learners can comprehend. An alien education is both unproductive and psychologically disturbing, often leading to a dangerous form of half-learning where children can answer questions on content yet do not fully understand what they are being asked or what they are answering, because it has little connection with their lives and experience.

RELEVANCE TO NEEDS

'Relevance to *needs*' though vital to quality is far from clear and at times is very ambiguous. In fact we are continually trying to achieve a sort of balancing act between different types and orders of needs.

1 Between 'our' needs, 'your' needs and 'their' needs

As we have noted, different persons and different groups of persons have different needs: townsmen and countrymen; traditional folk and modern folk; the middle class and the peasants; this language group and that one. A recent study on *Quality of Life* in India[27] illuminates stark differences in the goals set by different groups and classes, yet at the same time raises the fundamental philosophical question of whether education should merely satisfy the desires of a parent or child who has been conditioned to a relatively low aspiration, or whether it should seek to make him dissatisfied and aim higher. Moreover, what a government may hopefully assume to be the needs of a community (in the cause of maintaining the social and economic status quo), may be somewhat different from those the people themselves enumerate.

2 Between 'my' needs and 'our' needs

There is always a tension between the needs of the individual and the needs of groups. Individuals learn at their own pace and in their own manner. No education programme which neglects to provide for individual needs can claim to be truly relevant. But not only are individuals taught as a group, they also need to act and react and co-operate as a group if society is to function. Indeed it may be relevant to look at the record of various nations with similar economic and human resources and speculate as to why it is that some have developed faster than others. Many would consider social discipline and community cohesion (emphasised strongly in the national philosophy of Malaysia, the most economically successful of our five countries) as a major contribution to national progress.

3 Between 'now' needs and 'later' needs

It is tempting to look at school education solely as a preparation for life, and indeed it must do this, concentrating, as we have already stressed, on those qualities which enable learners to survive and adapt to change. But this is only part of a school's task. In many countries as much as half the population is below the age of fifteen.

'Quality of life' is not just for adults. A child has as much right to enjoy the time he is in school as an adult has to enjoy work and leisure.

Hence when young Musa says he is proud of his football team he is telling us something very important. Moreover schoolchildren, particularly in poor countries, have responsibilities to their families and the community – they play a crucial part in both. The Child-to-Child programme, which will be examined in later chapters, is an example of how such responsibility can be channelled, in this case towards providing better health-care of families and communities by harnessing the untapped power of children: older helping younger, peers helping each other and children as a group acting as health workers within a community.[28]

Education which keeps 'needs now' in mind may prove the best foundation for 'needs later'. It motivates children, builds on their direct experience and develops in them a sense of responsibility.

4 Between different levels of needs

Needs differ in importance and complexity. In the simplest analysis it is important to identify, as Coombs and Ahmed have done,[29] those learning needs which are minimum and which must be satisfied for all learners: a sort of educational driving test which needs to be passed if learners are to set forth with confidence and safety along the road of life. But categorisation of needs must be taken a good deal further and deeper than this.

Consider the nature of needs. At first it would seem sensible to express needs largely in terms of 'having'. We need to 'have' good health, food and employment and we need to 'have' the skills to attain these. However a little thought convinces us not only that 'having' is a most complicated concept but also that 'being' is just as important and equally complex.

The psychologist Abraham Maslow sees human needs as arranged in a series of levels which together contribute to a sense of wholeness and humanity.[30] In one sense, however, such needs are hierarchical because the 'lower' categories are necessary for mere survival. Maslow identifies:

Physiological needs

These are essential for physical growth and biological survival, such as food, water, air, activity, sleep, sex, shelter and sensory stimulation. Every organism needs these to survive, but in the case of the human organism, if the lower needs remain unsatisfied the individual remains preoccupied by them and his ability to be motivated by higher needs is thwarted.

Safety needs

They include not only the crude concept of 'saving one's skin' but also the need for security against uncertainty and anxiety. Lack of control over our future and its security, as well as lack of self-confidence, may

15

cause us to look up towards a 'strong man' of whatever beliefs and to embrace conservative or fanatical codes because they present a clear and ambiguous set of 'dos' and an even more emphatic list of 'don'ts'.

Love and belonging needs

At the more personal level these include the need to contribute to and be accepted into a group and community; at the larger level, the need to feel part of a wider fellowship – religious, cultural or political. This need becomes more and more insistent as modern life heightens

> ... feelings of alienation, aloneness, strangeness and loneliness which have been worsened by our mobility, by the breakdown of traditional groupings, the scattering of families and the generation gap.[31]

These words written with the USA in mind are equally valid for the growing urban areas in developing countries two decades later.

Self-esteem needs

These include first the element of self-respect, the need we feel to become a 'respectable' or useful member of society, but, beyond this the element of esteem we feel when we want to be recognised and valued. The desire we have to be known as a 'good farmer', a 'good parent', a 'wise person', a 'well dressed man or woman' comes into this category.

Self-actualisation needs

The final category of needs arises from the desire of humans to develop their humanity: to create a better pot or table; to make music or tell a story; to meditate or worship; to climb a mountain or break an Olympic record. As Maslow points out, such needs, being uniquely human, often transcend barriers of race and culture.[32]

When we examine these categories we realise that each has very important educational implications for every learner and that all need to be kept in balance. A school can easily, for instance, concentrate on the 'lower orders' of needs, giving children all the basic skills, all the security and happiness they need but without providing that extra dimension which develops the humanity in humans. A school may fail to contribute towards developing self-confidence and a sense of autonomy which are such important components in meeting safety, self-esteem and self-actualisation needs. A school may also fail to develop in learners the 'wholeness' which Maslow and other writers identify as so necessary for the mature human personality. We return to the implications of this wholeness in Chapter Three.

RELEVANCE TO HUMANITY

We ended our last section on a note emphasising the importance of developing the human potential in individuals. However the concept of *relevance* is also related to humanity as a species. To talk of a relevant education as one which helps to ensure the survival of that species may seem somewhat extreme, but, in our opinion, it is not. Many readers will be familiar with John Donne's famous words '. . . never send to know for whom the bell tolls; it tolls for thee'. But fewer of us can remember the full passage from which it comes:

> No man is an island entire in itself; every man is a piece of the continent, a part of the main; if a clod be washed away by the sea Europe is the less, as well as if a promontory were, as well as if a manor of thy friends or thine own were; any man's death diminishes me, because I am involved in mankind. And therefore never send to know for whom the bell tolls . . .[33]

No educationist today can ignore these words. Our lives and futures are now linked together as never before and an education which is not linked with the world issues and world priorities with which we began this chapter is not a relevant education.

BEYOND EFFICIENCY AND RELEVANCE: QUALITY AS 'SOMETHING SPECIAL'

Many would claim that the definition of quality as 'efficiency plus relevance' would serve our needs, especially if the word 'relevance' were interpreted widely enough. Certainly we have seen such a wide interpretation by Maslow when he emphasises the importance of fulfilling the human need to express themselves and become complete persons. Nevertheless we would recognise a side of quality which goes beyond the current definitions of efficiency and relevance.

It is that extra quality of inventiveness, stimulation, excitement, concern for others or happiness which is found but found rarely, in schools and teachers. It is a quality which must never be stifled and submerged by rules or bureaucracy. For it is through these special and unusual educational situations that general progress often comes.

Not that the paths that individuals of genius choose can be followed by all of us. A force like Gandhi or Paulo Freire or of Mother Theresa or the many thousands of less publicised individuals who have transformed classes, schools or communities is often too unique for common people to copy. But such a force always brings into the system aspects and insights of quality which can contribute to growth like buds upon a plant.

To a 'teacher of quality' or a 'school of quality' needs to be added the concept of a 'learner of quality'. In the last scene of Flecker's play *Hassan*, a caravan sets out from the East Gate of Damascus and the gatekeeper asks them who they are:

> 'We are the pilgrims, Master,' they reply. 'We shall go
> Always a little further . . .'[34]

An education of true quality must provide a gate through which schools and individuals can go a 'little further'.

SUMMARY

We have emphasised how urgent is the task of defining quality in education, and how vital is the role that education can play in preparing children to live their lives now, and to shape and take control of those lives and those of others to the demands of a complex and changing world.

Throughout the chapter we have emphasised that simplistic solutions expressed as slogans will serve us ill:

> 'Combatting falling standards'
> 'Modernising content'
> 'Education for production'

are all noble sentiments, but none of these even approaches a full answer to the challenges which face us.

Instead we have consistently stressed that both understanding quality and action towards its improvement are complex processes, dynamic and never entirely complete. But understanding *can* be improved and quality *can* be bettered provided we set our minds very seriously to the issue, provided we face uncomfortable realities and provided the capable and mature men and women whose day-to-day responsibility it is to make schools better are neither misled nor undervalued.

NOTES AND REFERENCES

1 Of course there are still countries where, because of poverty and unrest, enrolment percentages are still very low (Afghanistan, Ethiopia, Burkina Faso and Sierra Leone all being examples). In others (e.g. Pakistan, Morocco, Saudi Arabia) there are great imbalances between male and female enrolments but the rises in percentage enrolments over the past 20 years have been dramatic.

2 UNICEF, *Within Human Reach: A Future for Africa's Children*, UNICEF, New York, 1985.
    The report was written by P. Manzoor Ahmed with collaboration from a large team under the general guidance of Richard Jolly.

3 Young, B., 'The Primary Education Project' in *Education and Development*, CERID, Kathmandu, 1985. Also UNICEF, *State of the World's Children*, 1990.

4 Eshiawani, G. S., *A Study of Crowded Classrooms in Kenya*, Basic Education Resource Centre, Kenyatta University College, July 1984.

5 The British ODA report, *Education Priorities and Aid Responses in Sub-Saharan Africa*, HMSO, 1986, has a graphic and very disturbing table (p. 14) showing the widening gap between food production and consumption.

6 Barney, G. O., *The Global 2000 Report to the President: Entering the Twenty-First Century*. A report prepared by the Council on Environmental Quality and the Department of State, Washington DC, 1981, pp. 44–5.

7 'The Sinews of War. 5: Military Expenditures', *UNESCO Courier*, March 1982.

8 *Ibid*, p. 23.

9 Paulo Freire in *Pedagogy of the Oppressed*, Penguin Books, 1972, Chapter 2.

10 Botkin, J. W. *et al., No Limits to Learning. A Report to the Club of Rome*, Pergamon Press, 1979, p. 8.

11 Fuller, B., 'Raising School Quality in Developing Countries', World Bank Discussion Paper, 1985. Reports, research by Psacharopoulos and others. Psacharopoulos first introduced these comparisons in *Returns to Education: An International Comparison*, Jossey-Bass, 1973.

12 *Ibid.*, p. 9.

13 *Ibid.*, p. 31.

14 *Ibid.*, pp. 16–17.

15 Fuller, B., 'What School Factors Raise Achievement in the Third World?' in *Review of Educational Research*, Vol. 57, No. 3, Fall 1987, pp. 259–71.

16 For bibliographies which emphasise this point see *International Review of Education*, Vol. 29, No. 2, 1983 (special issue on the Universalisation of Primary Education), pp. 261–66.

17 These are called IKIPS (an acronym). There are 10 government and numerous private IKIPS as well as 13 universities with educational faculties.

18 At Malang in East Java.

19 As in reports presented in Malaysia (1979) and Botswana (1978).
    Both these countries have much reason to be proud of their
    education systems and consequently commissioned the studies. No
    studies have been made in systems such as Nigeria, Lesotho,
    Bangladesh or Nepal where the problem is at its most acute.

20 Such conditions exist in many schools in Nepal. The report of the
    task force for the Education Sector Survey (Maseru, November
    1982) records 176 teachers teaching Grades I, II and III at the same
    time in classes whose average size is 64.7.

21 Both the Kenyan curriculum for the new '8–4–4' structure of
    education and the Indonesian 'Curriculum '84' have come under
    criticism from the moment of their publication for these reasons.

22 As in Brazil. Discussed in Coombs, P. H., *The World Crisis in
    Education: The View from the Eighties*, OUP, 1985. Current figures
    for a number of other countries (including Nepal) are similar and
    from some, e.g. Bangladesh and Yemen, are lower (UNICEF, *The
    State of the World's Children*, 1990).

23 The World Bank development report 1980 gives the average ratio of
    costs of higher to primary education in sub-Saharan Africa as
    100.5 to 1.

24 Ministry of Education, Jamaica. Report in depth on primary
    education in Jamaica. (Chairman Murray, R. N.), Kingston, 1974.

25 Great Britain Board of Education. *Special Reports on Educational
    Subjects*, Vol. 4, 1905, p. 161.

26 Peters, R. in Beeby, C. E. (ed.), *Qualitative Aspects of Educational
    Planning*, UNESCO International Institute for Educational
    Planning, Paris, 1969.

27 UNESCO, *Quality of Life: Problems of Assessment and
    Measurement*, UNESCO, Paris, 1983.

    The study on India by Ramkrisha Mukherjee (pp. 52–109)
    highlights different expectations of a range of people from different
    classes, religions, backgrounds in Calcutta and rural Bengal.

28 See Hawes, H. W. R., *Child-to-Child: Another Path to Learning*,
    UNESCO Institute for Education, Hamburg, 1988.

29 Coombs, P. H. with Prosser, R. C. and Ahmed, M., *New Paths to*

Learning. Prepared for UNICEF by the International Council for Educational Development, New York, 1973.

30 In this section we draw on a very lucid analysis of Maslow's writings by al-Mekhlafi in a London University Ph.D. thesis entitled 'Relevance and the Curriculum in the Case of the Yemen Arab Republic', Institute of Education, London, January 1986.

31 Maslow, A. H., *Motivation and Personality*, Harper and Row, 1970, p. 44.

32 In his later writings Maslow explored the idea of meta needs' which we have here subsumed under 'self-actualisation'. The concept overlaps strongly with our last category of quality.

33 John Donne (1571–1631). The passage is from his 'Devotions Upon Emergent Occasions' (in this case the death of another).

34 James Elroy Flecker, *Hassan*, 1922. The full quotation runs:

> 'We are the Pilgrims, master, we shall go
> Always a little further: it may be
> Beyond the last blue mountain barred with snow,
> Across that angry or that glimmering sea
> Where on a throne or guarded in a cave
> There lives a prophet who can understand . . .'

QUALITY: WHO DEFINES AND WHO DECIDES?

The primary school at Sidahwa in Eastern Nepal is perched high up above the town. Most of the year it is enveloped in mist. Children attend when they can. Most of the teachers are untrained.[1] The headteacher, though holding a degree in education, has no experience or training in school management. The school lacks everything except children. Sitting in woollen caps they wait patiently on the matting for the lesson to begin.

The Kingdom of Nepal has no shortage of schools like this. And no monopoly either.

It is easy when describing schools such as Sidahwa's to equate lack of physical resources with no meaningful improvement in learning, to see things in pessimistic terms; and to succumb to a despairing fatalism that suggests little can be done to improve anything. Such a view would be mistaken because, as we suggested in the last chapter, it not only undervalues the responsibilities of those entrusted with teaching our children, but also masks the actual changes occurring in places like Sidahwa and elsewhere.

Such changes (and by changes we do not necessarily mean improvements) are not always glaringly obvious, especially to an outsider. Yet if we are to understand quality and action towards improving it, we surely need equally to understand the processes of change: how it occurs, who defines and decides it; the contexts and constraints in which it operates, and the forces, external and internal that shape it.

In the first chapter we defined the elements that we believe constitute quality:

efficiency (e.g. better use of available resources)
relevance (e.g. to needs and contexts)
something more (e.g. to journey a little further than mere efficiency and relevance)

We also stressed that understanding quality and action towards its improvement are complex processes in themselves, dynamic and constantly shifting in tune to new needs and changing conditions.

In this chapter we shift the focus away from a discussion of ends and goals to the means by which they can be achieved.

THE PROCESSES OF CHANGE AND DECISION-MAKING

It seems that the process of change is made up of three basic ingredients. First, an element of *choice* (or in some cases the absence of choice);

second, *decision-making* procedures enshrined in law or bounded by what is regarded as common or customary; and third, *power* or the ability to implement the decisions taken.

These factors when acting in consort become part of a process of decision-making that effects change. This process, however, does not take place in a vacuum. The contexts and constraints under which it operates (and which in many ways determine it) are equally important and will be discussed later in this chapter. What is certain is that *who* defines an agenda of choice and who decides which choice to follow is as important as *what* is chosen and *when* it is achieved. With much of our lives taken up with the operation of this process, added weight is given to the need for a balance in terms of quality being maintained between means and ends, process and product, decision-making and decision.

What we are saying, therefore, is that we wish to examine new ways of reaching our desired goals: more efficient, relevant and better procedures of decision-making that both accommodate constraints and contexts in which change operates and ensure that such change is neither considered solely for its own sake or for the ends it might bring.

Let us now examine a little more closely the three factors that constitute the decision-making process.

THE QUALITY OF THE DECISION-MAKING PROCESS

Within the process of change, choice, decision-making and power lie two distinct, though interrelated stages.

Firstly the stage at which agendas of choice are drawn up, perhaps in response to some immediate or long term need; and secondly the stage at which the decision is taken and then implemented. Power, as we shall examine later, operates throughout in determining all aspects of the process, and can best be viewed in ideological terms.

These stages, though distinct, are very much interrelated; particularly when one considers the fact that the implementation of one decision may in turn become a new choice on a fresh set of agendas.

Paulo Freire addresses these stages when he talks of a combined 'language of critique' and 'language of possibility'.[2] Considering options; discussing viable (and non-viable) choices; preparing the ground for deciding (hence the importance of improved education data-collection for decision-makers) – establishes a 'language of critique' in which reflection, understanding and consideration provide the 'vocabulary' of the moment. Priority is given at this stage to such things as: knowledge of present trends, grasp of current practice (perhaps models of good practice elsewhere) and consideration of likely consequences once the decision is implemented.

In the later stage, the 'language of possibility', Freire interprets change in terms of hope, involvement and responsibility of those participating in decision-making and those most affected by it. He suggests too that the latter be those substantially involved and in direct dialogue with the former.[3]

23

In sum then, quality decision-making is about two stages of a process; a critical understanding of the present situation followed by effective action for change.[4]

However, it is easy for those decision-makers working within a cumbersome bureaucracy (with poor communications and outmoded practices) to understand their function to be narrow, involving themselves in only one of the two decision-making stages or even just one particular role within that stage. One might have a situation, therefore, where those who draw up agendas and reflect upon possibilities absolve themselves of the responsibility for seeing the decisions properly implemented; while those entrusted with, say, providing feedback 'from the field' are excluded from the earlier critique stage when viable options, etc. were considered. Nobody is suggesting this is anyone's fault: in many ways it is a result of increased job specialisation and compartmentalisation of duties and responsibilities. Remedying this is not an easy matter and it is something we shall consider when discussing the concept of shared-control later. Hopefully we are also practising what we preach in our discussion of decision-making, i.e. establishing a critique of the present situation and then looking for new possibilities.

THE 'LANGUAGE OF CRITIQUE'

Any worthwhile critique relies upon knowledge (ideas, statistics, case studies, etc.) of the status quo, and it seems fair to suggest that at present most decision-makers have to operate with insufficient information about what is, and what is not, viable for consideration.

An important role for universities and other centres of higher learning would be to provide decision-makers with a deeper fund of knowledge: numbers of schools as well as true pictures of how many children attend them, what goes on inside them, who teaches and with what attitudes and approaches – information that might radically affect the quality of decisions taken. In Chapter One we expressed concern not only that universities were failing to fulfil this role for primary schools but that research being carried out was often too narrow. We should also like to see an improvement in the channels of communication between those traditionally expected to provide a critique, i.e. the universities; and those entrusted with 'deciding', i.e. practising educationists and teachers. Attempts to do so are beginning to emerge in Indonesia, Kenya and Lesotho and we shall encounter them later in this book, but they are no more than tentative first steps and the gap between the researchers and the implementers remains a wide one.

ESTABLISHING 'ROOM FOR MANOEUVRE'

Let us return to our classroom in Eastern Nepal for a moment and apply our language of critique to the landscape in which decisions are, or are not, taken.

Our learner, in his woollen cap and jerkin is more a receiver than decider, of what we referred to in the last chapter as Freire's 'banking concept' of knowledge.[5] Even if what he 'banks' is satisfactory in terms of efficiency and relevance, the passive nature of the delivery system soon teaches him that he has little control of *what* and *when* he learns.

His teacher, passing on the 'old' knowledge she learnt in her day (and probably in the same way) is more a transmitter than a decider, constrained by her limited knowledge of choices and the resources necessary to realise them.

The headteacher, though well qualified with his degree in education, decides little that is new or innovative, instead he acts as manager of rules and procedures that, though possibly containing and preserving what is good, leave little time or energy for improvement in areas such as in-service training of his staff, curriculum development or better school–community relations.

His immediate superior, the inspector of schools, though perhaps in a better position to advise on change, is unsure of her exact duties (she has recently been promoted from headteacher and has received little briefing and no training in her new post). She concerns herself with administrative matters, leaving such things as curriculum development and materials writing to specialist educationists working at institutions far away in the capital city.

At the top of the hierarchy is the government department heavily constrained by aid conditions. These are imposed, albeit benevolently (and with efficiency and relevance in mind) by donor agencies. On the one hand agencies represent richer nations anxious to assist the poor, but on the other they are equally anxious not to disturb a world economic order that centralises economic decision-making in western capital cities.

What characterises all the actors in this chain of command is the limited 'room for manoeuvre' each has, relative to those he or she comes into contact with. Equally, each may perceive his or her potential for achieving 'something more' in limited terms.

Making 'better use of existing capacity' refers, therefore, to human as much as material resources: to the capabilities and abilities of those working at each level of the education system.

We stress the idea of increasing this 'room for manoeuvre' particularly at *classroom* and *school* level. Evidence exists in many international contexts (and in some of the poorest countries) of teachers making 'more' of what they already have: examples of good practice, often involving no increase in material resources but which demonstrate that improvement can be achieved at both the critique and action stage.

Let us now look a little closer at those people, at each level, who define and decide what can be done.

WHO DEFINES; WHO DECIDES?

We are speaking of two things: the levels of decision-making (from centre to periphery, international through to local),[6] and the complex pattern of roles played out within the decision-making process.

The hierarchy we described earlier becomes more complicated when we realise that the actors at each level wear a variety of costumes, and perform various functions that may well traverse different levels vertically and horizontally. Our curriculum workers as *government servants* may well wish to preserve national culture and stop the drift to the towns. As *subject advisers* they may be seen to promote understanding of modern technology among the most able and urbanised of their pupils; a desire strengthened by their roles as *parents* of children whom they fervently hope will attain university entrance and achieve postgraduate study overseas. Our teacher, as a parent, will wish to decide (or not decide) issues concerning the individual children within her immediate and extended family. As a *teacher* though, she will need to widen her horizons and become responsible for making decisions, however prescribed, about many children, perhaps mediating between the conflicting interests of individual parents and schools.

If on another occasion she is called upon to act the part of *adviser* or *curriculum developer*, she may well be asked to give priority to longer-term decisions over short-term requirements and so on.

Quality of decision-making, therefore, is a priority. But as the horizons of the decision-maker widen so it becomes increasingly important to possess *knowledge* of choices available for consideration; *skills* in negotiation and communication; and *experience* and training in carrying through decisions in a manner that is both impartial and professional. Though great leaders may be born, good decision-makers usually learn their skills from training and experience. There seems no reason why such training should not start with the children themselves: in the classrooms.

Deciding at 'class roots' level

Part of the problem of teaching is that we teachers want to do everything. Once safely inside our classroom we become master on our own stage: we decide the knowledge that is to be learnt; we control what learners will do; we probably talk for four-fifths of the time; finally we push our charges through some form of assessment that is likely to have serious consequences for their futures.[7] Such a monopoly of decision-making is also an exhausting business and it is not unusual to find ourselves quickly worn out by the exertions of the talking, writing, instructing and deciding we have experienced in one day. Our pupils, on the other hand, feel tired for other reasons: they have sat and listened, maybe for five or six hours at a stretch; have competed for the occasional 'right to reply'; have switched from one lesson to another (having been told to 'finish it off for homework'); and have been threatened or encouraged by the prospect of the examination in the not too distant future.

We exaggerate, of course, yet there are many of us the world over who conduct ourselves in this way. Many reasons can be found for such behaviour: our attitude to knowledge ('there is nothing to decide – it is either right or wrong'); traditional methods of instruction ('chalk and talk); or insufficient training in available alternatives – what we call a lack of awareness of 'room for manoeuvre'.

A start is to provide a critique of the decision-making procedure at 'class-roots' level, carefully examining necessary decisions that must be taken by the teacher, and those decisions that can easily (and often more effectively) be undertaken by the children. We are all guilty of underestimating the capacity and ability of children to act responsibly in the management of their own learning. Evidence exists too, in Child-to-Child programmes world wide, that children are quite capable of educating each other.[8]

We are suggesting that decisions at classroom level become more of a shared activity (not totally child- or teacher-centred); that the teacher liberates herself from the exhausting straitjacket she so often wears; and that the children be taught how to decide things that matter to them and their community.

We shall return to this issue of sharing at a later stage of this chapter and elsewhere throughout the book.

It would be wrong to assume that each participant in the decision-making matrix (classroom or different educational levels) has equal clout: much will depend upon traditional political hierarchies and accepted social practices. What is certain is that decision-making in the educational system is a sensitive barometer of power relations in society.[9] To every question, 'who decides?' is another: 'who does not?'.

Not all decisions are taken in isolation from each other: one will define the 'room for manoeuvre' of another. In this way decisions cascade upon each other, creating an interdependent 'chain of possibilities' with a concomitant chain of actors, participants, definers and deciders.

Quality decision-makers, aware of the effects of what they do (or do not do) are those, surely, who seek to work in harmony with their co-deciders and consequently to achieve more. This is the language of possibility.

THE CONTEXT OF DECISION-MAKING

It would be naïve to believe that educational decisions can be taken unfettered from the historical, social, economic and political context in which schools exist. Such a context critically affects individuals' 'room for manoeuvre at every level.

The historical context

All five countries were, in times past, colonial territories and many traditions remain embedded within their education. Colonial systems themselves were full of contradictions. On the one hand they professed doctrines of adaptation to environment as stated so powerfully in the British Colonial Office's memorandum *Education Policy in British Tropical Africa* (1925).[10] On the other they were committed to a restrictive, but nonetheless effective, policy of providing an academic education designed to produce efficient junior civil servants. This education taught them to write, spell, add and multiply correctly, but did not dispose them to ask too many questions.

Both strands have survived but the second predominates, often corrupted in its transmission by one hardpressed teacher to another. Exhortations from educationists, new policies and new syllabuses cannot easily change such traditions. They are born of the teacher's need to survive in difficult circumstances, the reassurance of long practice, the security of formality.

The economic context

We have already indicated the stark economic and demographic realities in which schools and communities operate. A national economic survey (1977) of Nepal's rural poor found that 72% of the average family's total consumption expenditure was allotted to food and that a mere 2% went to health and education.[11] It is not surprising therefore that parents in rural areas like Sidahwa in Eastern Nepal 'decide' to keep their children (and usually the girls) at home.

Equally, it is natural that when the government is poor but some of its citizens have a little more (sometimes a lot more) that others, these will strive to better their children's life chances by investing in their education. Hence the existence of high-cost private schools in Kenya and Indonesia and of parental supplementation of books and educational materials in all five countries.

The political context

The extent of political power and political will also critically affect decision-making, as do political ideologies. Although all countries profess concern for quality in primary education and for the equitable division of resources, the differences between words and action are often very noticeable. Whereas Nepal's commitment to primary education accounts for only 29% of its national expenditure, socialist Tanzania regularly commits over 55%.[12]

The social context

In a later chapter we shall examine the influence of community traditions and values on decision-making. They are crucial. But other

TABLE III ADULT LITERACY RATES

	1970		1985	
	MALE %	FEMALE %	MALE %	FEMALE %
Nepal	23	3	39	12
Kenya	44	19	70	49
Lesotho	49	74	62	84
Malaysia	71	48	81	66
Indonesia	66	42	83	65

Source: State of the World's Children, UNICEF, 1990

aspects are equally important. First the literacy rates within a country, and closely linked with these the access of women and other disadvantaged groups such as the rural poor and ethnic minorities to education.

Though we argue that more people can learn and participate in the decision-making process, particularly at local level, to be able to do so in modern times requires *literacy*. To be literate is to immediately increase one's potential 'room for manoeuvre', and literacy of mothers is especially important. Interestingly the literacy data for our five countries reveal discrepancies not only between male and female but also between 'rich' and 'poor' nations.

The data from Lesotho shows the danger of generalising from education statistics. Not only are there more women than men reading and writing, but more girls than boys complete primary and secondary school than is the case in the average low-income country.[13] The migration of young boys to tend livestock and young men to work in the gold-mines of South Africa accounts for this anomaly.

Participation of girls in primary education and their retention is clearly vital to enable them to share in decision-making. The urban–rural divide is also important. If a male decision-maker from a high-income family is likely to be educated, he is also likely to be urban-based. Traditional perceptions of decision-making may well reinforce the importance and status attached to these categories, retarding the enfranchisement of the majority in terms of participation in the economic, political and educational life of the country.

Nepal, as we have said earlier, is a predominantly rural country with 94% of its people living in villages. In spite of laudable efforts to take schooling out to the localities, enrolment figures for the 'remote areas' remain around the 51% level, compared to a national average of 66% (with over 85% enrolled in the Kathmandu area).[14] Although overall enrolment figures for Kenya and Indonesia are higher, the same urban–rural discrepancies are present, not only in enrolments but in a number of other factors including standards of buildings, distribution of equipment and qualifications of teachers.

So far we have been suggesting that quality, in terms of educational decision-making, is not only concerned with efficiency and relevance but also *equity*. By making the system fairer in terms of enlarging the circle of those who decide and by creating a feeling that the provision of schooling and its improvement is the responsibility of us all, we will in the long run make better use of existing capacity. To become involved is to care.

PATTERNS OF CONTROL: WHERE DECISIONS ARE TAKEN

To understand where decisions about education are taken within the political system is a complex affair. The OECD (1973) identified four levels of control: national, regional, local and school. If control is taken to refer to locations where power is exercised then it is usual in less developed countries for power to be centralised, with regional authorities existing not as decision-makers but as administrators carrying out policies decided elsewhere.

We must, therefore, in any discussion of patterns of control, be careful to distinguish between decentralisation (decision-making actually moved away from the centre) and localisation or regionalisation (the administration of policies centrally decided).[15]

Kenyan government ministers, like their counterparts in Nigeria, often refer to their style of governing as one reflecting 'unity through diversity'. What this actually means in practice is not always clear. What does seem clear is that most decision-makers support the principle of a change in the pattern of control towards more decentralisation.

Reasons for this are many: to redress the balance of representation of groups in the wielding of power; to increase local participation in the decision-making process and cynically perhaps to then contain potentially dissenting groups; or to genuinely relocate power to different parts of the country where particular needs can best be decided at local level.

The emergence of different patterns of control are often the result of fierce battles by competing groups for power resources. If resource allocation is strictly controlled by the central authorities then responsibility for deciding how such resources are best employed is left to the local authorities – this being the context in which they operate with more or less 'room for manoeuvre'.

Some central authorities struggling to find these resources (Kenya and Nepal for example) call upon the locality to shoulder some of the burden of educational expenditure. In Nepal, the village communities are asked to raise forty per cent of all funds needed for buildings improvement; and in Kenya the *harambee* ('self-help') spirit is often evoked when the centre finds its resources stretched. As we shall see when discussing aid, this pattern is often repeated at the international level.

Once the subject of resource allocation and use has been decided, a vast array of other areas of concern, e.g. determination of subjects on the curriculum, improvement of learning materials, methods of teaching, can be seen as lying legitimately within the province of the lower levels of the educational hierarchy. It seems that, in practice, many systems operate an official trade-off situation: power to allocate resources at the centre is traded against teachers at the periphery, who decide over such issues as methodology and use of materials.

There is, of course, always a tension when resources are scarce, between the demands for decentralisation and the demands of accountability. Central governments may feel, often with some justification, that if they devolve control without adequate safeguards such power may be misused and limited resources misapplied. For this and other less valid reasons it is possible therefore, as Lauglo and McLean have stated,[16] for specific areas of the education system to be decentralised without full control of all elements of decision-making transferring to the locality. However, for any successful sharing of decision-making to occur it is essential that all partners have equal access to critiques of existing constraints and choices.

Such a raising of awareness is a necessary prerequisite to any change in the decision-making process. This 'language of critique' should not be interpreted as necessarily leading to a radical overthrow of existing procedures and practices. It might simply lead to initiatives seeking improvement in tried, tested and traditional means of control. Difference is not necessarily more efficient, relevant or better.

Rather than talk about 'decentralisation' or 'centralisation' it may be more useful to examine the quality of decision-making at different levels. A better question might be not 'who decides?', but who *shares* in the decision-making process? Given the complexity of the constraints facing parents, teachers and educational administrators, sharing control of education seems desirable if only on pragmatic grounds.

IMPROVING DECISION-MAKING AT LOCAL LEVEL

Decision-making, as we suggested at the beginning of this chapter, can be introduced to the classroom in such a way that it becomes a normal part of the school curriculum. Children can be guided into activities in which a set goal is making, implementing and evaluating decisions: learning in their own way the twin language of critique and possibility. We are also looking to a widening of the circle of decision-makers at local level, to include more representatives of those who are so often excluded: women, the poor, and those living in rural areas. The Seti Project in Nepal shows that increased participation in education of those in remote areas can have generous 'spill-over' effects for rural development generally.

TABLE IV
OPTIMAL LOCATION FOR MAJOR EDUCATIONAL DECISIONS

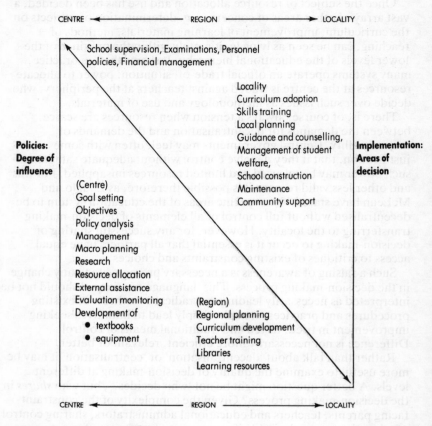

CENTRE ◄———————— REGION ————————► LOCALITY

School supervision, Examinations, Personnel policies, Financial management

Locality
Curriculum adoption
Skills training
Local planning
Guidance and counselling,
Management of student welfare,
School construction
Maintenance
Community support

Policies:
Degree of
influence

Implementation:
Areas of
decision

(Centre)
Goal setting
Objectives
Policy analysis
Management
Macro planning
Research
Resource allocation
External assistance
Evaluation monitoring
Development of
• textbooks
• equipment

(Region)
Regional planning
Curriculum development
Teacher training
Libraries
Learning resources

CENTRE ◄———————— REGION ————————► LOCALITY

Source: Noor, A., *The World Bank.*[17]

In terms of resources we are saying that rather than look to increases we must seek to 'exploit existing capacity' so that we: first, examine critically how we use what we have; and secondly, scrutinise how we can direct those resources to more efficient, relevant and 'better' ends.

In every locality we find one school that performs better than another. Equally, within schools, we discover some teachers and pupils making better use of the time, resources and opportunities open to them. Identifying these 'models of good practice' can help us decide ways in which we should improve the impoverished parts of the system. Through improved systems of information, communication and sharing of ideas, such good practice can be spread. We return to these issues in both Chapter Three and Chapter Seven.

IMPROVING DECISION-MAKING AT THE INTERNATIONAL LEVEL: THE QUESTION OF AID

In many ways the case we have been making for shared decision-making at local level can be made when we consider the control of international aid to education.

Quite often worthy projects, heavily funded by the large aid organisations, have failed to have any impact because at each stage of the development of the project scant regard has been paid to the involvement of local people in the decision-making process. Equally, mistakes are often made because those responsible for speaking the 'language of critique' (the university researchers for example) have little to do with those charged with implementing the decisions. This demarcation of roles may have something to do with our preconceived ideas about who traditionally decides what: the politician who analyses; the academic who implements; the local administrator who manages. By keeping each role and activity separate we are in danger of both wasteful duplication of effort and a misuse of existing scarce resources.

TABLE IV[17] shows an example of the possible division of roles and responsibilities.

Whether or not one agrees with this model, the concept of shared control and in particular sharing of resource allocation by centre and periphery is worthy of attention.

One of the particular problems of international aid is its propensity to engender passivity in its recipients. Paulo Freire, more eloquently, talks of the poor's 'culture of silence': a silence lacking any critical response to events enacted in their name. Whether schemes to 'share control' will rectify this is difficult to say, particularly as any rearrangement of control, be it educational or economic, will be seen by the privileged as an attack on their vested interests. If change in the external context is difficult, it seems all the more important for those working within the education system to strive for fairer patterns of control which in turn should lead to more efficient and relevant decision-making.

QUALITY: WHO DECIDES?

To understand the process of decision-making within an area as complicated as primary education requires both a 'language of critique', i.e. a knowledge of how decisions are taken, and a 'language of possibility', i.e. a knowledge of the part one can play in that process. The latter is more troublesome as it assumes certain philosophical and ideological positions, e.g. that one has a right to be involved, that one has something to offer, that the means by which decisions are made are as important as the ends. It is correctly argued that such positions are sustained or rejected by the culture from which they come. Many of the arguments of this chapter for example, draw upon the ideas and beliefs of the writers and the culture that has influenced them.

It has also to be recognised though that decision-makers do not work within a vacuum. Any praxis of reflection and action, critique and possibility operates within interrelated contexts both extrinsic and intrinsic to the education system of any particular country. For as we have seen, moves towards widening the circle of decision-making, increasing room for manoeuvre, exploiting existing capacity, etc. is constrained by a number of factors, most notably that of resources. However to stop there is to succumb to a negative, fatalistic view of change, to speak of critique without the hope of any possibility.

To do that is also to deny the existence of models of good practice, of efforts to share control, and of the need to work towards involving more people in the vitally important role of working towards improving the quality of education their children receive.

NOTES AND REFERENCES

1 Of the 32 259 teachers employed in the primary sector in 1982, 11 525 were trained. 78 of these held a university degree. *Primary Education in Nepal: a Status Report*, CERID, 1983.

2 Freire, P., *The Politics of Education. Culture, Power and Liberation*, Macmillan, 1985.

3 Mackie, R. (ed.), *Literacy and Revolution, the Pedagogy of Paulo Freire*, Pluto, 1980.

4 Giroux, H., *Theory and Resistance in Education: a Pedagogy for the Opposition*, Heinemann, 1983.

5 Freire, P., *Pedagogy of the Oppressed*, op. cit.

6 Lauglo, J. and McLean, M. (eds.), *Patterns of Control*, Heinemann/University of London Institute of Education, 1985.

7 Flanders, N. A., *Analysing Teacher Behaviour*, Addison-Wesley, 1970.

8 Hawes, H. W. R., *Child-to-Child: Another Path to Learning*, UNESCO Institute for Education, Hamburg, 1988.

9 Bowles, S., 'Towards equality of educational opportunity' in *Harvard Educational Review*, Vol. 38, No. 1, 1968.

10 Advisory Committee on Native Education *Educational Policy in British Tropical Africa*, Cmd. 2374. Reproduced in Scanlon *Traditions of African Education*, Columbia University Press, 1964.

11 Shrestha, G. M. *et al.*, 'Determinants of educational participation in rural Nepal' in *Comparative Education Review*, 30, 4, 1982.

12 Cooksey, B., 'Policy and practice in Tanzania secondary education since 1967' in *International Journal of Educational Development*, Vol. 6, No. 3, 1986.

13 LESOTHO: A Primary school enrolment ratio
                  102–127% (m:f), 1986–88 gross.
            B Secondary school enrolment ratio
                  18–26% (m:f), 1986–88 gross.
   NEPAL: A 76–35% (m:f) 1986–88 net.
            B 35–11% (m:f), 1986–88 net.

Source: *State of the World's Children, 1990.*

14 *Primary Education in Nepal*, op. cit.

15 See Stephens, D. G., 'Decentralisation of education in Northern Nigeria: a case of continuing "indirect rules"?' in Lauglo, J. and McLean, M. (eds.), *The Control of Education*, op. cit.

16 Lauglo, J. and McLean, M., op. cit.

17 Noor, A., 'Shared control of education: theory, practice, and impressions from education projects assisted by the World Bank', Unpublished Paper, University of London Institute of Education, 1983.

QUALITY AND CHANGE: THE QUALITY WHEEL

In the first two chapters we have stressed the importance of defining and improving quality in primary education in a world in which the citizens of developing countries can either seek to control their own futures or rest content to be controlled by other forces. We have warned against the danger of accepting simplistic and partial views of quality because they are easier, safer or more convenient to understand. (The blind man may be forgiven for failing to appreciate the elephant, but what of the sighted man who approaches the beast with his eyes tight shut.)

We have also uncovered a whole tangle of conflicting understandings and motives among those who seek qualitative improvement: motives which need to be uncovered, which may to some extent be harmonised with each other, but which can never fully be reconciled.

ATTEMPTS TO IMPROVE QUALITY

Developing countries attempt to better their primary education in three main ways.

More Schools

The first is, quite simply, by sending more children to school. For while it is dangerous to think of increases in percentage enrolments as synonymous with educational improvement and while we may need to look very sharply both at official figures and their interpretation,[1] there is no doubt that the figures showing increases in children attending primary schools are impressive, the more so because they have been achieved against the economic tide.[2]

These increases do not represent empty political gestures, but rather a genuine wish by governments and parents to give as many children as possible the right start. For however deficient a school is, the prospect of children meeting minimum literacy and numeracy needs out of school is far bleaker.

New goals and content

The second set of actions to improve quality are the genuine attempts in very large numbers of countries to plan and provide content which is both efficient and relevant, though the third element in our earlier definition, the 'something more', may often be given scant attention.[3]

Over the last decade, national statements of goals have become a

TABLE V
ENROLMENTS IN PRIMARY EDUCATION IN 22 SELECTED COUNTRIES
(IN COMPARISON WITH RATES OF ECONOMIC AND POPULATION GROWTH)

COUNTRY	GNP PER CAPITA IN US DOLLARS	GNP GROWTH AVERAGE GROWTH RATE % 1965–87	POPULATION GROWTH % PER ANNUM		INFLATION ANNUAL RATE 1980–87	GROWTH OF PRODUCTION (GDP)		PERCENTAGE OF AGE GROUP IN PRIMARY SCHOOL 1965–86					
			1965–80	1980–87		1965–80	1980–87	TOTAL	M	F	TOTAL	M	F
*Nepal	160	.5	2.4	2.7	8.8	1.9	4.7	20	36	4	79	104	47
Bangladesh	160	.3	2.8	2.8	11.1	2.4	3.8	49	67	31	60	69	50
Tanzania	180	-.4	3.3	3.5	24.9	3.7	1.7	32	40	25	69	70	69
Burkina Faso	190	1.6	2.1	2.6	4.4	3.5	5.6	12	16	8	35	45	26
Zambia	250	2.1	3.0	3.6	28.7	1.9	-0.1	53	59	46	104	112	101
India	300	1.8	2.3	2.1	7.7	3.7	4.6	74	89	57	92	107	76
*Kenya	330	1.9	3.6	4.1	10.3	6.4	3.8	54	69	40	94	97	91
Sudan	330	-1.5	2.8	3.1	31.7	3.8	-0.1	29	37	21	50	59	41
Pakistan	350	2.5	3.1	3.1	7.3	5.1	6.6	40	59	20	44	59	32
*Lesotho	370	4.7	2.3	2.7	12.3	5.9	2.3	94	74	114	115	102	127
Nigeria	370	1.1	2.5	3.4	10.1	6.9	-1.7	32	39	24	92	103	81
Sri Lanka	400	3.0	1.8	1.5	11.8	4.0	4.6	94	98	114	102	102	127
*Indonesia	450	4.5	2.4	2.1	8.5	8.0	3.6	72	79	65	118	121	116
Zimbabwe	580	.9	3.1	3.7	12.4	4.4	2.4	110	128	92	129	132	126
Philippines	590	1.7	2.9	2.5	16.7	5.9	0.5	113	115	111	106	107	106
Egypt	680	3.5	2.2	2.7	9.2	6.8	6.3	75	90	60	87	96	77
Cote D'Ivoire	740	1.0	4.2	4.2	4.4	6.8	2.8	60	80	41	78	92	65
Thailand	850	3.9	2.9	2.0	2.8	7.2	5.6	78	82	44	99	..	..
Botswana	1050	8.9	3.5	3.4	8.4	14.2	13.0	65	59	71	105	101	109
*Malaysia	1810	4.1	2.5	2.7	1.1	7.4	4.5	90	96	84	99	100	99
UK	10420	1.7	0.2	0.1	5.7	2.4	2.6	92	92	92	106	105	106
USA	18530	1.5	1	1	4.3	2.7	3.1	..	..	..	102	103	101

Source: World Bank World Development Report 1989

NOTE: With a population growth rate of 3.5%, population doubles in 20 years; at 2.4% it takes 30.

good deal sharper and better prioritised, though some countries such as Nepal have still to make progress.[4]

Consider, however, the examples from the four other countries associated with this study.

In Lesotho, a national debate was mounted in 1977 and 1978 to collect and summarise the views of the Basotho nation on the purpose of education.[5] This has been used as a resource in subsequent planning of content. Although current syllabuses lack a statement of general objectives, the task force appointed in connection with the Education Sector Survey in 1982 has some very precise ones.[6]

In 1977 Kenya mounted a national commission on educational objectives[7] from which many subsequent statements derive. Current primary syllabuses (1986) contain a thoughtful set of objectives for primary education as a whole, while most subject-syllabuses contain sets of specific objectives ranked in varying degres of precision and standards of assessment.[8]

Indonesia has elaborate and carefully formulated sets of aims and objectives, starting from statements of national goals and hence educational objectives and extending to general objectives for each subject; specific curricular objectives for each grade level; and instructional objectives for each unit in the curriculum. All these statements are reconsidered at each national curriculum revision exercise and are published in the national curriculum document.

Equally detailed and carefully worded formulations come from Malaysia and are reproduced in TABLES VI and VII.[9]

TABLE VI: GENERAL AIMS OF THE NEW PRIMARY CURRICULUM, MALAYSIA, 1981

1 Master Bahasa Malaysia satisfactorily, appropriate to its status as the national and official language of the country
2 Master the basic linguistic skills, i.e. to converse, read and write in the medium of instruction of the school
3 Acquire a strong foundation in mathematical skills
4 Acquire study skills
5 Understand, read, write and converse in English in line with its status as the second language
6 Develop desirable attitudes and behaviours based on the humanistic and spiritual values accepted and valued by the society as embodied in The *Rukunegara*, and to make these the basis of daily practices
7 Acquire knowledge of and understanding, an interest in, and sensitivity towards man and his environment
8 Interact socially, respect the rights and capabilities of other people and possess the spirit of co-operation and tolerance

9 Develop their talents, leadership ability and self-confidence to widen their knowledge and to improve their ability by using the basic skills already mastered
10 Show interest, understand, appreciate and participate in cultural and recreational activities that are within the context of the national culture.

Source: Kementerian Pelajaran, Kurikulum Baru Sekolah Rendah: matlamat, rasional, bidang pelajaran dan strategi pengajaran dan pembelajaran [The New Primary School Curriculum: aims, rationale, areas of study and teaching and learning strategy,] Kuala Lumpur, Kementerian, 1981, p. 4.

TABLE VII: OBJECTIVES FOR THE MALAYSIAN LANGUAGE CURRICULUM, 1981

1 Value and show pride in Bahasa Malaysia as the national language of the country and the instrument of national unity in accordance with the spirit and principles of The *Rukunegara*
2 Listen and understand conversations and broadcasts in daily life in and outside the school
3 Converse and express ideas using the appropriate language in a variety of situations such as in conversations with friends, teachers and parents, as well as in debates and lectures
4 Read aloud and silently to understand the contents of the passages appropriate to the maturity of the pupils and to make reading a habit for the acquisition of knowledge and for entertainment
5 Write compositions and letters that are accurate in meaning and relevant to the titles, and be able to fill appropriate forms for daily needs
6 Use Bahasa Malaysia in studying about man and his environment
7 Use Bahasa Malaysia as an instrument in widening knowledge and experiences
8 Appreciate prose and poetry.

Notes: In addition to the romanised script which is used throughout the school system, pupils will be taught to spell, read and write in the Jawi script from Year 4.
Source: Primary School Syllabus, Malaysian Language, Kuala Lumpur: 1981, pp. 1–2.

Such statements of objectives, now the rule rather than the exception, indicate that far more careful thought is presently being applied to the essential issue of deciding the purpose and direction of primary education. While cynics can point out that good purposes without subsequent actions do not get very far, it is equally true that without adequate goals action can be without direction.

New structures and policies

The third set of initiatives to improve quality are those attempts, evident over the past twenty years in almost every country, to set primary education on a new footing. These may be subdivided into three categories: smaller scale experiments; large scale primary improvement projects; and fundamental nationwide policy changes.

The first category comprises those projects, very frequently aid supported, which attempt to introduce innovative ideas and practices into primary education, even to 'break the mould' of current primary schools. Often these obtain greater publicity and honour outside their countries of origin than within them, and while they have frequently generated very important 'spin offs' in educational improvement there has always been a danger that the diet they provide would prove too rich and indigestible for national systems wholly to ingest.

Such innovations have included the Impact project[10] in the Philippines and its offshoots round the world,[11] the Namutamba and Bunumbu projects in Uganda and Sierra Leone[12] and many others. In the five countries surveyed in this study we can count the Model School project in Lesotho,[13] the Pahang Tenggara Integrated Education project[14] in Malaysia and the Development Schools Project in Indonesia.[15]

The second group includes those much larger 'Primary Improvement projects' which, though they are aid supported and sometimes even aid initiated, nevertheless receive full support and generate large scale commitment from the national government. Such projects usually aim to develop a substantial and critical mass of schools which can then be used as a platform from which to raise the generality of other schools until such time as all are following the new approach. They have included, in the past, very large initiatives such as the 'New Primary Approach' in Kenya[16] and the Primary Education Improvement Project in Nigeria[17] and in our own time are represented by a very considerable number of primary improvement projects in Zimbabwe, Botswana, Bangladesh, Andrah Pradesh and many other countries.

In Lesotho we see an example of such a project in the B.A.N.F.E.S.[18] programme, in collaboration with USAID and in Nepal the 'Primary Education Project' with UNICEF.

The final category comprises those instances where the government sets out completely to redefine both the goals of primary education and the approach to it, and to transform the system by putting its new policies into action. A classic and unfortunately not over-successful example of this was the attempt to introduce Education for Self-Reliance in Tanzania.

Such programmes sometimes result from fundamental changes in philosophy but, more often, as in Kenya, may represent an attempt to alter course to meet amended political priorities as well as new structures and patterns of control. However, even such less drastic approaches often require more planning and resources than they receive.

By contrast, the 1982 Malaysian reform which concentrates in almost equal measure on defining minimum 'standards' and ensuring that teachers approach their teaching in a creative and stimulating way, lacks neither resources nor support, and must be counted as one of the best planned and most successful attempts at primary school reform in Asia.[19]

INTENTIONS AND REALITY

There seems little doubt, therefore, concerning the *intention* in most countries to improve quality in their primary schools. There are those however who would argue that good intentions without corresponding effective action are not merely valueless but even positively harmful. This is because announced intentions may hoodwink people, including the policy makers themselves, into the belief that something very positive has been achieved by the ideas themselves however much they differ from what actually happens.

For, as we have indicated in our first chapter, there is a disturbing amount of evidence that in many systems the word and the deed are grossly at variance. That despite the increased numbers of schools, the curriculum changes, the experimental and large scale projects and the national programmes in primary reform, many, if not most, ordinary schools haven't changed substantially or may even have changed for the worse. This may be because practice has become more inefficient in the face of rising numbers and shrinking resources, or because content has become increasingly irrelevant to current needs or increasingly unteachable in the circumstances in which schools now find themselves.

Given the fact that so many planned innovations appear to have failed in their goals to better quality, should we just give up trying? Should we conclude that education, particularly formal education, is conservative and inert and that the best we can hope for is to nibble slowly away at current practices in the hope of achieving their gradual improvement?

This view is very commonly held, so commonly indeed that we have heard it advanced by aid donors as a reason for allocating resources outside the formal education section rather than to schools, but we should be unwise to accept it for a number of reasons.

The first is that the evidence presented is very partial. A great deal of the literature on the acceptance of innovation worldwide and practically all the literature on innovation in LDCs relates to the acceptance or rejection of *projects* rather than to programmes and approaches within the system as a whole.[20] Many projects are rejected because they are recognised for what they are, imposed by an outside interest group for their own motives and, for one reason or another, are deemed unacceptable or unsuitable in the schools for which they were intended.

41

Moreover, generalisations about these projects, pronouncing them successes or, more often, failures are often far too sweeping. Many already mentioned: the Impact project in the Philippines[10] or its Indonesian counterpart, Pamong,[11] and larger ventures such as the New Primary Approach in Kenya[16] and Northern Nigeria's Primary Education Improvement project[17] may not have reached the objectives they set themselves, but they are not in every sense failures. The Pamong project failed in its original intention to reduce costs and increase pupil ratio in Central Java (a province in which there is actual overproduction of teachers), but was taken up avidly in East Java where its modular approach was found very useful in accommodating dropouts who wanted to drop back into the formal system. The New Primary Approach failed to extend its activity-based methods into rural schools totally without the facilities to absorb it, but transformed Nairobi city schools which had adequate facilities. The Nigerian Primary Education Improvement project, with its emphasis on process skills in the classroom and on the use of mobile teacher trainers to improve quality in schools, was overwhelmed by the Nigerian announcement of universal primary education. But many of the materials it has generated have been used elsewhere in Africa and its experience in school based in-service training has proved valuable for planning new initiatives both in Nigeria and elsewhere.[21]

We should also be particularly wary in labelling systems as 'inert', 'conservative' or 'slow to change'. Such assertions are often quite demonstrably untrue, for people in those same systems have proved themselves capable of changing very swiftly when they understand that the change is in their own interests. Schools in the West have found little difficulty in accepting micro-computers and parents have proved happy to learn the skills for operating them from their children. Similarly in poorer countries the acceptance, in community health, of the message of immunisation (a very complicated concept with numerous cultural overtones) has proved far easier than anticipated. Here too it has been significant that the older generation has shown itself surprisingly willing to accept messages from the younger one. Consequently schools may well be in a position to change quite rapidly if they can be convinced that it is in their interests to do so.

Moreover it is certain that the experiences of the last decades, sobering though they may be, have added considerably to our knowledge of how and why change takes place and what inhibits it. Theoretically, at least, it should therefore be possible for those who seek to influence qualitative changes to profit from such experience and use it to shape policies and strategies. Possibly the best and most comprehensive analysis of such experience is provided by Hurst in a paper written in 1983.[22] Following a critical review of the literature he deduces seven important conditions for the acceptance of innovation: communication; relevance or desirability; feasibility; efficiency; trialability and adaptability. Later in the chapter when we present a model to explain the process of planned change we shall draw upon many of these concepts.

The final reason for not accepting this thesis is that we simply cannot afford to do so. Investment of money, time and hope in primary schooling is too great to be disappointed. Only through schooling can new ideas and attitudes quickly reach the great mass of the next generation. So while there is unprecedented popular concern that schools are not as they should be, virtually no one supports disestablishing them or disinvesting in them. The prophets of de-schooling called from the clouds. None heeded them.

A MODEL FOR THE ASSESSMENT AND IMPROVEMENT OF QUALITY

In order to guide our attempts to improve quality at primary school level we need a model which will reflect the complexity of the elements which determine quality and qualitative improvement and indicate their inter-relation and inter-dependence. For this purpose we have chosen the analogy of a wheel with a centre hub and two concentric rings to provide strength and enable the whole to roll forward (Figure I).

At the centre we locate the basic elements of quality common in any system: the categories of goals and basic principles of practice which determine relevance and efficiency.

In the 'inner wheel' we fix the conditions which determine successful implementation of qualitative improvement, a slimmed down version of Hurst's categories.

Finally, on the outer rim we place the agents of implementation who are to take action co-operatively if the wheel is to roll forward smoothly.

Thus the quality wheel looks like this:

Figure 1

43

Let us now examine these three circles one by one.

THE HUB OF THE WHEEL

(a) The goals of quality: a relevant education

Based on the analysis of the tasks which good education has always set itself, together with those new challenges we have identified as needing to be faced if we are to live effectively in the twenty-first century and beyond, we can isolate four comprehensive goals for general education which in our opinion subsume all others.

Education must:

1 Meet individual and community needs, both in respect of 'needs now' and 'needs later'.
2 Lay a foundation for lifelong learning and the ability to support change.
3 Provide whole learning, encompassing the different areas of experience which learners need to encounter as well as depth of experience necessary for the development of the mind.
4 Relate to the survival and development of the human species.

(b) Principles of practice: an efficient education

Alongside these principles of relevance we need to isolate four principles of practice and pedagogy which are necessary to ensure that such goals are efficiently transmitted from school and teacher to the learner. Thus education needs to be:

1 Learner-based.
 That is, sensitive to the physical, psychological, social and moral development of the learner.
2 Rooted in direct experience.
 That is, linked with the social experience and cultural values of the learner and devoted to building upon and widening such experience and values.
3 Sequential.
 That is, governed by effective principles of sequencing for individuals as well as for groups of learners.
4 Resource-based.
 That is, based upon those resources which are actually available in manpower, money, materials and time.

Let us examine the implications of these eight concepts one by one.

1 The elements of quality

1 Needs

We have already considered how complex is the task of identifying relevant needs. To balance individual with group needs, 'needs now' with 'needs later'; to identify different orders of needs from Maslow's survival needs through to his self-esteem and self-actualisation needs, is a daunting task. But this does not absolve planners from attempting it. People and societies *are* complicated and if we are to serve them we need to seek a better understanding of their nature.

Certainly there can be no doubt of the importance of recognising and agreeing minimum learning needs which need to be met by all schools. There have been a number of statements of such needs and that which follows is an adaptation of a list suggested by Coombs and Ahmed.

Every school should seek to achieve the following with *all* its leavers:

Positive attitudes towards helping families and communities; towards work and towards continued learning.
Functional literacy and numeracy – linked with opportunities for its continued development and use.
An introduction to logical and scientific thought and the elementary understanding of the processes of nature.
Functional knowledge and skills necessary to become a useful community member.
Functional knowledge of health care for self and community.

When such needs are addressed by schools they will have to be both carefully described and moderated to suit regional, local and individual differences. A goal of 'adequate literacy' immediately invites a host of descriptors:

In what language?
For what purpose?
What are the minimum
        average
          higher
            goals of attainment for learners of different abilities,
and different linguistic and social backgrounds?

Note also that they need to be addressed by schools and not solely through classroom instruction. Schools meet needs by effecting lasting behaviour change in children. To achieve such change depends upon the life and ethos of the school, the relationship of that school with its community and upon the competencies and personalities of the head and the teachers, to a much greater extent than it does upon the content of the syllabus or the lesson plan.

2 Laying a foundation for lifelong learning and the need to support change

This involves developing not only skills of learning how to learn but also the attitudes which enable learners to support change.

45

In many respects this goal overlaps with the previous one. Maslow's self-esteem and self-actualisation needs imply the development of autonomy. We need to consider it separately for two reasons. The first is that it is so vitally important and so commonly underemphasised; the second because it implies a different and wider view of the teaching/ learning process from that normally held by teachers and curriculum workers.

Commonly a school accepts the need to teach something (*content*) in a certain way (*method*) within the supporting framework of a good classroom and school environment. The success of the whole operation is measured by whether that 'something' is retained by the learner, and adjudged to be mastered by a test administered at a certain time, after which time its retention assumes less importance. The responsibility for success or failure rests centrally with the teacher. If, through some particular quality, a loving nature, a charismatic personality or a terrifying presence, that teacher manages to 'get results' then her method is commonly accepted as successful.

However, the educational goal of promoting self-learning turns the whole process inside out. The central element now becomes the method which learners acquire in order to gain new knowledge and skills and transfer them to other circumstances. The criterion for success is not the ability to perform well at school at a given time but to retain and extend the skills gained into further learning situations and life. The teacher's success is measured by her ability to organise learning rather than to inculcate knowledge and skills. The school's success is measured by its ability to develop autonomy in learners. There is therefore a tension, and not an unmanageable one, between the knowledge/skills-centred and method/approach-centred goals.

3 Providing whole learning for 'whole people'

An education of quality must seek to develop the whole mind and personality of learners and not just selective parts of them. This involves developing what we shall call 'breadth' and 'depth' in both thought and experience.

Breadth

'Breadth' involves knowing about a range of subjects and developing a variety of skills for learning and living; but it is much more than this. 'Breadth' involves an understanding of the different ways we approach and validate truth.[24] For the way we seek to establish truth in mathematics; in environmental science; in the study of people in history or literature; in motor mechanics; in religion or in art is fundamentally different. Hence the attempt of great educators, from Aristotle two thousand years ago[25] to educational writers such as Phenix[26] and Hirst[27] in recent years, to define the areas of knowledge necessary for learners to learn if they are to receive a 'balanced curriculum'.

It is vitally necessary that those who plan and deliver such a curriculum appreciate the meaning and importance of such a balance.

A child at primary school learns mathematics not only so that he can make change in the market but also because it develops the power to deal with abstract and exact relationships.

He learns social studies not just to gain important knowledge about his community, but so that he can learn to 'get inside other people' and thus begin to appreciate how people feel and why they act as they do.

He learns science not just to understand how scientific principles can help food production, but also to learn to apply a scientific method of thinking to solving life's problems.

He learns art not just to make things but to experience the excitement of creating.

Such different ways of approaching these truths are not necessarily linked directly to school subjects, especially at primary level, and they are certainly not confined to classroom practice.

Recently the Inspectorate in England and Wales have been using the useful phrase 'areas of experience'. They have noted nine such areas in the curriculum from 5–16: aesthetic and creative; human and social; linguistic and literary; mathematical; moral; physical; scientific; spiritual; technological.[28]

We might argue in favour of health as an additional area of experience, thus giving ten areas. But whatever the final list contains, the specification and analysis of such areas of experience is essential to understanding 'breadth' of knowledge and hence vital to quality. We also believe that such qualities are universal. A child in the Himalayas or the Drakensberg mountains needs to understand these ways of thinking every bit as much as a city child in Nairobi or Kuala Lumpur.

Depth

This necessary 'breadth' of learning is not enough. 'Depth' must also be developed through a disciplined initiation into processes of thought necessary to understand a complex world, solve problems and cope with change. Never before has it been more important for children to grow up with the ability to 'reason why'.

All of us recognise this fact in principle. But unfortunately once we realise that high-sounding catch phrases, 'training the mind', 'activity and experience', etc. do not really help us effectively to select the right content in the right order, we are again forced into examining and interpreting a very complex map of knowledge. The attempts of Bloom, Krathwohl[29] and their associates in the 1950s and 1960s to classify educational goals have been widely misunderstood and misapplied as an instrument for curriculum planners, but as a simple framework for understanding what we must seek to teach learners they have never been superseded. TABLE VIII gives some examples of how the six levels in Bloom's cognitive domain are gradually deepened and developed through a good primary school programme.

47

TABLE VIII BROAD CATEGORIES IN THE COGNITIVE DOMAIN OF BLOOM'S TAXONOMY OF EDUCATIONAL OBJECTIVES WITH ILLUSTRATIVE EXAMPLES FROM THREE PRIMARY SCHOOLS CURRICULUM AREAS

BLOOM'S CATEGORIES	EXAMPLES FROM MATHEMATICS	EXAMPLES FROM SOCIAL STUDIES	EXAMPLES FROM HEALTH
1 Knowledge as a Product			
(1.1) Knowledge of specific facts	Numbers 1–100	Names of towns in Kenya	Parts of the body
(1.2) Ways and means of dealing with them	How we measure weight (units and their relationships)	Sequence of historical events	Life cycle of a disease
(1.3) Universals and abstraction	Theories of Pythagoras	The concept of ecology	The concept of mental health
2 Comprehension			
(2.1) 'Translation'	Translating an oral statement into a mathematical one	Relating a picture to a map	Recognising signs of dehydration
(2.2) Understanding	Grasping relationships to enable learners to solve a problem in geometry	Understanding how pictures are made	Understanding why epidemics of diarrhoea happen in a population
(2.3) Going beyond the information given (inference and extrapolation)	Recognising a pattern and sequence in mathematical statements and predicting the next in a series: e.g. 4 – 9 – 19 – 39 –(79)	Inferring probable climate from a relief map	Predicting what might happen if child suffered from continuous attacks of diarrhoea

TABLE VIII   BROAD CATEGORIES IN THE COGNITIVE DOMAIN OF BLOOM'S TAXONOMY OF EDUCATIONAL OBJECTIVES WITH ILLUSTRATIVE EXAMPLES FROM THREE PRIMARY SCHOOLS CURRICULUM AREAS *(continued)*

BLOOM'S CATEGORIES	EXAMPLES FROM MATHEMATICS	EXAMPLES FROM SOCIAL STUDIES	EXAMPLES FROM HEALTH
3 Application	Using measurement to improve methods of planting	Finding one's direction with a compass and a map	Making a salt and sugar solution and feeding it to a child with diarrhoea
4 Analysis	Analysing the mathematics a builder needs to construct a house	Analysing and classifying occupations in a neighbourhood	Analysing and graphing causes of accidents in the neighbourhood
5 Synthesis (5.1) Production of a unique communication (5.2) Production of a plan	Making up one's own problems Planning the steps necessary in constructing a scale model of a house	Writing up a survey planned by the teacher Making an original plan of a survey of a pond or stream	Writing a play with a health message Planning a health campaign in a village
6 Evaluation (6.1) Evaluation from evidence given (6.2) Evaluation using broader judgements	Learning to find one's own mistakes in mathematical problems Judging whether a solution to a problem was the 'best', 'quickest', 'easiest' one	Evaluating whether a survey had achieved its purpose Deciding whether a community was 'living together well'	Evaluating whether an immunisation campaign had been successful Assessing how 'healthy' a community is

The process of analysis and progressive development of competencies extends inevitably from general goals to specific areas of experience. There are specific thinking skills and learning competencies applicable, for example, to science, language and moral education and there are no short cuts towards seeking to identify them and work them into a programme. The school cannot abscond from its prime task of teaching young people to think straight.

> A child who leaves school able to read an advertisement but unable to recognise the point of view of the advertiser.
> A child who can understand mathematics but is unable to apply its principles to farming.
> A child who knows scientific facts but is ignorant of how to reason scientifically.
> A child who knows religious dogma but ignores the moral principles which underlie it.
> . . . that child is anybody's football.

4 Relating to the survival and development of the human species

This goal overlaps with those already described but needs to be isolated both because of its importance and because of the particular nature of the learning it engenders.

For while, on the one hand, we are talking of developing skills and attitudes, whole people, thinking people, and autonomous people able to comprehend both the nature of development and the threats to it – we are, at the same time also referring much more crudely to the need positively to indoctrinate young minds, for youth does not automatically recognise the long term dangers of waste, over-population and aggression any more than it does the virtues of nationhood.

Thus just as children have been indoctrinated to love their countries and respect their past, so we submit that it is a major role for primary education through its content in all subjects, through the life of the school and the example of its teachers, to emphasise those development and survival priorities we described at the very outset of this book.

II Principles of practice

We stressed that in order effectively to communicate these goals to learners primary schools should provide content which is learner-based, experience-based, sequential – and resource-based. Let us now examine each of these.

1 Learner-based content.

Courses in child development and educational pyschology are part of the repertoire of teacher education courses all over the world. No educationist in our five countries would dispute that it is essential to design and deliver content which children are able to assimilate and willing to learn.

50

TABLE IX VARIATIONS IN UNDERSTANDING OF MATHEMATICAL CONSERVATION AMONG RURAL KENYAN CHILDREN (1977)

(Carried out by Mureria and Okatcha in rural schools 20 miles northwest of Nairobi.)

Fifteen boys and fifteen girls were tested from each of Classes I, III, V and VII. The average ages of classes ranged from 7 years 8 months to 13 years 9 months. Three tests were administered on conservation of **Length, Area** and **Volume.** The results were as follows:

They are expressed as a ratio of conservers to non-conservers thus:
Conservers (3)/Non-Conservers (12) = 3/12.

CLASS	I	III	V	VII
Length				
Boys	4/11	8/7	11/4	13/2
Girls	4/11	3/12	9/6	12/3
Area				
Boys	0/15	10/5	10/5	10/5
Girls	2/13	1/14	5/10	8/7
Volume				
Boys	5/10	4/11	9/6	10/5
Girls	0/15	3/11	7/8	7/8

But to do so is not easy as it looks for a number of reasons. The first is that far too little is known about learners and learning in different cultural contexts. Such a lack of knowledge is compounded by the considerable difficulties which psychologists appear to experience in simplifying and generalising their findings so that they can be made use of by curriculum workers, teacher educators and teachers. As a result, few if any simple texts are available in any of our five countries which summarise or incorporate relevant recent findings by national psychologists.[30]

Even when findings are clear they may prove embarrassing. Abstractions contained in social studies programmes based on national philosophies may turn out to be beyond the comprehension of younger children, yet they are retained because the government wishes them to be taught.

Research into the capacity of children to understand mathematical concepts may reveal, as it has done in Kenya (TABLE IX),[31] very wide variations in cognitive abilities among children of the same school: some children in the lower classes being able to 'conserve'[32] length, area and volume whilst others in the upper classes cannot. The implications of such variations in a system which offers universal primary education and operates of necessity a policy of automatic promotion are immense.

51

To devise content which is more learner-based will not, therefore, be easy. Nonetheless a number of strategies need to be tried if quality is to be improved. An essential preliminary is certainly to generate far more down-to-earth research on learning and learners in different contexts and cultures in relation to the tasks they are expected to perform. From such an analysis information of importance will emerge. It will undoubtedly be discovered that a proportion (we suspect an uncomfortably large proportion) of syllabuses, books and visual material presents difficulties in understanding to a considerable number of the learners for whom it is designed. Only once these difficulties are known is it possible to find ways in which 'a body of knowledge can be structured so that it can be more readily grasped by the learners'[33] or to find methods which can help to simplify the abstract and open doors between adult concepts and children's interest and understanding. Thus, as before, the language of critique must precede the language of action, while action itself starts at the 'class-roots' level with a rethinking of the methods with which teachers communicate to children.

2 Experience-based learning

The second vital principle governing the approach to good primary education is that learning needs to be rooted in a child's experience.

This does not imply a content which fails to broaden such experience but rather one which anchors learning in reality. A child whose first school-learning is fundamentally divorced from his home-learning may well maintain 'home-think' and 'school think' in separate boxes throughout his school life, with increasingly disturbing results to his effectiveness as a citizen and community member.

The 'half-learned' school-leaver has been the butt of writers the world over, not only because he is such a tragi-comic figure so easy for others to use but also because he is very common.

The divorce between school and home often starts with the very first books he receives. A child who learns to read in a language other than his own or, most particularly, in a language which he has never heard spoken before, begins his education at a serious disadvantage. So too does the child whose first lessons and first texts, as in Nepal, are full of examples foreign to his experience.

While these arguments are often accepted in a general way by educators in developing countries, traditions of centralisation, patterns of curriculum and instruction, and lack of resources often intervene to overcome them. These are analysed in later chapters. Meanwhile it remains certain that the mismatch between planned content and the experience of the learners remains one of the greatest single barriers to quality in primary schools in many developing countries.

3 Effective sequencing

No one would deny that learning should be effectively sequenced. At first sight this seems straightforward. We build up from the known to the unknown according to the logic of the subject and the level of understanding of the learners. It is not useful, for instance, to attempt geometrical problems unless learners can recognise shapes and know how to measure.

But, as so often, what seems to be simple at first turns out, on second view, to be curiously complex. In the first place principles of sequencing vary greatly between subjects and in many cases depend for their strength on a spiral approach, returning and revisiting concepts so that they are widened and deepened as children grow older. Moreover, sequence needs also to be influenced by the experiences available to a child which may vary unpredictably. Both these truths, for truths they are, make life more difficult for tidy-minded curriculum planners.

'Why teach about nutrition in Grade V,' they ask, 'when it has already been covered in Grade III?'

'Why change round a logically constructed programme to fit in to the vagaries of the weather or the unpredictability of national or international events?'

In the second place, and far more critically, we need to accommodate sequence to *learning* rather than teaching. It is the child, and not the teacher, who travels the path of learning and some groups and individuals do it much faster than others. This poses grave implications for the planning of content.

Let us for the sake of example represent learning as a ladder. Many programmes, particularly in skills subjects such as language and mathematics, are designed in a series of steps.

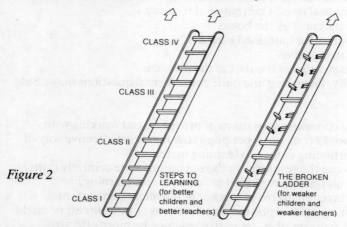

CLASS IV

CLASS III

CLASS II

Figure 2

CLASS I

STEPS TO LEARNING
(for better children and better teachers)

THE BROKEN LADDER
(for weaker children and weaker teachers)

Now suppose, as frequently happens, a class in first year only completes three steps instead of four, or some individuals in that class only just manage two steps. Such groups and individuals would have to try to jump the gap and start at the next section of the ladder where the new syllabus and textbook begins. But this they would find difficult or impossible because they are slow climbers anyway: the logical sequence of learning is broken and the class or the individual joins the ranks of the half-learners.

The solutions to these problems are, again, not easy and fundamentally affect current approaches to textbook design, school administration and testing; but they are very difficult to ignore. None of us as parents would readily send children up a ladder with broken or rotten rungs.

4 Resource-based learning

The importance of basing learning on the availability of manpower, money, materials and time is unquestioned. Those of us who have seen quite heart-breaking instances of children trying to learn book knowledge without books, or teachers attempting to teach what they cannot understand or classes trying to cover content which is by its very length and nature uncoverable, will have no doubt about the educational carnage such actions lead to. Moreover, anyone with a sense of equity will readily realise that in such situations it is always the children from richer and more educated parents who stand some chance of survival. The poor, as so frequently, have very little.

However, though the dangers of learning planned without heed to the resources available are plain to see, they are less easy to remedy given pressures of numbers and expectations, shrinking budgets and the effects of the diploma disease which forces schools and teachers to 'cover' topics whether or not they have the adequate resources to do so. So while solutions do exist which could ameliorate the situation, they are all fairly radical ones. Conventional responses:

'. . . let the parents buy the books'
'. . . run courses for untrained teachers'
'. . . prune the syllabus'

do not always strike at the root of the problem.

Additionally, disturbing and quite fundamental questions may need to be asked:

- Is the conventional pattern of providing and working with textbooks (one book per pupil) the most cost effective way of apportioning money to learning materials?
- How can the resources in the environment be centrally rather than marginally exploited as resources for learning?
- Do current patterns of teacher deployment and current teaching styles represent an efficient use of resources; or might some patterns of co-operative teaching be more effective?
- How can children be better used as peer teachers and generators of educational material?
- Do current principles of syllabus construction need radical overhaul to bring them into touch with the realities of use in schools?

We have now considered the eight essential components (four goals; four principles) which together form the hub of the wheel. Perhaps readers may think we have in so doing complicated the issue, but the hard fact remains that we can never achieve perfection in the design of a relevant and efficient content. We can only aim towards such a content. Our aim is likely to be the surer if we appreciate the difficulties we may encounter.

THE INNER WHEEL

The inner brace of the wheel contains those conditions which need to exist if we are to transform the principles outlined earlier into real practice in schools. Like Hurst we isolate certain categories (five against his seven) and although readers may find language we use slightly different, with one exception the principles outlined are similar.

Our five conditions for enabling qualitative innovation to happen are:

- Adequate information and communication.
- Shared goals of relevance and desirability.
- Participation at all levels.
- Realism in expectations and operation.
- Flexibility in relation to both content and mode of implementation as well as its timing.

Information and communication

It is difficult and perhaps even dangerous to order these five elements, so interlinked are they. Nevertheless, one is tempted to start with information and communication since if you don't know where you are, you are unlikely to be able to plan where you are going.

Many programmes designed to raise quality appear to prefer starting from where they hope they should be rather than where they are, thus confusing the 'language of critique' with the 'language of possibility'.

As we have already indicated, this is partly because when the truth does surface it either proves embarrassing or complicates the planning process by introducing more variables than a planner cares to cope with.

However the following questions would provide a necessary starting point:

What's going on now?
- the current 'curriculum as practice'
- life in classrooms
- school and community links

Who wants what?
What don't they want?
- aspirations of society and groups within it
- culturally acceptable and unacceptable approaches

Who is in a position to make decisions and are their agendas open or hidden?
What can the learners understand?
- language use and mastery
- experience and variations between groups
- broad generalisation in relation to cognitive development

What resources are there?
- manpower; money; materials; time
- including: those actually available
                      those potentially available

What else is happening?
- what parallel initiatives are in operation?

How far does the context for education vary?
How far is it the same?

Once this information is gathered it must be communicated up and back along a hierarchy from central planner to teacher and from teacher to planner. It is also vital for communication to take place *between* schools, teachers and the local society and infrastructure through which they work. Such co-operation is a basic feature of many projects aiming at qualitative improvement such as the 'Cianjur' project in Indonesia, described in some detail in Chapter Seven.

Shared goals

No reader who has gone along with us this far will now expect full agreement from all interest groups concerning either the purpose or the mode of qualitative improvement. Tensions between such groups are inevitable and even beneficial to the growth and development of education. However, a good deal of consensus can be achieved as to purpose, as we have seen in both Malaysia and Lesotho. And a great deal of consensus *ought* to be achieved on means. Three essential ingredients of 'goal sharing' are:

Negotiation

That is, sitting down together, trying to resolve tensions and discussing the roles that different partners at different levels in the system can play to achieve desired ends. It is vitally important that the limits of our 'room to manoeuvre' are here explored and defined.

Common criteria and models of excellence

If there is some agreement on the characteristics of a 'good Malaysian'; active learning in Indonesia; a 'good primary school in Lesotho'; 'key teacher behaviours to be encouraged in Kenya'; 'minimum acceptable conditions in Nepali schools' . . . then there is a common goal to aim for. It is essential that such criteria are fully understood by those to whom they apply. (It is only recently that inspectorates, including Her Majesty's Inspectorate in England and Wales, have released details of the schedules they use for evaluating schools.'[34]

Efficient and attainable goals

As Paul Hurst has reminded us, to expect teachers to respond in the manner of Marie Antoinette's finance minister,[35] 'If it is difficult it is already done, if it is impossible it will take a little longer,' is unproductive. Sadly we often mistake common sense for lack of commitment.

Participation at all levels

This follows inevitably from our last category, for mere sharing of information and goals is passive. So, to a great extent, is the negotiation of roles and exploration of room for manoeuvre. In the last resort those responsible for improving quality at every level have to *act* and, what is more difficult, accept the responsibility for action. Equally important for those in higher positions in a hierarchy is the ability to accept that those lower than them can take decisions which are just as important to learning even if they are more restricted in scope. In other words the chief inspector or curriculum co-ordinator must bring himself to accept that a good untrained teacher may question and modify the content of the national syllabus and that she would be right so to do. The process of participation is as important for the health and morale of a system as it is for its relevance and efficiency. It is only through allowing participation to happen that 'his' quality and 'their' quality become 'our' quality.

Realism

While no sensible planner will deny the importance of facing realities in planning for quality, or doubt that such reality is frequently and deliberately ignored, we need to be careful that in our responses to crises we do not close the door upon good dynamic education.

A class of eighty-five seven-year-olds, observed in 1986 in Lesotho failing signally to learn reading from an overpressed teacher with virtually no equipment, can invoke two types of response. Either to train the teacher to use mass education techniques more effectively and to make sure that all the children have a class text. Or to involve both children and parents (many of whom are literate in Lesotho) with the teaching of reading and at the same time attempt to bring in more individualised reading material into the classroom.

The 'no-nonsense' aid donor is likely to advocate the former;[36] the 'innovator' the latter.

In fact the best solution is almost certainly to try both, in the hope that gradually the much more interesting and potentially effective approaches suggested in the second alternative will become grafted on to the old.[37]

Flexibility

The final condition, that of flexibility both in the content and operation of approaches to raising quality, is rather less difficult than it appears. On first consideration the inflexibility of centralised syllabuses, examination systems and patterns of control seem totally incompatible with the wide difference between learners and communities, and with the unpredictability of world events. But adopt a new way of looking at content, at methods, at administration and at assessment and the problem becomes more manageable. We shall discuss these new approaches in the last chapters of this book.

THE OUTER RIM

On the outer rim of the wheel we have located the agents responsible for making plans for qualitative improvement actually happen and whose working together is so essential and so frequently lacking. Although a large number of categories could be identified, we differentiate five:

(i) The content choosers

Those who plan curricula, syllabuses and educational materials at all levels.

(ii) The people trainers

Those responsible for pre-service and in-service training of teachers and other personnel who supervise and organise teachers, supervise and manage schools.

(iii) The administrators and supervisors

Those who collect information, plan, administer, inspect and advise.

(iv) The community and its leaders

Who co-operate with the school, or stand apart from it; who accept its products, or reject them.

(v) The evaluators and examiners

Those who attempt to gain information to aid decision-makers on the efficiency and relevance of primary schooling and attempt to improve it, as well as those who examine pupil attainment both to assess progress and to allocate places to higher levels of schooling.

These categories are relatively easy to differentiate at the central level of educational planning and those who undertake the tasks: the administrator, the teacher trainer, the curriculum worker are often committed full time to them. As we move, however, from central through local to school level, both the roles and the persons who perform them become less discrete though they can often act and think differently once they transfer from one role to another.

We do not, of course, suggest that relations between these agents should be a continual round of sweet accord and co-operation. Human relationships do not work that way and when there is no tension it is usually because nothing much is happening. What we do stress and shall continue to stress throughout the remainder of the book is that through a process of maximising information, minimising conflict and encouraging argument, rather than armed neutrality, some give and some take: the wheel can roll.

CONCLUSION

Our quality wheel, therefore, now looks like this:

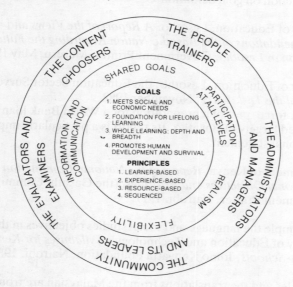

Figure 3

Assuming it is to roll forward, the agents on the outer rim need to be securely linked in with its inner structure as well as being effectively knit together; thus they are prepared to move in the same direction. How far they are able to do this will be examined in later chapters.

NOTES AND REFERENCES

1 Figures are averages. They often conceal high dropout rates. Moreover enrolments represent those 'on-role' not those who attend regularly. Occasionally, especially when times are hard, the figures just cannot be believed, for no country would face the ignominy of appearing to have falls in enrolments.

2 Figures extracted from the *World Development Report*, World Bank, 1989.

3 There is, however, rising concern particularly in South-East Asian countries that gifted children are not being sufficiently stretched. Indonesia and Malaysia both have specific programmes.
In other countries, sadly the only gifted children to profit are those whose families are sufficiently well off to send them to private schools.

4 At the time of writing, however, the Primary Education Project in Nepal is seeking to persuade the curriculum centre towards further action on goal definition.

5 Ministry of Education, Lesotho. *A Report of the Views and Recommendations of the Basotho Nation Regarding the Future of Education in Lesotho*, Government Printer, Maseru, May 1978.

6 Ministry of Education, Lesotho; the Education Sector Survey, *Report of the Task Force*, November 1982.
The task force, part of a preparation for a World Bank loan, was composed largely of Basotho. Its report is a particularly impressive educational statement.

7 Government of Kenya, *Report of the National Commission on Educational Objectives and Priorities*, (the Gacathi Committee), Government Printer, Nairobi, 1977.

8 For example the language and social studies objectives in the Ministry of Education and Technology's *Syllabuses for Kenya Primary Schools*, Jomo Kenyatta Foundation, Nairobi, 1986.

9 The tables and the translations from the Malaysian are from Siti Hawa Binti Ahmed's unpublished Doctoral thesis, 'Implementing a New Curriculum for Primary Schools. A Case Study from Malaysia', London University Institute of Education, January 1986.

10 Flores, Pedro V., *Educational Innovation in the Philippines. A case*

study of Project Impact, International Development Research Centre, Ottawa, 1981.

11 Cummings, William L., *Low Cost Primary Education – Implementing an Innovation in Six Nations*, I.D.R.C., Ottawa, 1986.

12 The project started in 1974 and terminated in 1982. It was an attempt to introduce modular-based learning into twelve pilot 'development schools' attached to colleges of education and attracted considerable interest in its early years.
A full description in English in Postlethwaite, T. N. and Thomas, R. M., *The Modular Instruction Project*, Office of Research and Development, Department of Education & Culture, Republic of Indonesia, Jakarta, 1977.

13 Described in UNESCO-UNICEF co-operative programme *Basic Services for Children – a Continuing Search for Learning Priorities*, Vol. 1 (includes case study of Namutamba), Vol. 2 (includes case study of Bunumbu). Both volumes UNESCO, Paris, 1978.

14 Operated in association with Durham University between 1972 and 1978. Although the project itself was wound up, the concept of model schools as centres of excellence remains in favour in Lesotho.

15 Attempts were made in the early 1970s to build a novel, integrated, community school curriculum to serve the needs of a newly resettled area.

16 Sifuna, D. N., *Revolution in Primary Education. The New Approach in Kenya*, East Africa Literature Bureau, Nairobi, 1975.

17 *Basic Services for Children*, op. cit., Vol.2.

18 B.A.N.F.E.S. stands for Basic and Non Formal Education Systems – the project, USAID assisted, started in 1985.

19 Siti Ahmed, op. cit.

20 e.g. Havelock, R. and Huberman, M., *Solving Educational Problems*, UNESCO, Paris, 1977.

21 For example, Young, B. L., *Teaching Primary Science*, Longman 1979. One of the best and most influential books on science methodology in Africa. It derives entirely from the experiences of the author in developing science curricula in the project's schools. Much other influential material could be cited from different curriculum areas.

22 Hurst, Paul, *Implementing Educational Change – A Critical Review of the Literature*, Occasional Paper 5, Department of Education in Developing Countries, University of London Institute of Education, 1983.

23 Coombs and Ahmed, op. cit.

24 Bacon's *Essay on Truth* (1597) begins as follows: ' "What is Truth?" said Jesting Pilate, and would not stay for an answer.'

25 He classified disciplines into Theoretical, Practical, and Productive. For an interesting discussion read Schwab, Joseph J., 'Structure of the Disciplines', in Golby, M., Greenwald, J. and West R. (eds.), *Curriculum Design*, Croom Helm, London, 1979.

26 Phenix, P., 'Realms of Meaning', 1964. Reproduced in Golby, Greenwald and West., op. cit., pp. 165–76.

27 Hirst, P. H., *Knowledge and the Curriculum*, Routledge and Kegan Paul, 1974.

28 Department of Education and Science: Curriculum Matters, *The Curriculum from 5 to 16,* HMSO, 1985.

29 Bloom, Benjamin S. et al (ed.), *Taxonomy of Educational Objectives: the Classification of Education Goals. Handbook I – The Cognitive Domain*', Longman, 1986. Krathwohl, David, *Taxonomy of Educational Objectives*. Handbook II the Affective Domain. Longman, London 1964. The words 'Taxonomies', 'Cognitive', 'Affective' and 'Psychomotor' have bewildered generations of students and teachers who continue, however, to use them because they sound so learned.

30 One useful and available book however is Ohuche, R. O. and Otaala, B. (eds.), *The African Child and His Environment*, Pergamon, 1981.

31 Mureria, Margaret and Okatcha, F. M., 'Conservation of Concept of Length, Area and Volume among Kikuyu Primary School pupils' in Okatcha (ed.), *Modern Psychology and Cultural Adaptation*, Swahili Language Consultants and Publishers, Nairobi, 1977.

32 'Conservation' in its simplest form means the ability to understand the concept in many forms however it is presented, e.g. one kilo of beans remains one kilo whether it is spread out on a table or packed tight in a bag.

33 Bruner, J. S. *Towards a Theory of Instruction*, Harvard University Press, 1966, p. 41.

34 Both the Inspectorate and the Department of Education and Science are now giving considerable publicity to the models they consider worth emulating. A useful recent publication is Department of Education and Science's *Better Schools – Evaluation and Appraisal: Conference Proceedings*, HMSO London, 1986.

35 He was a Swiss called Necker, called in just before the French Revolution to try to sort out the finances of a hopelessly insolvent government.

36 In fact this has already been done by the World Bank Textbook project now operating in Lesotho.

37 This strategy has actually been recommended by a national seminar in 1986. See Barnabas Otaala and M. Andrew Letsie (eds.) *National Teacher Training College Curriculum: A Review and Reappraisal*, Report of a Workshop (June 9–13 1986), Instructional Materials Resource Centre, N.T.T.C., Maseru, 1987.

THE CONTENT CHOOSERS

This chapter is about the content of primary education and the people who choose it. We have deliberately refrained from using the word 'curriculum'. In theory it is a suitable and familiar term; 'All the learning planned and provided for children at school.'[1] In practice people have been building too many fences round it. Curriculum as commonly understood is decided at curriculum centres, by or under the influence of 'curriculum developers', usually subject specialists. Curriculum development is almost exclusively interpreted as programme and materials development and curriculum implementation as spreading the word from the prophets at the centre to the faithful in the field.

There is however a wide gap between what is planned and what is provided and consequently there exist two very different curricula: the official curriculum of the centre and the actual curriculum of the schools. The gap between these two is not narrowing. So readers will permit us to stay with the more neutral word 'content' which describes both the intention and the reality, and thus the daily dilemma (which every good school and every good teacher faces) of trying to balance the two.

WHAT IS CONTENT?

To appreciate the complex nature of content in primary schools we need to examine the concept in some detail.

(i) *Content comprises all the learning experiences which children have.* That is:

The facts, concepts and skills they learn (often as a result of the syllabuses, schemes of work and textbooks they follow).

The mental processes and ways of thinking they develop (often as a result of the methods and approaches that teachers use).

The attitudes and dispositions they assimilate (largely as a result of the 'climate' of school and classroom and the influence and example of their peers and teachers).

Not all these experiences are necessarily beneficial. Children may be taught facts which are both trivial and wrong ('Eskimos live in igloos'); processes which exclude critical thinking (science experiments presented as verifying what we already know); or attitudes which are socially derisive (only girls cook). But they are nevertheless taught them.

(ii) *Content in schools is only partly divisible into separate areas of experience* (linguistic, mathematical, scientific, etc.) and even less easily divisible into subjects.

Many experiences learnt, especially those concerned with processes and attitudes, derive not from subjects but from individuals: from the way that Miss Ahmed teaches; from the size, organisation and social composition of Class IIIB; from the way Mr Okot, the headmaster, runs his school.

(iii) *Content cannot profitably be separated from 'methodology'*, for the way the teacher teaches and helps (or hinders) children's learning is critical in determining the educational experiences children have.

(iv) *Content taught and learnt in schools is thus fundamentally dependent on the social, human and educational context of each individual school*. Though a country may have a national syllabus, no two schools will cover it or interpret it in exactly the same way; no schools have the same environment or resources. No teacher will provide the same experience to her class. They are always filtered through the person of the individual.

(v) *Content in schools cannot easily be separated from the content of other educational experiences* which the learner has at the same time: from family and peers; from experience in the community; from radio and television. School content may complement, supplement or even seek to counteract such experiences but it cannot ignore them.

(vi) *Content in school is invariably dictated by a combination of present needs and past traditions*. No school and no teacher starts with a clean slate: some of the traditions and practices are accepted willingly and knowingly but many are merely absorbed, breathed in, as it were, with the chalk dust. Pupils and teachers have a complicated culture and folklore into which they initiate new entrants.

(vii) *Assimilation of content is only effectively measured by what learners actually learn*. What is provided is of relatively little moment in education if it does not change the behaviour of learners. Learners are not equal in experience, ability and motivation. They do not all learn the same content and never will, despite the fervent wish of planners that they might conveniently and tidily do so.

If we accept the truth of these seven principles – and they cannot easily be denied – it becomes very clear that the notion that we educationists can fully plan or control the content of school education bears little relation to reality.

To be sure we can and must seek to lay down principles of content and to apply pressure in the right way and at the right time to direct content towards the ends we seek to achieve. But inevitably the final result will be some form of compromise between the 'outsiders' and 'insiders' who choose the content, both of whom will be influenced not only by social values and traditions but also by practical and administrative expediency.

WHO CHOOSES CONTENT?

Consider in a little more detail the distinction between 'outsiders' and 'insiders'.

1 The 'Outsiders': society and the forces within it

Sociologists often describe the forces in society which influence and sometimes even shape the content of school education as the 'hidden curriculum'.[2] We find this word somewhat misleading because such influences are so diverse and range subtly from the overt to the covert; from what is seen as noble and desirable to what might generally be construed as less socially acceptable. They are spread both through educational traditions (mathematics has a higher status than health education); through school practice (competition pays off better than co-operation); and through role modelling (on other children, teachers or successful community members).

Moreover, these forces contain a mass of complexities and contradictions. A child aspires to go to the city and make money. If he succeeds and starts a shoe shop, he is regarded as a successful enterpreneur demonstrating the initiative and the skill which a nation needs to modernise itself. However, if he is less fortunate and ends up shining shoes he may discover that he has 'deserted the land' or 'abandoned his cultural heritage'.

The models which society offers may differ according to the class, sex and upbringing of the child. One 'ideal' girl may complete a basic education, marry at sixteen to raise a family and serve her husband. Another may prolong her studies and defer marriage to serve her community. A youth may be rewarded for bringing 'modern' influences and attitudes into the home or he may be resented for it. But hidden or open, confusing or clear there is no doubting the strength of these messages or the importance of recognising and confronting them. One way of doing this is for 'insiders' to recognise that they are at the same time 'outsiders'. The teacher, the textbook writer, the curriculum worker are often parents and always community members. A headteacher may deplore the influence of 'examination fever'[3] in the school yet buy his child a present when she has received a particularly good grade. A curriculum worker may strongly support the renaissance of the mother tongue in schools yet send her four-year-old to an English-medium nursery school. Such actions are not deplorable; they are realistic given the pressures of society. Once this is realised it is far easier for the 'insiders' effectively and realistically to plan content.

2 The 'Insiders': content chosen by education workers

Of course, a great deal of the learning planned and provided in schools *is* chosen by those who work with them and for them. But here too the picture is complex and the 'choosers' are many and various.

They also make a variety of different choices. One of the best detailed descriptions of a school curriculum is provided by Dave (1974)[4]. He divided the curriculum into five components:

> **Aims and objectives:** aims being interpreted as desired directions of educational progress; objectives as more specific and well-defined targets of achievement. Aims and objectives are formed at various levels, from the Minister of Education down to the individual teachers, parent and child.

> **The curriculum plan** which relates to both content and process. The plan itself is presented in written documents of various types, prepared and used at different levels, including syllabuses, schemes and timetables. Systems vary widely as to the amount of decisions taken at various levels.

> **Teaching methods and Learning activities** include all those, formal and informal, which take place in school, in class and out of it: inter-school activities; activities planned in the school, but carried out in the community (like health campaigns and social work) as well as activities generated in the school by societal agencies outside it.

> **Learning materials** refers to all written, audio and visual material used in schools, both commercially and locally produced; to learning materials deriving from the environment as well as to out-of-school resources such as libraries and museums.

> **Evaluation** refers primarily to pupil assessment (though it also includes procedures for guidance). It may be formal or informal and is carried out during a school year, at the end of it and at the end of a school stage, by students themselves, by the school or by agencies outside it.[5]

Each of these categories invites choice: 'this aim'; 'that syllabus'; 'these methods'; 'those materials'; 'this method of testing rather than that one'. And these choices are made at different levels of the system by a variety of different interest groups: politicians; curriculum developers; teacher-trainers; inspectors; local education officers; headteachers; teachers and parents – to name just some.

These 'choosers' have differing degrees of power to influence content. At first it would appear that such power would be directly related to position in the education hierarchy. The centrally-based curriculum developer would have access to power, the classroom teacher would be denied it. But a careful analysis reveals a much more interesting and complicated picture.

In the first place, power derives from social position and is influenced by individual initiative, or lack of it. A college principal, inspector or head who combines dynamic energy with good political connections, can achieve a great deal more than one who lacks both. (This provides a very strong argument in favour of using models of better practice as a means of influencing change.)

Secondly, once we analyse Dave's five components we discover that *access to learners* is just as important a source of power as access to policy-makers. The head of the curriculum centre can choose what appears in the syllabus; the teacher cannot. But it is the teacher, and only the teacher, who has the power to transmit that content in such a way that the learners understand it and change their behaviour in consequence.

To understand the complexity of choice and the reality of power-sharing consider the grid we present in TABLE X. For simplicity's sake we have divided the 'choosers' into only three levels,[6] though in reality there are many different and distinct categories.

Once this complicated pattern of choice is appreciated the whole process of planning and implementation assumes a different light. It is no longer just the business of curriculum developers. They must share power and negotiate co-operation not only with the teachers who stand between them and the users of the content they have planned, but also with a critically important band of middlemen: the teacher trainers, the local administrators and the inspectors whose contribution to quality is described in our next two chapters.

IMPROVING CHOICE: MORE EFFICIENT AND MORE RELEVANT CONTENT FOR SCHOOLS

While nobody denies the efforts or the commitment of current 'content choosers' (particularly those at the curriculum centres) to provide the 'best' content for schools, we would still argue that the process of choice leaves a great deal to be desired if it is to become truly efficient, relevant and equitable towards different children and communities.

Better efficiency

In Chapter One we identified three aspects of efficiency: meeting standards, raising standards and standards of efficiency. School education needs to set attainable standards and ensure that learners reach them.

Unfortunately this is far from being the practice in many education systems. One of the crudest measures of attainment of standards is the school retention rate. If a certain standard of attainment is expected by the end of Class IV, let us say the attainment of effective literacy and numeracy,[7] then learners who never make it to Class IV are unlikely to achieve it and learners who drop out or are pushed out at the end of Class I or II have no chance at all.

If we look at the retention figures in Lesotho and Nepal we find an alarming number of these early dropouts and if we extend the analysis worldwide we find evidence of a horrific waste of time and effort.

TABLE X THE CURRICULUM: WHO MAKES WHICH CHOICES?

	CENTRAL LEVEL ● MINISTRY ● CURRICULUM CENTRE ● CENTRAL EXAMINATIONS BOARD	LOCAL LEVEL ● LOCAL AUTHORITIES ● INSPECTORS ● TEACHERS' COLLEGES	SCHOOL LEVEL ● HEADS ● TEACHERS ● COMMUNITIES
AIMS AND OBJECTIVES	Sets and refines national aims.	Sets local economic and cultural aims. Interprets aims to teachers.	Sets affective aims and objectives – eg codes of behaviour in school. Interprets aims and objectives to pupils.
CURRICULUM PLAN	Writes national syllabus and decides time allocations.	Introduces variations in national syllabus. Creates local timetables. Recommends community participation.	Makes schemes of work. Emphasises or omits parts of national syllabus. Controls co-curricular activities.
METHODS AND APPROACHES TO LEARNING	Recommends approaches to be used.	Trains teachers in the use of certain methodologies. Moderates methodology through supervision practices.	Practises different methodologies. Determines to what extent schoolteaching relates to local culture and community life.
MATERIALS	Commissions and writes textbooks. Issues books to schools.	Teaches students to make materials. Initiates locally relevant materials. Chooses books and other materials for local schools.	Controls use of textbooks by pupils. Chooses some materials or recommends parents to buy them. Uses (or ignores) materials from environment.
EVALUATION AND EXAMINATIONS	Sets central examinations and standards expected.	Trains teachers in testing techniques. Evaluates schools and teachers and sets standards. Sets some local examinations.	Evaluates affective growth of students. Sets all internal tests and examinations. Marks work and keeps records according to certain principles.

The fact that figures for retention in the poorest countries show some improvement[8] over the past decade can only give us very modest consolation, especially when coupled with the significant lack of measuring instruments to actually prove whether basic skills have been attained.

Of course the situation in richer countries such as Indonesia and Malaysia looks much brighter. Dropouts are far less, in some cases negligible, and we can suppose that a very large proportion of children leave school both literate and numerate. In Malaysia, in particular, recent curricular emphasis on the basic skills has led to a standard of child literacy probably as impressive as anywhere in the world.

But a closer look at the standards being achieved will convince us that there is little cause for complacency: mastery of very basic literacy and numeracy skills is one thing but mastery of the skills and content expected by the official curriculum is quite another. Standards in relation to those demanded by the highly ambitious syllabuses, particularly those in mathematics and English (as distinct from local languages) leave very much to be desired. Final leaving examinations set in both Kenya and Lesotho record an alarmingly low mean of achievement particularly in mathematics. Passing is, of course, norm-referenced depending on places available in higher institutions and pass marks are jealously guarded secrets. But there is talk in both countries of pupils 'succeeding' to gain secondary places with pass marks of 40% in mathematics, which given a multiple-choice format and the possibility of achieving 25% marks through random guessing, suggests that large numbers of the learners who survive into the final class of primary school are virtually devoid of *any* significant mastery of content in the subject.

Even in Malaysia, where systematic evaluation of the attainment of learners in the new curriculum has reached Class IV, the evaluation section of the curriculum development centre are both concerned and disappointed with the levels of mastery that their tests are revealing and have had to face up to accepting levels of 60–70% instead of the 80–90% originally hoped for. The reason for these disappointing results lies to a great degree in the design of syllabuses for basic skills. Levels expected are often unrealistic, being those which can be achieved only by the more favoured urban schools.

Moreover, there needs to be considerable concern about the *kind* of standards being set and achieved as well as who are achieving them, for despite a certain amount of lip-service paid to the need to promote skills of problem-solving and developing dispositions toward creativity, in practice many influences combine to prevent these from being developed:

- overloaded programmes
- overcrowded schools
- national, computer moderated examinations

- unchallenging textbooks and (in Malaysia at least) workbooks
- undertrained and overworked teachers

All these combine towards emphasising definitions and patterns of mastery which contribute greatly to Freire's knowledge in the bank.'[9]

Moreover when we look at *who* are attaining the standards, even in the sense of building up good, 'bank accounts', the issue of equity becomes very apparent. Two brief studies may illustrate this.

First join us[10] in a rural school in the lowlands (by which we mean not-so-highlands) of Lesotho. It is winter and there is snow upon the higher hills. Children in their blankets huddle in large unpartitioned school buildings. They are divided into grade groups: 80(I); 60(II); 50(III); 45(IV). We attach ourselves to the forty-five Grade IV children (clearly survivors from a large number). The difference in their 'survival potential' is only too apparent. It is true that thanks to the World Bank all have access to a language and mathematics book (sets are kept in a cupboard and issued at appropriate times. They are not to be taken home). But let us examine what the children have in their bags. The fatter, better dressed and warmer looking children have a supply of exercise books. Some even have reading and mathematics books of their own. These are the survivors. We asked one girl to read her book, she does so confidently with no difficulty. But here are some colder looking children. They possess no books and only a single exercise book each, in which they write everything that comes along: rough and fair notes; exercises; Sesotho; English; maths; social studies; religious knowledge. The World Bank books come out. The cold boy next to us attempts to read the 'exercise for the day' to us and makes very little of it.

Halfway across the world in a hotter and richer community just outside Kuala Lumpur we drop into a large, well-built and well-equipped school in the heart of what looks to be a middle-class area. But appearances are deceptive. There is a squatter settlement just down in the valley and forty per cent of the children come from there. The Grade I teacher faces a problem for which she can see little hope of a solution. These children over here (the majority, the ones with the wrist-watches and the workbooks) already knew how to read before they even came to school. Some were even proficient in English. But that group over there could do neither. Faced with these disparities the teacher had divided the class into ability groups (which almost exactly corresponded to the social origin of the children).

Would the gap between the groups become less? we ask.

'Unlikely'.

Would it widen?

'Probably'.

Were the squatters' children very poor?

'No, not really so poor. Their parents are uneducated. They don't spend their money on the right things. That is why their children don't do well.'

Finally let us look at the efficiency of the content in meeting the needs of individuals rather than groups. In a book written ten years ago one of the present authors offered the following allegory:

The allegory of the swimming pool

HUGH HAWES: How then do the children of Africa pass through their first school?

SOCRATES: I would have you imagine a swimming pool. It is long and the bottom slopes downwards. At the one end it is very shallow and at the other end it is deep.

Into this pool plunge rank after rank of children chained together. They are of different heights: some are short and some are tall. At the edge of the pool stand guardians with spears. They force the children forward at a steady pace. After a time the shorter children become submerged and the number underwater increases as the ranks go forward.

HUGH HAWES: What happens to these?

SOCRATES: Some drown and are hauled out of the pool and left on the edge. Still more are forced to walk on underwater, oblivious of the world outside. By the time they reach the end of the pool they are too exhausted to climb out.

HUGH HAWES: What of the tallest children?

SOCRATES: They reach the end of the pool without difficulty but very slowly for they must march in step with their weaker and shorter fellows.

HUGH HAWKES: The end of the pool, then, represents the final examination; the lines of children are the pupils of different ages and abilities; the guardians, I suppose, are the textbook writers, syllabus makers and educational administrators.

SOCRATES: Just so.[11]

Few who have read this conversation and laughed at it have denied its truth, but nearly everyone has concentrated on the plight of the shorter children. Spare a thought for the tall boys and girls for they should be equal objects of concern. They are the leaders of the future and if an education fails to develop in them their potential for leadership, for creative and critical thinking and for decision-making then that system cannot be described as efficient.

Relevance

Relevance, we may recall, demands a balancing act of considerable difficulty:

- balancing needs and demands from many interest groups
- balancing individual with social needs and eventually both with the broader needs of humanity
- balancing 'needs now' with 'needs later'
- balancing simple and immediate needs such as the need to eat, to be healthy or to work with deeper and more complicated ones such as the need to be esteemed, the need to achieve one's potential or the need to create and express oneself

The issue of relevance is a daily preoccupation of curriculum centres and some of its aspects are both well understood and imaginatively tackled, though inevitably the interpretation of relevance is affected by the social origins and experience of the curriculum writers themselves.

Syllabuses do on the whole reflect social goals and are related to perceived occupational needs, sometimes, as in the 1986 syllabuses in Kenya, very closely related.

Books increasingly seek to avoid stereotypes:

- all the parents in wage employment
- all the action taking place in or near the town
- all the homes spacious, permanent and obviously middle class

There is room however for further analysis and subsequent improvement (consider, for instance, the images of women presented in African textbooks).[12] There is also an increasing national acceptance of the need to define areas and topics in the curriculum where local interpretations and variations would be considered desirable.[13] Nevertheless once we take a more searching look into the relevance of primary curriculum to needs of learners, schools and the society they serve, five disturbing aspects emerge:

I   Relevance is interpreted almost invariably in relation to 'needs later'. Because 'needs now' are neglected the essential link between education and direct experience is often lost.

Let us take a very simple example from mathematics. The measurement of weight.

'Needs later' requires that children understand their tables of weight, how to manipulate them and how to solve written problems in which weight is a variable. This will enable them to pass their examinations.

A good teacher will take them further. Children will learn to weigh and measure in the classroom and thus acquire practical skills which pencil and paper tests cannot measure.

'Needs now', however, suggests a new cluster of learning experiences. For instance children might need to:

- Learn by investigation how weighing takes place in the market and what constitutes fair and false weighing
- Learn to relate weight to volume (most goods are sold in measures or piles): thus learn to estimate weight
- Learn to relate weight to important tasks in the home; e.g. to the weighing of babies and young children in relation to their development: this leading into questions of child rearing and nutrition

At first sight our second list of 'needs now' appears merely an extension of the first: relating learning to life skills. In fact it goes much deeper. In the first place it adds to the content elements of enquiry and assessment based on life experience. We learn something in school. We try it out in a real situation and assess how far it works. If it does not serve us, always assuming it to be useful knowledge taught correctly, it is likely that we have not properly understood it and therefore need to learn it better.

Secondly, it creates a vital link between two forms of education: education in home and community and education at school. By constantly relating experience of one to another, both forms of education are strengthened.

Finally, if properly managed, the association between 'needs now' and 'needs later' can make a book-bound education far more lively to children.

Desirable though it may be, the introduction of a content which favours emphasis on 'needs now' is not without difficulties. It makes for more flexible timetabling and requires more inventive teachers. Nevertheless in many school subjects and a number, though not all, of topics within them, a methodology based on the following five-point sequence may be well worth considering. We have taken as examples topics from three different areas of the curriculum: Mathematics, Health Education and Social Studies.

(i) *What is the problem?*
   e.g. Measuring weight; preventing accidents; living together peacefully.

(ii) *What are the basic facts and skills which bear upon the problem and its solution?*
   e.g. Units and methods of measurement.
   Causes of accidents and principles of first aid.
   Concepts of government; law and order, etc.

(iii) *How can we find out more about the applications to our daily life?*
   e.g. How do people measure in our community; where and for what purpose?
   What accidents happen in homes and communities, to whom and why?
   How is the local community made up; how governed; what difficulties exist in living together?

(iv) *How can we apply the ideas and skills we have learned in our personal and community life?*
   e.g. Weighing and measuring in the market and the home.
   Identifying and eliminating causes of accidents and providing first aid.
   Social action in a community, taking social responsibility towards different groups in society.

(v) *How can we assess the effect of our knowledge?*
e.g. Easier and more confident use of measuring in home and market.
Less danger of accidents: even less accidents.
Better understanding of, and relations with our neighbours.

II   Relevance is generally understood as concerned with relevant knowledge and the skills associated with that knowledge. Rarely are deeper issues of developing thinking skills, to enable learners to cope with change, given sufficient attention.

The curriculum planner in social studies may rest content, for instance, if a child 'knows' the history and geography of a local area, can read maps and manipulate ways of measuring time. Her colleague in science may be equally satisfied if a learner has understood soil components, local farming practices and nutritional problems in an area and is equipped with the knowledge, skills and motivation to do something about these.

These aspects of relevance are desirable and necessary but they are not enough. The deeper challenge remains. Learners must be grounded in the 'process skills' to enable them to handle new and changing knowledge in different areas of experience.

The reason this aspect of relevance is neglected is because process skills are less easy to define, and less easy for both curriculum planners and teachers to use and identify than simpler concepts. To teach someone to read for inference, assess evidence, extrapolate from it, hypothesise, control and manipulate variables – all sounds rather high-flown and abstract when compared to down-to-earth tasks like writing a job application, mapping the local area, or learning how to keep poultry.

Yet developing 'process skills' remains, possibly, the most crucial and most relevant task which a teacher undertakes in primary schools:

- It offers the one clear solution to the dilemma of how to deliver a national content to learners of different abilities and backgrounds.
- It represents a very effective means of linking 'needs now' with 'needs later'. The ability to solve problems and argue logically serves the learner as well at home as it does in school.
- It represents the one educational activity which schools can do rather better than the other agents of learning with whom they co-operate (or compete).

Arguably, the radio or television may do a good service in teaching background knowledge. Work experience teaches vocational skills

better than school does. The family and the peer group may have a
stronger influence than the school in teaching social skills and moral
dispositions. But only a school (and a good one at that) has the means to
help children to acquire learning skills and the ability to think in a
disciplined and logical way.

Most important of all the development of process skills may represent
the only defence of the 'powerless' against those who seek to dominate
them. Dictators have always feared thinking people.

'Yon Cassius', says Shakespeare's Caesar, 'has a lean and hungry
look. He thinks too much. Such men are dangerous . . . He reads much.
He is a great observer and looks quite through the deeds of men.'

Dictators come in many disguises today, from the army officer to the
advertising agency, but it is still essential for the individual to 'look quite
through the deeds of men' and recognise them for what they are.[14]

*III   Relevance is interpreted very largely as relevance to economic and
employment needs. The essential element of learners' 'self-esteem' and
'self-actualisation' needs is too often ignored.*

Although there is some rhetoric concerning the preservation of culture,
on the whole, creative and cultural elements in the curriculum are still
accorded a relatively low priority. It would be hard to find support for
the view that art, dance, drama or the writing of stories or poetry were
of the first order of importance in primary schools. They are accepted, it
is true, but in a strictly subordinate category to the 'real purpose' of
primary education and with the unspoken assumption that when the
going gets tough it is these elements which are most expendable. (Who
could possibly imagine the World Bank giving loans for the distribution
of art materials?) In fact it is precisely in those tougher situations
characteristic of the developing world where the need for self-
actualisation is most crucial.

*IV   Relevance is communally rather than individually assessed.
Appropriate and entirely feasible opportunities to follow lines of thought
and action interesting and relevant to individual learners are very
frequently missed, as are opportunities to stretch their abilities.*

This relates to the plight of the 'taller children' in our swimming pool
allegory. For on the one hand we have a catalogue of missed
opportunities for pupils to follow their own interests and so meet their
needs for self-actualisation; on the other a real lack of challenge to more
able children to measure progress against their own abilities. Children
who answer set questions correctly and consequently score high marks
are left to rest content with their achievement. Yet it is precisely these
children who should be given the opportunity to reach out, to create
and, in many cases, to seek to apply the content they have mastered to
'needs now' within their environment and community.
Finally:

V   Relevance of school content to issues which affect the preservation of humanity as a whole – international as well as local and national are, in many countries, sadly underemphasised.

Such issues are apologetically introduced as if problems of peace, population, deforestation, erosion and pollution should be confined to 'activists', with children kept in happy ignorance of the realities which could threaten their lives as adults. Nobody with a sense of arithmetic who has read some of the projections included in Chapter One, and who works out that children who are in primary school now will reach the age where they will begin to make important decisions in their communities (say forty) by the year 2030, will doubt the need for a very heavy emphasis on these issues now and a chance to think constructively about possible solutions.

TOWARDS BETTER CONTENT
1 Understanding the task.

If content is to be improved, that is made both more efficient and more relevant, it is first necessary to comprehend how complex is the task of improving it.

However, once we start examining such a task we begin to realise that a great deal of the knowledge we seek and the action that such knowledge implies may have political, social and educational implications which are so potentially threatening that we may wish we had left them alone. The more deeply we examine the content the 'hotter' it becomes. We can distinguish three levels, the lower far hotter than the upper.

TABLE XI
LOOKING AT CONTENT IN SCHOOLS: 'HOTTER' AND 'COLDER' LEVELS

COLDER

Level III	CONTENT OF INDIVIDUAL SUBJECTS	*Warm* Gets uncomfortable if you hold onto it
Level II	CONTENT OF THE SCHOOL PROGRAMME AS A WHOLE	*Uncomfortable* Sometimes easier to leave alone
Level I	CONTENT OF SCHOOL EDUCATION IN RELATION TO REAL NEEDS OF SOCIETY	*Very hot* to handle. Easy to get burnt!

HOTTER

LEVEL I, where the fires rage fiercest, is where the bravest among us might seek to examine the content of school education in its social and political context: where we look at what the school wants to teach and can teach alongside what others want it to teach and alongside what else is being taught to learners at the same time; where we take an honest look at the competition between the official curriculum in the school and the hidden and not-so-hidden curriculum outside it; where we uncover the way in which certain interest groups use the schools system, limit it and manipulate it. An almost inescapable conclusion of such a survey will be that school education on its own has little prospect of transforming the social order, even by slow degrees. Only through action which is at the same time political and educational is such radical change likely.

But such a realisation need not lead us to the barricades. If we are prepared to accept the reality that school education *does* contain and perpetuate both questionable influences and social inequalities, we can seek to soften them and strive conscientiously to improve the lot of those who are most disadvantaged. What is fundamentally dishonest, though often politically expedient, is to pretend that such influences and inequalities do not exist: that children will value 'serving their country' in preference to making a decent living, that labour under the hot sun is inherently noble and that the child of a doctor and a peasant start school on an equal footing.

Investigation at this level, involving, as it does, a comparison between real social and political needs of citizens and what is being planned and provided for them is both hot and hazardous. It is therefore not surprising that while in many countries universities may be prepared to seek out and argue from such information, curriculum centres, on whom lies the task of translating the findings into practical action, are likely to prefer leaving such investigation to others.

LEVEL II, where the temperature may still be uncomfortably warm, is where we take a look at the school curriculum *as a whole* in the light of manifest national priorities such as:

> the need for individuals to become fully and functionally literate and numerate (including, where possible, technological literacy and numeracy)
> the need to produce job makers rather than job seekers
> the need to develop true qualities of autonomy and self-reliance so that learners can both support and manage change
> the need to contribute to the evolution of co-operative, socially·minded and disciplined individuals.

Common to all these priorities is the fact that they are developed through the school as a whole and through the curriculum in its widest sense.

The implications of such an analysis is not quite so threatening as in our lowest level but can also lead us towards some fairly radical rethinking which would deeply disturb many interest groups, especially those oriented in established school subjects.

It might imply:

A re-examination of the curriculum 'map' as a whole both in regard to the number of subjects taught as well as the internal links possible between them. It was this process which led to the complete reorganisation of the lower primary curriculum in Malaysia based on just three areas: language; number; and cultural and creative subjects.

An enunciation of qualities desirable in learners at the end of a school cycle and possibly at the end of certain stages of it expressed, possibly, in terms of the major concepts, learning processes, skills and attitudes which might be developed . . . and how these might, in turn, imply the use of certain educational strategies and approaches.
The generation of a list of such qualities is, of course, relatively easy. What is particularly difficult is to limit such a list to what is significant, important and therefore manageable. Several attempts have been made to create such profiles, among them the Jamaican statement *Functional Education in Jamaica* produced in 1972, where some sixty teachers and other educators sat down to talk through and list the outcomes of nine years of schooling. These outcomes were unwieldy but valuable nonetheless.[15]

It would be a mistake however to think of this activity as best done nationally. Its value as a focus at teachers' group or even school discussion level would be very great since the process of getting schools and teachers to think across the curriculum is very likely to substantially change their whole attitude towards teaching and learning.

A realistic and searching analysis of the backwash effect of testing, examinations and record keeping on the school curriculum, together with discussions on how policies of assessment, marking, grading and, where appropriate, streaming or ability grouping can be reviewed in consequence.
If a child and his parents are aware, for instance, that an enquiry into some aspect of environment (let us say, how rice is grown) will be encouraged and rewarded in school, then co-operation in such useful and stimulating learning will be assured. If, however it becomes apparent that the only marks awarded will be on weekly multiple-choice tests, then co-operation is unlikely to be forthcoming.

An attempt to look at and moderate the school programme from a wider perspective than mere classroom teaching . . . involving discussions of such aspects as:

- the role of language across the curriculum and within the informal activities in the school
- the planning, purpose and evaluation of co-curricular activities

- the guided use of the school or class library as a resource for learning. (Such a resource may be non-existent in poorer contexts such as those in Lesotho and Nepal but in richer ones such as Malaysia and Indonesia or, indeed, in city schools in Nairobi it is a powerful educational tool)
- school approaches to methodology and to the setting and moderation of tasks for children.

LEVEL III, still warm, but relatively easy for anyone who cares to enter is where we take a long hard look into the content of the subjects or areas of experience currently designated in the curriculum.

Such an analysis made at national, local or school level could aim to clarify:

- Minimum specified competencies in the subject which could be attained at different levels
- Process and learning skills to be developed
- Fundamental concepts in the subject which need to be widened and deepened, often profitably expressed as questions:[16]
  e.g. How do living things grow?
  How do we measure length?
  How did people learn to live together?
  or with slightly greater precision:
  What food do we need to grow and protect our bodies?
  How do we know if children are getting enough food?[19]
- Dimensions for flexibility necessary and possible so that the damaging effect of the combination of a single syllabus and textbook, inequalities in backgrounds of children with a system of automatic promotion can be counteracted. In this way the dangers of what we have heard described as 'progressive cycles of ignorance' may be avoided
- Remedial and enrichment activities (particularly the latter) which may be devised in the subject, not only for individuals but also for groups of learners
- Links that can and should be built within the subject with other subjects
- Links possible and necessary which can be made into the environment, especially with the child's 'needs now' as part of a family and community.

Such a process of reassessing subject content is relatively unthreatening. It could easily be undertaken, for instance, by the mathematics panel in a curriculum centre, a subject association in mathematics, an imaginatively designed in-service course or a teacher's panel meeting in a teachers' advisory centre.

However when the discussion moves on to the implications of findings for action at ministry, college or classroom level then they are revealed as a good deal hotter than they look since they will almost inevitably call into question:

- Current curriculum content: revealing it to be overloaded
- Current syllabus and textbook presentation: too strong an emphasis on factual coverage rather than strengthening of skills and processes; too inflexible
- Current school approaches: too classroom-based; too divorced from community needs
- Current separation of content from methodology: rather than appreciating that methodology itself constitutes content
- Current 'territoriality' within subjects: too unco-ordinated; too inflexible.

REVIEWING AND IMPROVING CONTENT: WHOSE TASK IS IT?

We have indicated earlier in this chapter that different decisions about content can, and must, be made at different levels. Let us, therefore, go a little deeper into this matter and examine who does what in relation to some of the priorities discussed earlier in this chapter.

National Review Groups

One obvious strategy is to invite a weighty body of wise men and women to sit upon the curriculum and deliver judgement upon it. This strategy has been quite properly used in many nations including three countries examined in this book. Variations on the theme have already been mentioned in Chapter Three and include:

- The setting up of a commission to examine national objectives in Kenya[17]
- The mounting of a national forum on education in Lesotho (1977)[18]
- The setting up of a cabinet committee in Malaysia whose report (in 1979) was the result of five years study into the content of education in the nation's schools.[19]

Such reports are often seminal in their effect on the planning of educational content, but they have two main weaknesses. The first is that they are often reflective of the interest groups which set them up, what might be styled the 'enlightened establishment', and thus they are quite unlikely to give an airing to views which are too young, too radical or too uncomfortable to live with. They speak with measured, middle-aged, paternal voices: others more strident need to be heard.

Their second weakness is that they tend to deal in headlines. There is often need to spell out the issues in considerably greater detail. Therefore we also need thoughtful investigations of primary school content by groups with more time and less weight. The results of such studies could then be used as a guide to planners at every level in the system. Examples of such reviews might be the British Schools' Council publication *Primary Practice* (1983)[20] or the Australian National Curriculum Centre's *Core Curriculum for Australian Schools*.[21]

The curriculum centres

Even though, as we have earlier indicated, curriculum centres do not exercise the sole power of choosing content for schools, there is no doubt whatsoever of the prime importance of such centres in a centralised system of education. The two important documents mentioned in our last paragraph both emanated from central curriculum bodies and it is hard to imagine who else in Kenya, Malaysia, Lesotho, Indonesia or Nepal could commission such investigations. Nor should anyone doubt the excellent quality of work which can and does emerge from curriculum centres all over the world, as, for example, the primary science material from Kenya and Indonesia, the language programmes from Malaysia, the individualised mathematics materials from Lesotho or the health education materials from Nepal.

Yet there are still very serious weaknesses affecting the work and thinking of curriculum development centres, many of them attributable to fundamental weaknesses in the structures and policies of the centres.

Four main problems exist:

The *first* is the low commitment and investment which they place on research and situational analysis (our 'language of critique').

This is partly because research was thought to be the job of universities whose practical help to the content choosers has been sadly wanting; and partly because research was always conceived as a long range, 'fundamental' enquiry: research with a big R.

In fact research with a big R is only a small part of what curriculum centres need. Rather than a small number of trained doctors with their 'instruments', they need a large number of individuals drawn from the ranks of their own curriculum workers and those who implement the curriculum in the field, who have the will and the skill and the modest financial support necessary to conduct such essential activities as:

- needs assessment at national and local level
- investigations into classroom realities
- content analysis of present and projected materials
- investigations into learners' interest in and comprehension of school materials.

Additionally they require a structure and policy which would make it possible for such personnel to be given the time and the incentive to undertake such enquiries. Because they lack both the basic knowledge and the manpower to gather it, programmes and materials very frequently fail to meet the needs of the learners for whom they were designed.

The *second* problem that curriculum development centres face is the very fragmented and even adversarial nature of their structures and management. The basic unit in a curriculum centre tends to be the subject group, department or panel, often largely composed of teachers. Such groups often meet irregularly and sometimes sporadically. When co-ordination takes place, it is usually to reconcile the needs and interests of these various groups.

Co-ordinating committees usually exist but these will almost invariably be composed of heads of subject divisions concerned largely with defending their own interests. Apart from the enunciation of very general aims and principles there is very little pre-planning of content as a whole and little opportunity for independent groups to be constituted to examine essential issues prior to panels starting enthusiastically upon their specific tasks. These weaknesses in structure are undoubtedly very largely responsible for the lack of cohesion in the planned content of school education as well as for the gross overloading in content noticeable in country after country.

The *third* inherent weakness in curriculum centres is the failure to marry theory with practice.

Both theory and practice are valued, but almost, as it were in different breaths. This is partly a result of lack of training or an even more fundamental lack of understanding. The full time 'curriculum developer' from the centre may be relatively happy with the theoretical ideas she is using, but she is usually in a minority, working with a panel of teachers who may have difficulty in distinguishing between 'affective' and 'effective' or who may even hold the belief that 'psychomotor' has something to do with driving a car.

Since nobody wishes to admit these uncertainties (or for anyone in the panel to lose face) theory is swiftly passed over and the more familiar task of arranging topics in a time sequence commences.

However the root of the problem lies with the scholars rather than the curriculum workers. In the first place there are very few books available which face the task of expressing curriculum theory in simple and useable language which the average intelligent panel member can work from. Moreover when such material does emerge as, for instance, in the work of Robert Mager,[22] it supports a fundamental untruth, that one approach to curriculum design is possible and profitable in all situations and for all subject areas. For though the logical technological approach based on the framing of objectives is essential in some areas (imagine being operated on by a surgeon with creative ideas about anatomy) it is quite inappropriate in others (imagine a firm of publishers laying down sets of objectives for a great novelist).

Planning content of education at every level needs an appreciation of the truth that there are no technological solutions, only technologies which the mature and informed men and women who choose content can call upon to help them shape and sequence content properly.

TABLE XII LOCALLY-PRODUCED MATERIALS COMPATIBLE WITH A CENTRALLY PRESCRIBED SYLLABUS: A REVIEW OF OPTIONS AVAILABLE

TYPE		COMMENT
New locally relevant reading material for pupils	e.g. 1 Stories and other supplementary reading materials written for pupils and sometimes by them.	Reading material can be very simply and cheaply produced using duplicators or table-top offset litho printing. (seen in *West Indies*).[23]
	2 Local histories, geography, biography.	Local historians can be contacted and oral traditions collected. Teachers' college and university students may be used as informants (used in *Uganda*).
	3 Materials in local languages.	Especially important to produce additional reading materials to supplement official texts. Teachers' groups and centres can contribute.
	4 Local cultural and vocational materials.	Including 'how-to-do-it' books on crafts and activities such as local workbooks (Bunumbu–*Sierra Leone*).
Supplementary guides for teachers	1 Guides on adaptations of syllabus to local conditions as in geography, biology, agriculture.	List of plants with their local names. Examples of local places where physical geography may be exemplified. Locally relevant farming practices. Other agencies, e.g. Agricultural and Health services may assist.
	2 Guides to assist teachers in areas of special difficulty identified by local inspectors.	Such guides may profitably be written during in-service training with teachers and heads. Teachers' colleges may take a lead in generating such materials (as in Milton Margai College, *Sierra Leone*).[24]
	3 Guides for teaching of local cultural and vocational activities.	Such as songs, dances, local games; local productive activities such as fishing, weaving (as in *Sri Lanka*).

Worksheets and other activity materials

e.g.
1 Worksheets and cards for use by individual children, especially slow learners.

2 Worksheets for use by groups of children detailing how group activity may proceed.

3 Activity material related to practical tasks, e.g. school health or agricultural activities.

Material produced by individual teachers may be shared and 'banked' for future use (seen in *Malaysia*).

Teachers' groups may devise and share such materials and discuss their use (as in *Indonesian* project 'Active Learning through Professional Support').[25]

Child-to-Child health activities in various countries, e.g. *Zambia*, Gujarat (*India*), *Uganda* encourage the design of such activities, e.g. conducting health campaigns, preventing accidents.[26]

Audio-visual materials including real objects and real performance

1 Locally relevant audio visual material, e.g. maps, tapes of stories and songs, diagrams of industrial processes.

2 Locally produced teaching equipment including individual equipment.

3 Stimulus material produced by teachers and other community members not only pictorial but also tapes and drama performances.

4 Material produced by children either for others in school or for younger brothers and sisters at home.

5 Combination materials (teachers and children), particularly in community drama, radio broadcasts etc.

Resource centres at teachers' colleges can be effectively used – many have been set up, some (e.g. *Botswana* (Francestown)) have developed towards producing material for school.

Much inexpensive material can be designed particularly for early teaching of language and number. Local industry can be effectively used.

Particularly valuable if linked with adult education programmes. Drama and puppet theatre in such areas as health and environmental conservation has use for formal and non-formal education.

In school, children in upper class can produce reading and mathematics apparatus for those in lower classes. Similarly toys and games for child development can be made (as in *Jamaica, Botswana*).[26]

'Child power' especially directed by teachers has a very great impact on performers and audience alike, as in 3 above. Particularly effective in, say health campaigns and so used in *Guatemala, Uganda, Zambia, India* and elsewhere.[26]

TABLE XIII LOCALLY-PRODUCED MATERIALS COMPATIBLE WITH A CENTRALLY PRESCRIBED SYLLABUS: A REVIEW OF OPTIONS AVAILABLE (*continued*)

TYPE	COMMENT
Improved materials for testing and evaluation	1 Assignments, homework and other class practice materials collected by teachers. 2 Test questions and effective multiple-choice questions.	Teachers require assistance in setting useful tasks for their pupils and materials which enable them to do so are potentially very valuable. Many countries use local teachers to produce mock examinations, e.g. *Kenya, Nigeria, Indonesia*. Fewer have got round to banking them.

The *fourth* and final weakness in curriculum centres is their relative isolation from other bodies with whom they share the choice and moderation of content for schools, those responsible for teacher education, administration, evaluation and examinations. This point needs little elaboration at this stage. We return to it at the end of this chapter and throughout the remainder of this book.

Choice of content at local level

At a time where decentralisation of educational administration and management is so often written and talked about, discussion of the responsibilities of local bodies for choosing content is still relatively muted. In fact, as TABLE XII shows, there are a large number of open possibilities for local initiatives which can easily be reconciled with the concept of a central curriculum document and centrally prescribed textbooks.

There is far more to content selection at local level than the identification of local variations needed in central programmes and the generation of materials to suit such local needs.

- Each time a local education committee takes a decision about priorities (say, to strengthen language teaching and the teaching of reading in schools in the district)
- Each time a teachers' group discusses approaches to methodology and generates cyclostyled material for its members
- Each time locally-based efforts are planned by the inspectorate to assess and improve standards in schools
  – then quality is affected.

Should anyone doubt the effect of initiatives by local educational leaders on quality, let them compare the record of adjacent districts with similar resources but different commitment and management. We return to these issues in Chapter Seven.

The schools

At first sight it may seem that primary schools, particularly those in difficult circumstances, are relatively powerless to make content choices. Nothing is further from the truth and the proof lies, of course, in the quite staggering variation in achievement between adjacent schools and the very striking difference in attainment between children in different classes at the same level. The argument is developed at some length in Chapter Seven when we consider the key role of the headteacher in promoting quality. Here, it is perhaps worth reminding ourselves of the variations possible and present between individual teachers in a relatively rich country (Malaysia) and a relatively poor one (Lesotho).

In Malaysia, despite some overcrowding in classrooms, school resources are generally adequate and the Ministry actively supportive of schools and teachers who encourage active and problem-oriented methods in the classroom. The importance of remedial and enrichment programmes are also stressed. In this environment the contrast is between the teacher who profits from this encouraging climate and makes the most of the better designed and more imaginative materials available, who attempts to get the most out of individual children, who sees out-of-school and out-of-class activities such as the school library or youth groups as both important and worthwhile; contrasted with the teacher who for lack of energy and initiative has retained the same stolid, boring, classbound and testbound routine which has served her and her predecessors for years.

For trained observers such as ourselves the contrast between entering classes (and schools) where two such different approaches obtain is arresting. It is not merely a matter of difference of output, though test results and exercise books demonstrate this clearly. It is much more a sense of excitement against a sense of boredom, a sense of purpose against one of confusion, and above all a sense of happy involvement by children against a dull and muddy feeling of stagnation. All of these contribute to very significant differences in quality between one class, one school, and one teacher and another – differences usually well appreciated not only by those who administer the system but by the parents who use it.

At the other end of the resource scale, in Lesotho, the context is vastly different but the sharp contrasts in quality are just as apparent. Where the contrast in Malaysia is between living and dead learning, that in Lesotho is between hope and despair. Although the common lot of primary schools in Lesotho is that they are short of everything except children there are still schools where teachers are resolutely determined to retain their part in decision-making and to seek to surmount the difficulties which face them: selecting effectively from an overcrowded syllabus, sharing out scant resources, making the most of their communities and environment, suiting their class management and methodology to the realities of their environment. Others, by contrast seem overwhelmed by the difficulties which confront them, and during the limited periods when they actually attempt teaching seem resigned to covering the ground recommended by the syllabus, whether it is manageable or not, for the benefit of a handful of children in their large classes (whom one strongly suspects would educate themselves in virtually any circumstances).

In every country, therefore, choice of schools and teachers is vital to the quality of education that children receive. Despite the manifest power of schools and teachers to select content and influence quality, the myth of their impotence to do so remains, for like many myths it serves certain people well.

Choices at different levels

The last pages have attempted to develop a theme introduced earlier in the chapter. Choices of content at different levels need to be articulated, negotiated and so far as possible harmonised. To expect sweet agreement between all parties who choose content is neither realistic nor productive; but to hope for better understanding of the process of choice and better communication between the choosers is realistic. So too is an understanding that the myth of the powerless school is a dangerous untruth.

It is not always necessary to think big and national in order to improve quality. For whereas no one would question the need for certain changes in approach and emphasis at the level of the curriculum development centre, no one, equally, should overestimate the ease and speed at which such reforms can take place. On the other hand, the advent of a new and dynamic district inspector can change the quality of educational provision in his area in a few years, a head can transform the school in a matter of months and a new class teacher can raise the quality of learning available in her classroom from the very day she sets foot in it.

Content choosers in partnership

In this chapter we have established that the choice of content is not the purview of a group of specialists, but rather a complicated series of interrelated choices at every level from the minister to the children and their parents. Equally we have implied that content choosers are related at every stage with other agents of implementation. By defining methodology and assessment as important aspects of content we have linked in teacher educators and examination designers. We have indicated how administrators and supervisors critically affect the choice since it is they who set priorities, plan in-service education, authorise variations from national content. Above all it is they who choose the heads who play such a key role in maintaining quality at school level. We have further identified how the community has to be accepted as a partner in the choice of content if the hidden curriculum is to be brought out into the sunlight and if 'needs now' are to be reconciled with 'needs later'.

Nor have we underestimated the difficulties in achieving such a working relationship. Tensions and even mistrust between these agents will undoubtedly occur but these may be minimised if the initial leadership comes from the curriculum centre. Once teachers' colleges, local administrations and above all schools are assured by the centre that their role in the choice and improvement of content is recognised and welcome, they are far more likely to respond willingly and positively.

A most useful preliminary towards establishing such a working relationship would be for the curriculum centre to organise national and regional seminars to discuss the control of the curriculum. Although such a seminar has not yet been held in any of the five countries on which we base our examples, the ideas, we understand, might be welcomed in some form in all of them.

NOTES AND REFERENCES

1 An adaptation of John Kerr's famous definition, 'All the learning which is planned or guided by the school, whether it is carried out in groups or individually, inside or outside the school.'
Kerr, J., *Changing the Curriculum*, University of London Press, 1968.

2 The phrase probably originated in 1968 in Jackson, P. W., *Life in Classrooms*, Holt, Rinehart and Winston, 1968.

3 See Dore, Ronald, *The Diploma Disease; Education, Qualifications and Development*, Unwin, 1976.

4 Reproduced in Hawes, H. W. R., *Lifelong Education, Schools and Curricula in Developing Countries*, UNESCO, Institute of Education, Hamburg, 1975. Quoting from unpublished working papers by R. H. Dave.

5 *Ibid.*, p. 31.

6 There are many ways of arranging such a grid and marking the divisions.
Lawton (1983) suggests examining: curriculum, pedagogy and evaluation at national, regional, institutional, departmental and individual levels.
Lawton, Denis, *Curriculum Studies and Educational Planning*, Hodder and Stoughton, 1983.

7 Conventional wisdom seems to accept four years schooling as being the period necessary to establish permanent functional literacy and the figure is frequently quoted. We have been unable to trace the source of this belief.

8 A comparison of tables in UNICEF's *State of the World's Children 1989* with those of 1984 shows an increase in retention rates in most poorer countries. But figures are still dismal: in thirty countries including many large ones such as India, Pakistan, Bangladesh and Brazil less than half those who start school finish it.

9 Freire, op. cit. See Chapters One and Two.

10 In this case Hugh Hawes and Barnabas Otaala, accompanied by the
    head of the Curriculum Development Centre's language panel.

11 Hawes, H. W. R., *Curriculum and Reality in African Primary
    Schools*, Longman, 1979, p. 104.

12 A useful M.Ed. dissertation in 1983 by Adelaide Sosseh, 'Images of
    Women and Girls in Gambian Primary School Textbooks' at the
    London University Institute of Education, examines this issue.

13 Recently (1987) a seminar at the Indonesian Office of Research and
    Development met to examine just this issue.

14 *Julius Caesar*, 1.ii.

15 Ministry of Education, Jamaica, curriculum development thrust,
    'Functional Education in Jamaica' Kingston, 1972 (unpublished).

16 A number of curriculum projects in health education have adopted
    this technique such as the British Schools' Council projects *Health
    Education*, 5–13 and 13–18, also *Home Economics*, 8–13.
    Key questions include, for instance:
        'What is growing?'
        'What helps me grow?'
        'What is food?'
        'How much food should we eat?'.

17 Government of Kenya. Report of the National Commission on
    Educational Objectives and Practices (the Gacathi Committee),
    Government Printer, Nairobi, 1977.

18 The Kingdom of Lesotho, Ministry of Education, *Report on the
    Views and Recommendations of the Basotho Nation Regarding the
    Future of Education in Lesotho*, Government Printer, Maseru, 1978.

19 The Cabinet Committee report is in Malaysian but its findings are
    described in Mukherjee, H. and Singh, J. S., 'The New Primary
    School Curriculum Project Malaysia' in *International Review of
    Education*, Vol. 29, No. 2, 1982, pp. 247–58.

20 Schools Council, *Primary Practice*, (Working Paper No. 75),
    Methuen Educational, 1983.

21 Curriculum Development Centre, Canberra. 'Core Curriculum for
    Australian Primary Schools (1980)' in Horton, T. and Raggat, P.,

Challenge and Change in the Curriculum, Hodder and Stoughton, 1982, pp. 104–17.

22 Mager, R. F., *Preparing Instructional Objectives*, Fearon, Palo Alto, 1962.

23 Produced during the 1970s by the Jamaica Reading Association, Box 20, Kingston. These little books, duplicated on both sides of two A4 sheets, stapled and folded were produced in hundreds and written by the teachers themselves.

24 Milton Margai Teachers' College in Sierra Leone operates its own Centre for Research into the Education of Secondary Teachers which regularly publishes useful material.

25 Described in Chapter Seven.

26 The Child-to-Child programme at the London University Institutes of Education and Child Health furnishes descriptions of these activities on request and describes them in its newsletters.

CHAPTER 5

THE PEOPLE TRAINERS

This chapter is concerned with those we consider central to our drive to improve the quality of primary education: the teachers. For if we are to change schools we must keep at the forefront of our proposals the idea of changing teachers, *while* they are working in schools.

Central to our discussion are two questions: first, 'What makes a good teacher?' and second, 'What constitutes good teaching?' In this chapter we shall be specifically concerned with identifying the characteristics of good serving teachers[1] and good teaching, 'good' being defined in terms of effectiveness, i.e. knowledge, efficiency, relevance and flexibility. We will also give 'conditions of acceptance' needed at the chalk face for qualitative reform to succeed. The relationship of the teacher to change will therefore concern us.[2]

Any discussion of the teacher's role in the education system will inevitably concern the professional training of teachers both pre- and in-service. As a prerequisite to this discussion it should be said that the division between pre- and in-service teacher education is not always as clear as it may seem.

For many unqualified teachers in-service training may be the only training they receive. For others, pre-service education may well have been of a general kind, an extension of their secondary education with some study of education thrown in for good measure. In-service education (if they are fortunate to receive any) therefore may constitute their only source of *professional* training.

We will therefore be viewing in-service training, *not* as an extension of what was taught at the pre-service stage (and, therefore, understandably used as an avenue for personal advancement) but as an *activity* located in the school and concerned with what the teacher does. We will also suggest that current divisions between 'pre-service' and 'in-service' training may prove increasingly unprofitable to maintain and that we may do well to evolve a more unified and more flexible concept of 'Teacher Education and Training'.

If this isn't complicated enough, it seems logical when analysing the place of the teacher in relation to her training to consider the role of teacher educators and those responsible for *their* training. For it appears curious that so little attention has been paid to the trainers of trainers.[3] One possible reason may be the apparent and widely-held belief that university and college educators require little specific training for the job, educationists included.

As we stated earlier, it is not just the quality of the teacher that is central to our concern but what the teacher knows and what the teacher does with that knowledge. To a very considerable extent, therefore, *what* we teach cannot be separated from *how* we teach.[4]

We might also note that as much as the teacher acts *in loco parentis* so all adults, and even many older children, particularly in developing countries, are cast in the role of teacher.[5] When discussing a classroom teacher's methodology we need to keep in mind the general child-rearing practices considered appropriate and legitimate by the culture in which the teacher works.

This is particularly important when we consider ways in which we want the teacher to change her behaviour. For it may be that we are in fact asking a society to change its general attitude to the way all its adults interact with the children for whom they are in some way responsible.

THE TEACHER *IN SITU*

Twenty-five years ago a body called the World Confederation of Organisations of the Teaching Profession (WCOTP) surveyed the 'status of the teaching profession' in twenty-three African countries:

> The status of the teaching profession in Africa is low. Recruitment has been haphazard, while training has been inadequate. The teacher often does not get a salary which keeps him contented comparable to that of others having the same qualifications. He often has to work in conditions which would daunt the bravest of spirits.[6]

Low status, inadequate training, poor working conditions and little prospect of improvements in conditions of service, these 'realities' are what frame and constrain the situation in which many good teachers work.

What seems to have happened since WCOTP's survey is that the teacher, far from being seen as central to the design and implementation of innovation and reform, has become marginalised by non-teaching educationists working within centralised planning units and curriculum development centres. The teacher has often been left to implement changes designed elsewhere and, given the demands of day-to-day teaching, has fallen back on well-tried traditional practices. We will return to this when discussing methodology.

What we are saying, therefore, is that we must seriously consider the day-to-day working experiences of serving teachers (and their views of what constitutes realistic change) highlighted by the WCOTP survey when discussing such grand issues as teacher effectiveness or the relationships of teaching styles to the quality of pupil outcomes.

A GOOD TEACHER

Let us address our first question: what characterises a good teacher? The following characteristics can be identified:[7]

1 Teaching experience

As the common man would suggest, it appears from research all round the world that 'the more experienced teachers are, the more their pupils appear to learn'.[8] Experienced teachers in Africa particularly, were rated as being more committed to the teachers' instructional role than those with only a few years work under their belt. It may be that good teachers are by definition those who have decided, for one reason or another, to stay within the profession. The negative aspect of this characteristic is teacher turnover. Maybe an understanding of why new recruits leave the profession prematurely will give us a clearer view of how to improve the quality of education generally? For it would seem unfair to blame high turnover on teachers' selfish pursuit of a career outside teaching.

In 1978 Koguna[9] studied 560 Grade II teachers in Northern Nigeria who left the profession during the period 1970–76, attributing their departure to eighteen factors which mirrored the picture revealed by the WCOTP survey. We can group these factors into those relating to:

(a)   personnel policies and practices (5 factors)
(b)   working conditions (3 factors)
(c)   administrative and supervisory issues (4 factors)
(d)   community (2 factors)
(e)   personal (4 factors)

Of these factors all but six (two community and four personal) were possibly avoidable in that they resulted from actions of, or neglect by the State Ministries of Education and/or Local Education Authorities. Furthermore, the research suggested that the community factors could have been alleviated to some extent had education officials made an effort to improve the image of teachers and the teaching profession within the community.

2 The attitudes, opinions and beliefs of teachers and their expectations of pupils

Common sense would also suggest that teachers who don't understand and empathise with children will be neither very effective nor very happy in their work. Research bears this out, indicating a strong relationship between teacher attitude towards pupils and teaching generally and pupil outcomes.[10] Further research therefore needs to be conducted on training teachers how to develop positive attitudes towards pupils and how to give them accurate, helpful and positive feedback.[11] How far such a change in teacher attitudes would go against or reinforce widely-held cultural attitudes to learning and the behaviour of teachers raises further interesting questions.

3 Teacher-processing of information

If teachers are to become, as we would wish, central to the reform process, it seems important to understand the way in which they develop their views and process information they receive, particularly that emanating from other agencies of our 'quality wheel'.

What research[12] seems to suggest is that serving teachers often either only pay lip-service to change filtering down from above or unknowingly think that they have made significant changes in behaviour or pedagogy, when in fact little meaningful change has actually occurred. It has been noted in Malaysia where the primary curriculum reform enjoins group teaching that a very large majority of teachers, having arranged their children in groups, then proceed to deliver their lessons in much the same way as they had always done.[13]

As Hurst says, with large classes, few textbooks, little or no equipment, high noise levels and hot climates, rote-learning 'delivers a relatively high rate of return for a modest work input'[14]. But rote-learning is not the only option open to the beleaguered teacher. What the authors of this book wish to stress is that teachers *can* change their approach to teaching and improve the quality of what they do in the classroom without necessarily making their work more difficult. In fact, if anything, what we suggest is that change, if it is to work, must reduce the burden placed upon teachers and liberate them so that they can begin to take more control over what they do. We shall return to this issue later when specifically discussing methodology.

What does seem clear though, is the need for more understanding of how teachers process the advice and new information given to them and the constraints upon them in the implementation of that change. One characteristic of what constitutes a good teacher seems to be the ability of the individual to master this process. That ability and the ability to teach is related very much to the teacher's own 'knowledge-base', and in particular his or her knowledge and mastery of the language of instruction.

4 The teacher's knowledge

We might ask the basic question: what do we expect a *good* teacher to *know*? His subject areas surely (and he might develop a particular expertise in say science or language); his own pupils' lives and interests most certainly; and without doubt knowledge of the craft of teaching. We might add to that list knowledge of the language of instruction, knowledge of developments in education and knowledge of good practice that is happening elsewhere.

Central to learning knowledge is the issue of doubt, uncertainty and *not* knowing. Perhaps one thing teachers can do for their pupils is to show them that it is possible to live with a degree of uncertainty, that there are not necessarily cast-iron answers for everything.[15] Perhaps, as teachers, we also need to reveal and celebrate the fact that we, like the pupils, are also learning. But in sober fact there is a limit to the extent that even the most self-critical teacher can admit not knowing, and by and large the less confident the teacher is the lower that limit will be.

This means that pre-service, in-service and staff development programmes need to focus not only upon developing a teacher's *skills* but also his or her knowledge-bases. Such foci might be framed around the following type of questions:

- what 'new' **knowledge** in mathematics and history does our primary school teacher need now?
- are there new **approaches to teaching** health education that primary level teachers now (or will) need to know?
- are there new **approaches to classroom organisation** that teachers need to know before they can introduce new knowledge in other areas?
- how much **knowledge of the local community**, existing **resources**, the children's **out-of-school life**, etc. does the teacher possess which is not being effectively integrated into the world of books and 'in-school' practices?

Knowledge breeds confidence, improves status, and enhances the capability of the teacher to take more control over the teaching-learning process (in particular the use and adaptation of resources). As we said earlier, it seems that *how* one teaches is closely bound up with *what* one teaches.

5 Age; Sex; Status

Though what the teacher knows and teaching experience are important factors in the quality of the teaching force, it appears that a teacher's age, sex and socio-economic status have little consistent effect upon teacher effectiveness.[16] There is some evidence that 'male teachers are more effective in Science and Mathematics and older teachers with secondary pupils',[17] a fact that may have more to do with pupils' cultural expectations than any teacher-related factors.

6 Training

Our sixth and perhaps most controversial characteristic of what determines a good teacher is training. Does a teacher's training make a difference to how she performs in the classroom? We will examine this issue in our next section.

GOOD TEACHING

We have examined the good teacher, but what of good teaching? Let us apply four criteria we have used earlier in defining quality: efficiency, relevance, flexibility, and striving for 'something more'.

(a) Efficiency

At the start we asked the question, who is a good teacher? One answer might be: a teacher who works efficiently at her job; her job primarily being the improvement in the standards of learning of her pupils. To be efficient in doing such is to be effective. Joyce, Hersh and McKibbin studying education in selected industrialised countries[18] identified two broad categories of attributes which, they suggest, are characteristic of an effective school. These are social organisation and instruction, and instruction and curriculum. The table below lists the different attributes under these two heads.

TABLE XIII ATTRIBUTES OF EFFECTIVE SCHOOLS

SOCIAL ORGANISATION	INSTRUCTION AND CURRICULUM
Clear academic and social behaviour goals	Higher academic learning time
Order and discipline	Frequent and monitored homework
High expectations	Frequent monitoring of student progress
Teacher efficiency	Coherently organised curriculum
Pervasive caring	Variety of teaching strategies
Public rewards and incentives	Opportunities for pupil responsibility
Administrative leadership	
Community support	

Commenting on this list in relation to less developed contexts, Dove notes that 'these attributes would appear to be important in *any context*' (our italics). She goes on, 'the attributes of effective schools seem to depend on the way teachers conduct themselves'.[19]

What this would seem to imply is that the teacher is very much the agent of her own development, and that at the heart of an improvement in teacher efficiency and effectiveness is the ability of the teacher, with support, to take personal initiatives in raising standards of teaching and learning in the classroom.

A casual glance at the attributes listed in the 'Instruction and Curriculum' column would seem to require not a heavy input of resources but rather more time, effort and commitment on the part of the teacher. It may be that teachers are more willing to perform such tasks as 'monitoring student progress' and the setting of 'homework' once these activities have become common practice within schools and an accepted part of pre- and in-service training. Ask teachers to take more responsibility and maybe they will! Support them and we are sure they will.

It may also prove worthwhile to examine how much time the average teacher actually spends teaching in the classroom. A foreign adviser visiting schools in rural Nepal witnesses the following:

> I must admit that I have been shocked during my visits to schools by the extremely low level of motivation and commitment of teachers in rural areas. On visiting schools it is the rule rather than exception that the teacher is not teaching.[20]

And, of course, we all know of the opposite: of many teachers labouring to be as effective as local conditions permit. If teacher 'time on task' is important in assessing effectiveness then a similar study of time spent by pupils on their learning tasks might also tell us something about the relevance of what they and the teachers are doing for forty or more hours per week, thirty to forty weeks a year.

(b) Relevance

Many changes suggested by policy-makers may sound well, in theory, but prove difficult to implement because they take little account of what parents, pupils and more than likely the teachers too consider relevant to 'doing well' and 'getting on in life'. It means, therefore, that if we are going to suggest that child-centred, heuristic learning is *more* relevant to a child's needs (and we are), we need to take account, as Turner[21] suggests, of whether the proposed changes:

> ... will increase the possibility of pupils climbing the education ladder to higher status and an improved standard of living or whether they will lock the children into their own situation of deprivation by teaching only those low-level skills which enable them to function in a rural situation or as urban labourers.

School pupils in particular, he goes on to suggest, will want to know if such changes will give them access to higher educational institutions. Teachers will be asking whether their own status in the school is being threatened by possible changes decreed from a distant ministry and they may, understandably, feel that more is being demanded of them than they are able to deliver, with consequent feeling of insecurity and anxiety. Heads may feel particularly threatened, since they are expected to provide leadership without any clear perception of how exhortation can be translated into implementation. Teacher educators will, in Turner's words, 'be asking questions about the impact of new ideas on the structure of the college ... and at the Ministry questions may be raised about the cost of implementing the new programme'.[22]

It seems, therefore, that relevant teaching is about 'needs now', e.g. giving the teacher new strategies for dealing with large classes, and 'needs later', e.g. relating those new practices to what parents, pupils and the community want from schooling, be it technical proficiency, better use of leisure time or academic success.

(c) Flexibility

The third criterion of good teaching, flexibility, is no less complex than issues related to efficiency and relevance. The ability to be flexible is surely linked to an understanding of what 'room for manoeuvre' exists: what necessary conditions exist in which teachers feel confident in responding and reflecting upon change. Hurst believes that the ability of the teacher to respond flexibly will also depend upon how centralised or decentralised control of policy is within the education system.

His seven conditions of acceptance mentioned in Chapter Three are in effect prerequisites of teacher effectiveness in the process of qualitative improvement of education:

1 Teachers must have information about changes.
2 The teachers' value systems must coincide with the outcome of qualitative change or at best only cosmetic change will occur.
3 Teachers will need some evidence for believing the changes will work. They should be consulted far in advance of implementation.
4 Teachers will only be able to modify their practice when the necessary resources have been provided. We might add that if no resources are forthcoming then this should be taken into account before any reforms are considered.
5 Teachers will need to feel the effort required of them is worthwhile. The efficiency ratio of yield to input must balance in the teachers' favour.
6 Teachers must not be inundated with too many changes. Such a situation will undercut any foundations on which to build.
7 Teachers should be encouraged to see implementation of reform in terms of trial and adaptation. Such a view (and a recognition that experimentation is a legitimate activity) will reduce anxiety and help keep things in proper perspective.

Given these 'conditions of acceptance' it is more likely that teachers will act, as we wish, in a flexible and reliable manner and will also feel part and parcel of any drive to improve the quality of education.

(d) 'Something more'

Good teaching seems to need 'something more' than just efficiency, relevance and flexibility. Perhaps the process of change involves teachers responding to real practical situations by repeated cycles of analysis, observation, solution, design, application and reflection. This cycle can be seen in the context of our earlier framework of moving from a period of critique towards a position of possibility.

One aspect of our 'something more' is perhaps the motivation on the part of the teacher to want to make such a move: to care enough about his or her responsibilities to seek to 'design, apply and reflect' upon the possibility of change; and to be encouraged and supported in the belief that education is more than just a mechanistic means of training our young but is something more meaningfully related to developing the whole child.

But 'something more' also relates to the teacher's power to influence the minds, the characters, the lives, the very souls of learners. Great teachers, great 'gurus' were not revered in the past because they had passed examinations in content and methodology, but for the way in which they had 'educated' (led out) young people from ignorance to enlightenment, led them out in many different ways and by many different paths. If we neglect this aspect by equating quality of teaching with level of training or by insisting on one 'right' methodology we shall be doing education a disservice. Exceptional and effective teachers, whether or not they are school teachers, whether or not they have academic or professional certificates, must be recognised and encouraged.

Let us now return to the controversial question of training generally, and to start with, the specific question of whether teachers' training actually makes any difference to their effectiveness.

THE TEACHER-IN-TRAINING: PRE-SERVICE

In 1975, Alexander and Simmons questioned the 'effectiveness of conventional investments in teacher education . . . for raising student achievement levels'.[23] They went on to say that the central question was 'whether trained teachers do improve student improvement'. Even to raise such a question angered and concerned professional educators at all levels and left teacher educators in universities (already sensitive about their role as 'neither academic nor practising teacher') feeling decidedly uncomfortable.

Two major studies on the relationship of teacher training to student achievement were conducted:

1 The World Bank-funded Institute of International Education (IIE) study by Husen, Saha and Noonan in 1978.[24]
2 The International Development Research Centre (IDRC) study in Canada by Avalos and Haddad in 1980.[25]

The former reviewed 64 studies in 32 separate reports while the latter based its findings on 589 studies in a number of developing countries. The IIE report reduced the discomfort of teacher trainers a little when it concluded that teacher credentials had positive effects on student achievement. The IDRC report made a similar conclusion but added that the relationships between teacher qualifications and training and pupil achievement were 'complex'.

Emerging from the research we may ask two important questions:

- If training does make a difference generally, why are there significant examples of countries in which teacher education seems to have little effect 'at the chalk face'?
- Is there therefore an important distinction to be made between good teacher training and poor tertiary level education, masquerading as pre-service instruction?

It seems, therefore, that it is the *quality* of education at teacher training level that is decisive. This appears more important than trying to prove a relationship between training (of any sort) and pupil effectiveness.

The major fault of most pre-service teacher education is that it does not address itself to the needs of the schools in which its graduates will work.

Nepal is a good example where, frankly, the situation over the past few years has deteriorated to such a point that the Institute of Education, responsible for pre-service teacher education, has been threatened with closure unless drastic steps are taken to redress the situation.

In a nutshell, the weaknesses of the training seems to be:

The quality of students entering teacher education

In Nepal, 'students, in general, rank this programme (i.e. teacher education) as their last preference'.[26] Teacher educators are therefore working with poorly motivated students who are entering the profession as a last resort.

The quality of teacher educators

'Most teacher educators of these (i.e. outlying campuses of the University of Tribuvan, Nepal) campuses had no experience in school teaching'.[27] It seems a curious paradox that, whereas a great deal of attention is paid to the relationship between teacher training and pupil learning, very little attention is paid to the relationship of teacher educator training and the performance of teacher trainees. One way forward may be to provide teacher educators with an opportunity to return to (or enter for the first time) the primary classroom and work alongside existing teachers. Teacher tutors will then have 'recent and relevant experience', which will help student teachers relate practice to theory.

The quality of pre-service training of teachers

At issue seems to be finding the balance between what the beginning teacher needs to know (principles of child development, new approaches to teaching agriculture, etc.) and the development of *strategies* (involving skills and the affective domain) that will be most appropriate in making most *use* of that knowledge.

Given that significant teacher training occurs within university Departments of Education it is easy to see how a situation can develop where the 'study of education' as a discipline *per se* predominates. The recently established B.Ed. degree in Primary Education at Kenyatta University in Nairobi illustrates this point. During the lengthy validation procedure the Senate of the University whittled down many of the innovative aspects of the proposed degree, substituting them for requirements of a more traditionally academic kind. Supporters of this action might in many ways rightly claim that a necessary balance must be maintained between the continued education of the teacher-in-training and the training in professional skills, but too often, as in Kenyatta, certain highly academic content is equated with 'standards' and professional skills become marginalised in the process.

At a London University conference held in 1979 entitled *Teacher Education in Developing Countries: Prospects For the Eighties*,[28] Peter Williams noted 'four strands in the thinking of those who would like to see change' in the direction of teacher education in developing countries:

(i) Teacher training institutions need to be more in touch with other professional training centres, perhaps sharing courses and facilities with only the final stage as a specialist course. Such a change it is suggested would raise the status of teaching and mean that those who entered the profession were more committed to teaching.

(ii) Teacher training institutions need to be 'in closer association with school practice; to make courses more relevant to the classroom; and to use the motivation and experience of those who have taught in the actual process of their training.' Children need to be observed in their 'natural habitat' by students and for that observation to be related back to knowledge given in areas such as psychology and sociology of education.

(iii) Teacher training institutions need to consider 'alternative patterns of initial training', e.g. part-time training with untrained teachers remaining in schools, thereby easing the problem of staffing at primary level. Such innovations would need to be 'properly staffed' with adequate professional support services to avoid the danger of producing under-trained teachers. But there is a strong argument for suggesting that more training needs to be done in school by serving teachers well supported by the college or university.

Teacher training institutions need to consider phasing training over the teachers' career, i.e. a process of continuous professional development. It is recognised that such a change, with teachers moving between employment and training, might escalate the opportunity-cost involved but if seen in terms of 'part-time refresher courses' then a useful balance between the two might be maintained.[29]

These concerns and ideals were widely shared by those who listened to him.

IDEALS UNDER SIEGE: THE CASE OF LESOTHO

Attempts have not been lacking to transform the kind of ideals urged by Williams into reality. In Africa as early as the 1940s the Institute of Education at Bacht er Ruda[30] in the Sudan exemplified many of them. In the early 1970s UNESCO stimulated and funded a number of innovative projects in teacher education including those at Bunumbu in Sierra Leone and Namutamba in Uganda.[31]

The fact that so little success was achieved by these and other initiatives in breaking through towards a more effective, relevant and imaginative concept as teacher education may stem from the fact that a powerful combination of forces appear to be ranged against change.

In an attempt to analyse these, let us examine the case of the National Teachers' Training College (NTTC) in Lesotho. This college was established in 1975 and supported in its initial years by a consortium of donors, both international and bilateral, co-ordinated by UNESCO. The new college, designed to replace the small uneconomic mission colleges, was founded with high hopes and high ideals. It was to serve both pre-service and in-service education; act as a focus of curriculum reform and materials production; and link schools and college through the novel system of an 'internship year'. During their second year in the college students would spend their entire time teaching in schools. They would be helped and supported by members of staff, designated as internship supervisors who would operate from special centres established throughout the country where resources, advice, and a venue for in-service training would be locally available for students (and serving teachers).

As the former principal of the NTTC states, these goals (incorporated in the 1978 *Staff Handbook*) make satisfying reading for progressive educationists. The needs of trainers are characterised as follows:

(a) the need for a teacher-training institution not only to initiate the trainee in his instructional role but also to prepare him for the variety of responsibilities which he may be required to assume in a changing and developing society;

(b) the need to prepare trainee teachers in the effective use, for the benefit of the learner, of all the resources afforded by the social and cultural environment;

(c) the need to give the student-teachers an opportunity of experiencing some of these new roles and responsibilities during their period of training through participation in the decision-making process within the College; through the establishment of closer links with various educational institutions in Lesotho and elsewhere; and through the provision of a practically-oriented programme designed to develop the students' initiative, adaptability and resourcefulness in the face of changing circumstances, and thereby to prepare them for the challenge of the future;

(d) the need to provide for and ensure the student-teachers' personal and professional self-development after they have left the College by developing in them a positive attitude to lifelong education and the need for recurrent professional updating while in service;

(e) the need to provide not only an adequate preparation in the subject matter of each branch of study and the pedagogy related thereto but also a conceptual framework encompassing all the disciplines so as to accommodate and support the continued growth of knowledge;

(f) the need to make provision for professional development, both theoretical and practical, which should not be limited to the student's acceptance of what is passed on to him, but should include an introduction to the notion that he or she, given an enquiring mind and some elementary research techniques, can contribute to our knowledge of teaching and learning;

(g) the need to familiarise the teacher-to-be with the educational applications of technology, including the mass media.[32]

In 1986 the staff of the College met again to review these noble goals and assess how far they had been achieved. During the course of a week's intensive discussion the following disturbing facts emerged:

1 Because staffing proved difficult and because relatively high academic standards were required of tutors, few of those recruited had any experience in primary schools, fewer still had a knowledge of schools in rural areas and a substantial number had never taught at all.

2 Because staff were recruited from university graduates in particular disciplines and because the College was divided into faculties each largely autonomous, the goals of inter-disciplinarity remained unmet. Instead of concentrating on developing the student as an individual, far more emphasis was placed on covering ground with students in subject or professional areas. As a result of this territoriality the autonomy of students was eroded: they had heavy timetables, virtually no free time and consequently virtually no personal 'room to manoeuvre'.

3 Because the standards in College were equated to standards in universities with a view that College graduates who wished to study further could be granted certain exemptions, College tutors continually kept university syllabuses in mind. Many of these had little in common with the knowledge and skills needed by a primary teacher, yet suited the interests and capabilities of the tutors themselves.

4 By contrast, those with school experience and often slightly lower paper qualifications found themselves employed permanently as internship supervisors on a slightly lower salary and with a considerably lower status than their academic colleagues.

5 Finally the 'sandwich' approach to internship, so apparently rational in theory, proved inconvenient for academics and bureaucrats alike. It interfered with academically-orientated studies, upset school staffing plans, raised costs and delayed the output of teachers into the system. It has been replaced by a more conventional pattern of school practice.

It is to the great credit of the National Teachers' Training College that they have been deeply concerned at the erosion of their noble goals, as reflected by the agenda and outcomes of their discussions in 1986. One particularly interesting outcome of this seminar was the report of a group which set itself the task of 'dreaming' the future policy and orientation of the College by the end of the next decade. They came up with a highly innovative model which combined in-college and in-school training and far greater interchange between College lecturers and good school teachers.

INITIAL AND IN-SERVICE TRAINING

Increasingly, therefore, we may need to question the old division between pre-service and in-service training: in colleges throughout developing countries what is pre-service for some may be in-service for others. For there is an increasing tendency to draw college entrants from the ranks of the large pool of untrained teachers since at least these have showed themselves ready and willing to enter classrooms.

We should not deplore this trend. Rather we may welcome it and, indeed, as Williams implies, begin to consider some very radical changes in practice towards a redistribution of resources for training over a teacher's career even though this may result in the cutting down periods of initial training. With this in mind it may be appropriate now to turn our attention to the in-service training of teachers (often called INSET), for it combines and extends many of the issues raised in our discussion of the teacher *in situ* and the teacher-in-training. We will also consider the relationship of INSET to what is termed 'staff development' in schools.

The teacher-in-training: INSET

More than 50% of Nepal's primary teachers are untrained. In Kenya and Lesotho the figures are marginally better at 31% and 30% respectively.[33] In West Africa the figures rise to 71% for Liberia, 68% for The Gambia and 61% for Sierra Leone.

And it is not just percentages but the numbers involved that is worrying: Kenya's unqualified teaching force numbers close on 32 000, with Nepal having to cope with approximately 21 000 untrained primary teachers.

In Nepal selected serving teachers are removed from schools and given a lengthy campus-based, degree-oriented training at the Institute of Education. Underqualified or untrained personnel deputise for them, often ending up as the permanent replacement, whilst the now upgraded teacher moves on to a more lucrative post in the secondary sector.

As Shrestha notes:

> The built-in career ladder in academic training has, in fact, made in-service training only an upgrading programme for teachers.[34]

This undesired end result of in-service teacher education reflects less on the quality and relevance of the training given and more on the differentials in conditions of service, status, etc. existing between primary and secondary sectors (quite apart from the greater differences between teaching generally and other professions).

We are therefore dealing with a number of constraints in our efforts to raise teacher training to a minimally acceptable standard, two of the most important being: maintenance of the link between serving teachers and their schools; and the retention of those teachers within the profession.

Given that we can provide a critique for the situation, what can we do about it?

We have identified five ways forward, approaches that are grounded in successful innovation in a variety of national contexts:

(i) We need *more* in-service education. If we believe *in situ* training is important we need more of it. The Indonesian initiative in West Java (officially styled Active Learning Through Professional Support but often referred to as 'The Cianjur Project') is described in Chapter Seven. It has succeeded in constructing a working INSET model that places at its centre the teacher *in situ*. It has stressed the professionalisation of head teachers and advisors, the development of locally-based training for serving teachers (often in 'teachers' clubs' held on school premises) and the encouragement of a more active and process-based style of learning and teaching in schools supported by locally produced materials for teachers and supervisors.

If we could have *more* of these sort of teacher support initiatives we might find it easier to ask the serving teacher to shoulder responsibilities associated with change.

(ii)   We need a *new philosophy* of in-service education. Most of all we need to get away from a 'deficit theory' of training which is informed by a belief that INSET is only 'training the untrained' and nothing more. For the experienced teacher INSET is more a matter of professional *staff development*. Smith[35] considers that such development 'might begin with teachers considering what they do well, and would like to do more, or even take as its starting-point intuitions about ideals rather than recognition of problems'. What we would be doing therefore, in Lesotho, Kenya, Indonesia, Malaysia, Nepal and elsewhere is to illuminate teachers' existing *strengths* rather than highlight their weaknesses and alleged needs.

Such activity would build up a bank of good practice which might well form the basis of in-school workshops attended by both strong and 'beginner' teachers.

Nepal's local teachers' resource centres as part of their Primary Education Project, Indonesia's model schools within the Active Learning Project and Kenya's 'Teacher Advisory Centres' are examples of such foci upon good practice.

(iii)   Our third way forward concerns the need for a *revised curriculum* of in-service education. Throughout this book we have emphasised criteria of flexibility, teacher autonomy, relevance and efficiency in the improvement in the quality of primary education. These criteria need to guide us in the design and implementation of INSET and staff development programmes.

Perhaps if participants were given more of an opportunity to design their own courses, e.g. tailor content to teacher needs now, adapt methodology to allow for peer group demonstrations, adopt a more problem-solving approach, we might see an unleashing of great potential and a closer working relationship of educationist (curriculum developer, planner, lecturer, etc.) and client-teacher. Such an approach has been referred to as 'participatory teacher education'.

(iv)   We need a more *decentralised* approach to INSET. The further INSET occurs away from the classroom, the more difficult it is to keep it relevant and applicable. Our aim must be to look to local self-help initiatives. The Headteachers' Training Programmes in Malaysia, the Active Learning through Professional Support Project in Indonesia, the B.Ed.

(Primary) programme in Kenya are efforts to move in the right direction. As we mentioned in Chapter Two, though, for teachers to assert themselves over the decision-making process is difficult, given centralised bureaucracies and traditions of political control that have marginalised teachers' governance of education. But, as we have seen, there are an increasing number of examples of good practice which do not threaten existing political hierarchies and *do* improve quality.

(v) Lastly we need to consolidate and develop the links between all those directly or indirectly involved in boosting the teacher's knowledge and expertise once *in situ*. Such important links include:

- The link between teachers' college and any in-service programme occuring outside the college. A weakness of the Indonesian project is the lack of involvement of local teacher training colleges.
- The link between in-service centres (teacher advisory centres [Kenya], resource centres [Nepal], etc.) and existing schools, thus encouraging a 'spill over' effect and effective feedback.
- The link between those responsible for research and development (curriculum development centres, institutes of education, etc.) and those charged with supporting change, e.g. headteachers, inspectors/supervisors.
- The link between the headteacher and teachers within schools. It may seem strange to emphasise these links but it seems crucial, from the experiences of Nepal and Indonesia, to qualitatively change the nature of the links between headteachers and teachers so that the former redefine their role and become the centre of school-based in-service education; and in the process build up communication links with other heads doing similar work. With strong headteachers taking on this role (with minor administrative tasks delegated to others?) it will mean that schools can initiate the business of quality improvement at source.

Learning from models of good practice nationally and internationally; the establishment of support services for the serving teacher; the strengthening and development of links between parts of the system; and the redefining of existing roles of headteacher and supervisor are just a few ways good in-service training can lead to better quality in primary schools.

THE TRAINING OF TRAINERS

In a recently-completed research project, *Training Third World Educational Administrators: Methods and Materials*,[36] which had as its

109

focus the 'training of trainers' and the 'management of educational change', Hurst and Rodwell identify five problem areas in the training of educational administrators. Their findings would seem to have import to our concern for improvement in the training of teacher educators.

1 Inadequate budgets

'Some of the new institutes are run on a shoestring . . . it is essential to create an impression on administrative trainees that the training institute is itself a model of efficient organisation.'

2 Undertrained trainers

'The trainers . . . have inadequate knowledge and experience of alternative training methods and techniques; their style and approach is frequently of the teacher rather than the trainer.'

3 Shortage of suitable training materials

'Trainers often have timetables that leave insufficient time for generating materials, and this increases the pressure on them to use traditional methods.' As a result of this it appears that few trainees at teachers' colleges have any instruction in materials production. There would seem to be sense in 'training trainers' in the designing and production of basic teaching-learning materials and using locally available resources.

4 Neglect of research

This neglect extends to training needs and impact of training, 'Evaluation consists all too frequently of enquiring whether trainees found the course useful and which bits they found most useful.'[37] One can pose a question: how many institutes of education/teachers' training colleges require their trainees to evaluate their own training and then discuss those findings at an end-of-year staff meeting?

5 Lack of a coherent training policy

'Lack of any coherent training policy . . . and poor co-ordination and integration of training provision.' There may well be much to be gained by institutions in one particular area (perhaps a university, polytechnic and several teachers' colleges) forming a regional/national board of training and meeting at timetabled regular intervals to discuss common problems, the sharing of resources and improved lines of communication.

Hurst and Rodwell's research (in Thailand, Sri Lanka, Mauritius, Kenya and Malta primarily) reached a main conclusion that:

> a key problem facing a materials research and development project such as ours is the need to attend to issues of training of the trainers and institutional support for implementation.[38]

If the starting point, for them, is the training of trainers then a second priority is the appropriateness of alternative methods and techniques in different contexts, a priority we shall consider in the final section of this chapter.

The Kenyatta University B.Ed. programme referred to earlier is designed to improve the quality of experienced personnel in primary schools who may well, in turn, become teacher trainers and principals of teachers' colleges. Some thought has also been given to training the university staff concerned with the new degree, and as previously stated, careful attention given to the production of training materials. A logical next step will be to extend the process into teachers' colleges with graduates from the University providing leadership and encouragement to primary school trainers and local teachers attending in-service courses.

THE TEACHER AND TRAINER: APPROPRIATE METHODOLOGIES

Earlier in this chapter we asked two questions: What is a good teacher? and What is good teaching? In many ways they are two sides of the same coin for a good teacher could be defined as someone who teaches well.

In spite of all the interesting research conducted into teacher effectiveness it is probably true to say that we all have a view of what constitutes the fundamentals of good teaching: learning to do something from experience; help and encouragement from others; the exploration of knowledge; the discovery of something new; the practice of something in order to be able to do it better. Others among us may have a different vocabulary, utilising phrases such as: life skills, enjoyable activities, holistic learning, but whatever terms we employ it does seem that real learning is more concerned with doing than with being told, with experience than with passive listening, with interaction with those in a similar position than with sitting all day on the same very hard chair.

Yet if these 'fundamentals' are so well known why is it that the common methodology found in classrooms all over the world is the teacher-centred, lecture type relying on rote-memorisation and evaluation through end-of-session examinations? Is it training of teachers (or lack of it), inadequate resources, teaching styles handed down over generations, problems of pupil control, classroom management, teacher status?

It is not enough to say that there are no models of good practice around; rare they may be but all of us can cite examples where good committed teachers are promoting sound, sometimes exciting and innovative learning.

The major question appears to be why are there not more teachers behaving like this? One of the things we have stressed in this book is the fact that quality, or the improvement of quality, is less a result at the end of a production line (e.g. an examination pass) but more a process in which experience and experiential learning for both teacher and pupil are key determinants of improvement. This means that if we want the pupils to use better, alternative methods in their learning processes we must support, instruct and encourage the teacher in his or her methods; and if we want the trainer to behave differently we must focus attention upon his or her process of training, and so on. We are all part of a human chain engaged in similar activities, with shared responsibilities in improving the end product and providing a better teaching/learning process for all participants.

Such worthy sermonising though has little impact if left at this level. What is needed are concrete examples of good practice in which this 'process-chain' has been seen to have been significantly improved.

The following is an extract from a paper, written by one of the authors of this book as part of the preparatory phase for a major programme of teacher improvement described in more detail in Chapter Seven. It lists seven types of teacher behaviour and seven sets of activities that could be (not should or must) encouraged by a supervisor or, for that matter, a teacher educator, without any extra financial expenditure.

TABLE XIV Changing teacher behaviour – behaviours and activities identified by supervision seminar (1979)

Desired Behaviour	Example of an activity which could be encouraged by the supervisor
1 Towards more logical and flexible planning of work	1.1 Sensible lesson preparation in units rather than individual lessons
	1.2 Ability to modify preparation as a result of feedback from children
2 Towards encouraging children to think critically	2.1 Developing a line of questions which encourage thought and response from children
	2.2 Encouraging children to ask questions
3 Towards better recognition of individual differences between children and the range of ability within classes	3.1 Competent and systematic marking of children's work
	3.2 Setting appropriate tasks for children
	3.3 Additional relevant work set for brighter and slower children
	3.4 Better and more individualised questioning

TABLE XIV (*continued*) Changing teacher behaviour – behaviours and activities identified by supervision seminar (1979)

Desired Behaviour	Example of an activity which could be encouraged by the supervisor
4 Towards encouraging creativity in children	4.1 Encouragement of methodologies, i.e. drama and role playing which allow children to develop individual talents
	4.2 Encouragement in the display of children's work, e.g. in art and craft
5 Towards encouraging children to link learning with living in the community	5.1 Setting of practical tasks
	5.2 Use of local examples in teaching
	5.3 Use of the community as a 'laboratory' involving pupils studying outside the classroom as well as in it
	5.4 Use of local community members as resource people in the school
	5.5 Use of the school building for community purposes
6 Towards differentiating the needs and interests of older and younger children	6.1 Use of activity methods for young children
	6.2 Awareness that younger children have a shorter attention span than older ones
	6.3 Awareness that younger children cannot understand abstract concepts (like diagrams)
7 Towards encouragement of co-operation and mutual self-help among children	7.1 Good grouping practice involving opportunities for children to discover things together instead of singly
	7.2 Opportunities for better children to help weaker ones

If these are the kind of behaviours which need to be encouraged in teachers and children, there are clear messages for the methodology which needs to be adopted in colleges.

It is interesting that a number of the activities recommended necessitate more a change in attitude to learning than any increase in resources. 'Encouraging children to ask questions', 'lesson preparation in units rather than individual lessons', 'use of local community members', etc. are all asking for a change in the way teachers and trainers perceive their role. Such a change, to judge from the research of Hurst and Rodwell, must be *managed change*, discussed, trialled and then evaluated by the practitioners themselves.

There are many real problems faced by potentially very good teachers: large classes of eighty or more, a supply of dated and inadequate textbooks, an elitist secondary selective entrance examination, etc.

Acknowledging the existence of these classroom realities is half-way to devising strategies for their solution. There has in the richer Northern hemisphere been much talk of 'school-based curriculum development' in which the school, under the leadership of the headteacher, establishes working groups, INSET programmes, etc., to tackle problems that were once the purview of a centralised schools council or regional local educational authority.

Efforts of this kind require training and support taking many forms from school clusters, teacher advisory centres to weekend and holiday 'refresher courses' held at a local teachers' college.

Curriculum development centres and INSET workshops have, in the past, devoted a great deal of time and money to matters of *content*. Much good work has been done particularly in the field of indigenisation of syllabus content. What is now needed is for similar effort to be directed to making more effective the way in which teachers handle such content, given the 'real' problems indicated above. A suggested start would be for a headteacher to gather his staff together one day and focus attention upon, say, 'effective strategies for teaching large classes.' Initiatives like this might well produce quite unexpected results, particularly if staff from more than one school and with different levels of experience could be brought together.

In a nutshell what we are saying is that the focus at school and college level must move from an emphasis upon content to one of *process*. It may be helpful at this point to consider a recently developed teacher training model which seems flexible enough to be of use to us.

Avalos[40] argues that teacher trainees, supported by teacher supervisors (who might be lecturers visiting a student on teaching practice or an inspector assessing a beginning teacher during his or her early years of teaching) can, with information about alternative modes of behaviour, change or add to their teaching skills.

There are five suggested phases of the process:

(i) Stimulation of initial teacher awareness

A raising of the trainee/in-service teacher's level of awareness. Avalos, like Paulo Freire, suggests teachers analyse classroom behaviour, keep 'teaching diaries', examine pupil work for evaluative purposes, etc. We would wish to add a further dimension to this phase: awareness of the social and material *context* of the homes and communities from which children come and the schools in which they teach.

(ii) Presentation of information

Knowledge of teaching methods *appropriate* to context, task, ability level; information on performance in the classroom. She suggests this be achieved by a mixture of lectures, group discussions and the use of structured materials. If such information can be supplied by those with recent and relevant experience of primary schooling, again, the gap between theory and practice will be narrowed.

(iii) Demonstration and modelling of the teaching pattern or skill

Through observation of lessons, use of stimulation exercises, games, etc. Again, there is much to be gained from reassessing the relationship of teaching practice to the overall course of teacher education. We would again stress that such modelling should place emphasis on the reality of teaching situations.

(iv) Practice and feedback

Practice of a teaching model or skill rather than focus upon the transmission of knowledge in a traditional way. Avalos suggests that microteaching workshops and peer observation would be one way of doing this but it must be remembered that the technology associated with some models of microteaching is beyond the reach of many poorer countries. What seems important, particularly in the teaching practice phase, is that trainees meet together and learn from each other's experiences.

(v) Coaching

Support through regular contact between supervisors, teacher trainees, and the school in which the practice is occurring.

The merit of Avalos's model seems to lie in its holistic approach to training and its emphasis upon the acquisition of professional teaching competencies through participation in a process. It will work quite as effectively in a situation where trainees face one hundred pupils with few resources as it will in more favoured circumstances, but only if our language of critique remains honest. We must train teachers to face the tasks we know they will have to perform and not those we hope they may encounter.

CONCLUSION

In this chapter we have attempted to place teachers and their educators at the centre of a process taking the raw recruit through the pre-service training years to a position where he or she is supported in the classroom by in-service education and programmes of staff development. We have, throughout, tried to examine what constitutes a 'good teacher' and what might be termed 'good teaching'.

We have also attempted to apply our criteria of quality (e.g. flexibility and relevance) to such teaching and have examined the training contexts of pre-service, in-service and that applying to 'trainers of trainees'. Throughout, we have stressed the importance of the teacher learning *in situ* and from models of good practice.

Finally, we have given some thought to the issue of methodology and the call for an approach that emphasises process rather than product.

We might conclude with an extract from a recent survey of Her Majesty's Inspectors in England and Wales which looked into the question of *Quality in Schools: the Initial Training of Teachers*.[41]

> The training of a teacher is a complex undertaking, and one that should be seen as a continuous process occupying the full span of professional life. Building on what the students bring with them, good initial training sets out to lay firm foundations for a lifetime as a teacher that will stretch into a future at best only dimly perceived, and be carried out in a thousand-and-one different situations. The student's experience in this formative period will go far towards shaping his or her attitudes and understandings; it should provide a body of knowledge and a range of skills that will meet immediate professional needs; and it should encourage an open mind and a desire to go on learning and developing. The initial training system cannot give the teacher everything he or she will need as the years unfold, nor can it be expected to. The teacher is only at the beginning of what should be a process of continual professional growth and renewal, with induction into the profession followed by a pattern of in-service training (INSET) across the years. The success of the initial training system must be measured by the quality of the foundation it lays, and by the thoroughness with which it prepares students for their professional responsibilities.

The challenge faced by countries with limited resources is to interpret these truths within the material and human constraints in which they find themselves. Once it is realised that the major role of both pre-service and in-service education is to enable teachers to help themselves and help each other, our task becomes much easier.

NOTES AND REFERENCES

1 Avalos, B., 'Training for Better Teaching in the Third World: Lessons from Research' in *Teaching Education*, Vol. 4, 1985.

2 Hurst, P., 'Some Issues in Improving the Quality of Education' in *Comparative Education*, Vol. 17, No. 2, 1981.

3 Hurst, P. and Rodwell, S., *Training Third World Educational Administrators – Methods and Materials*, Final Report, University of London Institute of Education, 1986.

4 Smith, R., 'A Philosophical Overview: Quality at the Timberline' in 'The Quality of Teaching': a special issue of *Scottish Educational Review*, 1988.

5 Dove, L., *Teachers and Teacher Education in Developing Countries: Issues in Planning, Management and Training*, Croom Helm, 1985.

6 W.C.O.T.P., 'Field Report on the Survey of the Status of the Teaching Profession in Africa' by Jones, S. H. M., 1961, pp. 1–3; quoted in Fafunwa, B. A., 'Teacher Education in Nigeria', paper presented at the 1969 National Curriculum Conference, Lagos and reprinted in *WAJE*, February 1970, p. 20.

7 See Avalos, B., 1985, op. cit.; Dove, L., 1985, op. cit.

8 Avalos, B., 1985, op. cit.

9 Koguna, S. H., 'The Causes of Teacher Turnover Among Grade II Teachers in the Primary Schools in the Kano State of Nigeria', Ph.D. Thesis, Ohio University, 1978.

10 Avalos, B., 1985, op. cit.

11 Dove, L., 1985, op. cit.

12 Lopez, G., Neumann, E. and Assael, J., 1984, 'La Cultural Escolar: Responsable de Fracaso?' in Avalos, B., 1985, op. cit.

13 Siti Hawa Binti Ahmed, 'Implementing a New Curriculum for Primary Schools: a Case Study from Malaysia', Ph.D., London, 1986.

14 Hurst, P., 1981, op. cit.

15 Smith, R., 1988, op. cit.

16 Dove, L., 1985, op. cit, p. 196.

17 Dove, L., 1985, *ibid*.

18 Joyce, B. R., Hersh, R. H. and McKibbin, M., 1983, *The Structure of School Improvement*, Longman, in Dove, L., 1985, op. cit.

19 Dove, L., 1985, op. cit.

20 Bennett, N., 'New Education for Old Problems: Can Education be Made a Force for Rural Development in Nepal?', Seminar Paper, Ministry of Education, Nepal, 1980.

21 Turner, J., 'Educational Policy and Teacher Education' in *International Journal of Educational Development*, Vol. 4, No. 2, 1984.

22 Turner, J., 1984, op. cit., pp. 123–4.

23 Quoted in Guthrie, G., 'Current and Distance Education' in *Teaching and Teacher Education*, Vol. 1, 1985, pp. 80–9.

24 Husen, T., Saha, L. J., and Noonan, R., 'Teacher Training and Student Achievement in Less Developed Countries', *Working Paper No. 310*, World Bank, Washington, 1978.

25 Avalos, B. and Haddad, W., *A Review of Teacher Effectiveness Research in Africa, India, Latin America, Middle East, Malaysia, Philippines and Thailand. Synthesis of Results*, IDRC, Ottawa, 1981.

26 Shrestha, K. N., 'Teacher Education in Nepal: A Glimpse' in *Education and Development*, C.E.R.I.D., Kathmandu, 1980, p. 161.

27 Shrestha, K. N., 1980, *ibid.*

28 Quoted from Gardner, R. (ed.), *Teacher Education in Developing Countries: Prospects for the Eighties*, University of London Institute of Education, 1979.

29 Williams, P., 1979, op. cit., p. 41.

30 Griffiths, V. L., *Teacher Centred: Quality in Sudan Primary Education 1930 to 1970*, Longman, 1975.

31 Hawes, H. W. R., *Curriculum and Reality in African Primary Schools*, Longman, 1979.

32 Otaala, B. and Letsie, M. A. (eds.), *National Teacher Training College Curriculum: a Review and Reappraisal*, Instructional Materials Resource Centre, N.T.T.C., Maseru, 1986, pp. 31–2.

33 Greenland, J. (ed.), *In-service Training of Primary Teachers in Africa*, Macmillan, 1983, p. 4.

34 Shrestha, K. N., 1980, op. cit., p. 175.

35 Smith, R., 1988, op. cit.

36 Hurst, P. and Rodwell, S., 1986, op. cit.

37 Hurst, P. and Rodwell, S., 1986, *ibid*.

38 Hurst, P. and Rodwell, S., 1986, p. 13.

39 Hawes, H. W. R., 'Professional Support for Teachers in Schools: An Indonesian Case Study' in *EDC Occasional Papers 3*, University of London Institute of Education, 1982.

40 Avalos, B., 1985, op. cit.

41 HMSO, *Quality in Schools: the Initial Training for Teachers*, HMSO, 1987.

THE SCHOOL AND COMMUNITY

INTRODUCTION

> Education [in Africa] should aim to render the individual more efficient in his or her condition of life, whatever it may be, and to promote the advancement of the community as a whole through the improvement of agriculture, the development of (indigenous) industries, the improvement of health, the training of people in the management of their own affairs, and the inculcation of true ideals of citizen and service.[1]

These sentiments ring as true today as when they were written in 1925 by the British Colonial Office. Projects to improve the relationship of school and community initiated during the colonial period have remained a prominent focal point for post-independence governments.[2]

The African Ministers of Education meeting in Lagos in 1976 made specific reference to education systems being adapted to meet 'the real problems and preoccupations of the community',[3] a call reiterated and emphasised during the Harare Conference in 1982.

In fact, the idea of the primary school having a community orientation has met with increasing support in the reform discussions of the past decade.

The *Bunumbu Project* in Sierra Leone, the *Namutamba* experiments in Uganda and Tanzania, and *Impact* and *Pamong* in the Philippines and Indonesia[4] are examples of projects[5], and so often only pilot projects at that, where the intention, if not the practice, has been to narrow the gap between a western-style school and the community in an effort to make education more meaningful, relevant and accountable to those it serves.

The issues of quality outlined in earlier chapters lie at the heart of the school-community relationship, and in exploring this relationship we shall pick up once again our concern with quality as *relevance* and consider again strategies to increase our *'room for manoeuvre'*. Equally, we will draw upon our languages of critique and possibility when looking at interactions between school and home, school and community and government and community; particularly in an area of current interest the community financing of education.

COMMUNITY AND SCHOOL: PROBLEMS OF DEFINITION

One of the reasons why community education is often 'more urged than implemented'[6] may lie with the difficulties in defining 'community'. For one writer the term conjures up images of 'a relatively small and homogeneous group of people working together in close proximity, knit together by interdependence, close personal relationships, a common history and shared value systems, and aware of its own identity.'[7]

As King and others have commented, this image can easily be countered by others[8]: the urban communities of sprawling cities like Bombay and Lagos; the nomadic communities in which identity is located not in place but way of life; and the 'communities within communities', the ethnic and religious groupings of people newly arrived and unassimilated into the 'host' community.

Some go as far as to be suspicious of the term 'community' altogether.[9] For them it is a concept that has been exploited by politicians and bureaucrats who freely use expressions such as 'But I'm doing this for the community' to legitimise dubious bandwagons which are, in reality, more about self-ambition and profit than local prosperity.

But if the term begs many questions we can be fairly sure of certain things. That it can generally be defined as a group of people, usually found in one locality, who share common social, economic and cultural interests. Its members recognise social obligations to each other and identify with each other as 'we'. They may well have some collective interest in shared institutions.[10] They feel they 'belong'.[11] However, within the communities to which we belong we plan different roles and may well adhere to different value systems, depending on which community roles we are playing.

Communities and sub-communities can be seen[12] as being determined by one or a combination of the following factors: geography, e.g. village or urban suburb; ethnic, racial and religious groupings, e.g. Brazilian-Indians in Sao Paulo, Christians in Lebanon; sex and age, e.g. women's groups, youth centres; occupation, e.g. schools built by tea estates for their workers; and family concerns, e.g. parental associations and mother and baby 'communities'.

What communities, therefore, seem to have in common with each other is their complexity and variety; each layer overlapping with another, with members of one belonging or deciding firmly *not* to belong to another. To say now that we wish to make schooling 'relevant to the community' raises the questions 'which community?' and 'relevant to whom?'.

Before we look in more detail at the relationship of school to community and vice versa, we might complicate the situation further by suggesting that the term 'community' and 'community education' mean different things in the West than they do in the less developed parts of the world. 'Community development', in terms of educational provision, in say suburban London may refer to special remedial language programmes aimed at newly arrived Asian women workers. In Africa, on the other hand, where basic education is still not enjoyed by all, 'community education' takes on different and more central functions relating to the *development* and *extension* of services previously reaching only a few.

At this point it may be useful to widen our discussion and examine the relationship of school and community from both angles; and then to

121

consider ways forward that will enhance the quality of both partners and
the relationship itself.

THE SCHOOL AND THE COMMUNITY

When we talk, as the African ministers talked in 1976 and 1982, of
bringing schools closer to the community, we, like they, are not thinking
of the non-formal, traditional sector where for decades tens of
thousands of schools, many attached to mosques, have been much more
intimately involved than their counterparts in Europe.[13] We are
concerned instead, with an alien, transplanted immigrant institution
grafted onto an indigenous community and from its inception
deliberately kept separate from the day-to-day activities of the
surrounding society.

Whereas the traditional, non-formal mosque or 'bush' school had as
its *raison d'être* the socialisation of young men and women into useful
members of the immediate community, the modern, so-called 'western-
style' school is characterised by a different set of values and functions:

- education is youth and future-oriented with emphasis upon
  preparation for some further stage *after* schooling
- knowledge, in the form of the curriculum, is prescribed and
  selected to fit the wider rather than local society
- learning, with its emphasis upon literacy, has become a
  vicarious experience moving away from the 'observing and
  doing' of traditional schools
- training for a vocation remains important though it is gradually
  becoming generalised and related to work needing literacy and
  numeracy rather than practical skills
- the process of learning has taken on a discriminatory
  characteristic with the more talented being labelled and
  identified via mechanisms of examination and certification
- schooling is modern-sector oriented with a view to preparing
  children for work in the national rather than local community
- control over education has passed from the hands of locally
  elected leaders to those in the central bureaucracy charged with
  'directing' national education
- the attitude to what constituted legitimate knowledge has
  changed with education being seen as an important *agent of
  change*, consciously setting a distance between the child and his
  local culture. In such a way it was understood that a school
  graduate might lead his community to better things by
  possessing knowledge and skills acquired from without.

Western-style schooling was, therefore, established with anything *but*
the community in mind. Rather, the activities of the school tended
naturally to be focused beyond and outside the local community and its

tendency was to divorce the child from community and culture. The building of schools apart from the community, the use of boarding facilities, and the propensity of teaching in an alien non-community language, reinforced the idea that formal schooling was not, and should not be, a communal activity.

It is against this background that we must examine calls for making schools more 'relevant to the locality'. Ironically, it is often the parents and pupils who are most adverse to changing the basic orientation of schooling. However, having said this, there is still a good case for inching schools towards a more community-oriented role if only on the grounds of relevance and efficiency.[14]

This process could well involve some fairly fundamental changes in:

Patterns of organisation and decision-making	**towards**	more local commitment and responsibility
Nature and type of programming and enrolments	**towards**	more varied and flexible times and flow of pupils
The curriculum, including methodology	**towards**	more experience-based and practical study
The role of the teachers	**towards**	acting less as pedagogues and more as *animateurs*
The use of buildings and land	**towards**	more community use
Patterns of financial provision and control	**towards**	greater local investment and accountability.

All these will be examined later but we should note that how far and how fast such changes are made and, indeed, whether they are made at all depends initially on the community's opinion of what constitutes the best use of a school and hence *their* interpretation of the terms 'relevance' and 'efficiency'.

If quality primary education is defined solely as making the best academic use of the school and its resources in order to 'get results', then the community orientation of that school will be limited to that end. It can easily be argued that children learn best when their learning is related to their own direct experience and their 'needs now'. Hence such relevant content may well be encouraged in academic subjects provided it contributes towards raising academic standards, but in most other respects the school and its teachers will retain their traditional roles separate and apart from the community.

If, on the other hand, 'more relevant' and 'more efficient' use of schools is interpreted to mean more flexible use of resources, i.e. teachers and buildings, with the establishment for example of 'multipurpose skill centres' for school and community use, we might see some of these changes made. As King has noted, one of the most striking features of school systems in Africa is their apparent under-use by anyone other than full-time students.[15]

The movement towards community financing of education is another area that is beginning to be taken seriously in places like Kenya. We shall discuss this later in some detail.

Before considering strategies for moving schools closer to the community, let us briefly examine the relationship from the other perspective:

The Community and the school

Community development has become widely associated with such issues as political empowerment of local communities, co-ordination of social services, economic development, citizen participation, continuing adult education and the extended use of institutions, such as schools, for these purposes.[16]

If we take two of these areas: involvement by the community in the *economic development* of the school and community participation in *school curriculum* issues we gain a clearer idea of the complexities involved.

Economic development of schools

The table below indicates different forms of support for primary schools rendered by members of a community; in this case those residing in the anglophone provinces of Cameroon.

TABLE XV CONTRIBUTIONS BY THE COMMUNITIES FOR THE REPAIR AND MAINTENANCE OF PRIMARY SCHOOLS

Type of expenditure	Primary Schools	
	No.	%
Cash resources	59	75
Work by community members	54	68
Building materials (modern)	20	25
Local materials (building, timber, roofing, etc.)	15	19
School furniture	4	5
Others	7	9

Source: Bude, U., *Primary Schools, Local Community and Development in Africa*, DSE, 1985.

Economically, at least, the quality of the physical resources of schools seems greatly determined by what the community can offer. The official instrument of community participation in these schools is the parent-teacher association: a body with often very hazily-defined roles and responsibilities. Raising cash, as we shall see later when discussing community financing of education in Kenya, and providing manual labour is acceptable it seems, not only because it is desperately needed, but because it is politically and educationally 'neutral', having little to do with how the school is actually run.

Could communities, therefore, move from a position of providing not only bricks and mortar but involvement in the curricular life of the school?

Community and curriculum

There are at least three areas in which the relationship of the community to the school curriculum seems obvious. In the first place, as already noted, the community needs to serve as a source of direct experience; as a laboratory where children can practice basic skills and develop key concepts in language, mathematics, science and social studies.

In the second place, the cultural curriculum needs to be community-oriented. Few would argue, for instance, that local songs, dances, crafts, customs and traditions should not form part of the learning planned and provided for children at school.

Finally, the community needs to be involved in the productive and economic aspects of the curriculum.

> Villagers who are skilled in craftwork may help children to learn crafts; priests may help children learn about hygiene; agriculturalists may help children learn about crops and animals; and store owners may help children learn about commerce.[17]

The advantages of such involvement are observable in Kenya where the new 8 : 4 : 4 system calls for the eighth year of the primary cycle (and for many the terminal year of schooling) to be devoted to acquiring technical and vocational skills, the kind possessed by local craftsmen and women.

The previously cited research in Cameroon raised a number of complexities and problems in involving community members in this way, notably that with limited resources *all* round, i.e. in community and the school, a 'trade-off' situation might need to be arranged in which teachers are trained for specific developmental tasks while community members instruct the schoolchildren in local craft, etc. The issue of remuneration for services is also problematic, as is the possible problem of hesitation by those possessing a monopoly of skills and services to pass on their knowledge to others.

Moreover, the issue of community participation raises fundamental questions over who decides what children learn, since it is likely to invite on the one hand participation of elected or delegated representation in the design and evaluation of practical school activities, and on the other for teachers of geography, science, woodwork and other subjects to take up local problems and integrate them into the learning process.

Such activities, of course, involve balancing efforts to implement national educational policies with 'relevant local' community-oriented education. They involve those who design curriculum at central level giving over some of their power to control what schools teach and hence learning to cope with the untidiness of alternatives. Equally, this it could potentially lead to a situation where schooling becomes manipulated to serve the interests of particular groups and therefore be to the unfair advantage of the richer and more enlightened members of the respective communities.[18]

When discussing the community's involvement in schooling it is easy to generalise and overlook the fact that each school student is a member of both a nuclear and extended family (some being large enough to be described as 'communities' in their own right) and as such is a natural conduit for community involvement in the school, even if it is only through the age-old support of children's learning at home.

This raises the important issue of corporate versus individualistic orientation of both school and community. Schooling in western capitalist nations mirrors the belief that human dignity and progress depends very much upon inalienable individual rights, suggesting that communities exist primarily to serve individual interest. Translated into the educational arena we see the legitimisation of this through the highly competitive nature of the examination system. Helping repair a school roof or contribute to a fund to acquire equipment for the whole school can be viewed as less important than assisting in the progress of *one* child through the school.

If, on the other hand, development and dignity are seen as deriving from relationships among people forged through collective associations working together, for example, to achieve better school provision for a disadvantaged group or a fairer examination system, we have a far richer climate for the nurturing of school-community relations.[19]

The education-through-self-reliance and *harambee* movements of Tanzania and Kenya respectively grew out of such a philosophy of development. As we shall see, they are tested when confronted with the issue of community financing of education.

Let us now look specifically at strategies, long-term and short-term, for improving the relationship of school to community and vice versa.

COMMUNITY AND SCHOOL: STRATEGIES FOR IMPROVEMENT

It is easy to criticise schools for not playing a greater part in community development. But if we consider the purposes for which *western style* schools were established (and we have listed some of these characteristics earlier) we can appreciate the difficulties they face in adapting to new roles and expectations, particularly of those new functions which are at odds with their established *raison d'etre*.

Yet educational institutions have made efforts through innovation and reform to move away from their founding image and towards a more community-oriented role. We will now examine three such innovations:

The first such innovation is the revival of interest in the *community school*. The introduction of maternity and child-care centres to schools in the Philippines in the 1950s; the attachment of small *shambas* (gardens) to schools in East Africa in the 1960s; the 'continuation' school approach introduced into selected Ghanaian middle schools from 1969, in which pupils spend one day a week doing practical work; and the concern expressed at the Lagos and Colombo Conferences of 1976 and 1978 respectively, for increased 'community relevance' of the primary school curriculum, illustrate the interest.[20]

In theory, depending on the proportion of the curriculum changed, then the 'community school' becomes the interface between formal, western-style schooling, traditional learning and non-formal education.[21]

In practice such reforms can be criticised on a number of levels. For one critic, the concept of the 'community school' reminds him of Philip Foster's famous 'vocational school fallacy', in which

> some would-be reformers seek to change education to make it more relevant to poverty-stricken communities. But what often happens is that the people either reject these institutions (which effectively condemn them to remain at the bottom of the political and economic structure), or the community schools eventually mutate into conventional institutions.[22]

Thompson[23] also warns of problems of uneven curricula development, particularly in countries with traditionally centralised education systems; the difficulties in avoiding discriminatory practices; and the headaches that would come in trying to evaluate and assess such practical, locally-oriented learning for examination purposes.

These problems might be overcome if schools become more flexible in their organisation and purpose and shifted somewhat towards a role as community training centre. This might involve *some* continuous assessment in some subjects; the employment of *some* local craftsmen to help with the teaching of vocational areas of the curriculum; the participation by members of the community in the management and decision-making processes of the school; the use of the school building for the learning needs of the adult community (literacy, health care, etc.); the use of teachers and children to *some extent* in outreach activities such as community health campaigns; the linking of the school with the world of work. All of these are *some* of the measures which, without an excessive amount of change, may prove acceptable to the community, and thereby be sure of a degree of success.

If relevance, efficiency, and something more are yardsticks by which we measure quality, the need for *flexibility* and *balance* (between academic and community-oriented curricula for example) seem to follow close behind.

What we are suggesting, therefore, is that schools attempt a number of reforms, some short-term, others long-term, some concerned with the curriculum offered to *all* children, others concerning particular programmes offered to a particular target group, for example illiterate adults.

If we look at the curriculum offered to *all* children (and thereby avoid the trap of segregating 'non-academic' children into second-class 'community schools') and apply the principle of balance and relevance, we might in the short-term make efforts to relate both academic and vocational subjects to community life, for example push to introduce local history into the examination syllabus; orientate mathematics to solving 'real' problems in, for instance, health or agriculture; and in the long term, look to producing a more flexible curriculum related to the individual and group needs of children. So often, in so many primary schools, *all* children are taught *all* things with the result that little account is taken of special needs, mixed abilities or likely future careers. Developing separate institutions to cater for such needs and differences only exacerbates the problem and leads us back to Foster's 'fallacy'.

However, the success of such changes will only be realised when teachers are trained, encouraged and supported to make such changes, then to integrate those changes into their classroom behaviour. The role of the 'people trainers' and 'content choosers' is to build into the fabric of schooling and teacher education opportunities where pupils and teachers can develop 'room for manoeuvre'.

Initially there may be a price to pay in terms of changing strategies and exploring possibilities; in the long term the learning taking place may in fact be more efficient because it is more relevant to a variety of needs and therefore results in less 'wastage' and less repetition.

There is equally an argument, if the concept of 'community school' is to grow into something more than just a pilot project, for teacher trainers, teachers and curriculum developers to be prepared to develop a working relationship with community members. If we want to involve craftsmen and – women in the teaching of, say science and environmental studies, these impromptu-teachers will need support and assistance from both teacher and trainer.

This brings us to our second innovation, a move towards teachers, and to a certain extent pupils themselves, becoming *animateurs* and instructors in the service of community development.

A viable way forward may be to focus attention on particular target groups that a school may be able to assist. To do this it may be more effective to identify the skills and qualities a teacher already possesses and then attempt to apply them to community development projects requiring those particular competencies. Many teachers do already, outside their school life, spend a great deal of time acting as secretaries to rural communities, assisting with the mobilisation and organisation of self-help groups, or acting as an official in a religious organisation. More recently the role of teachers as agents to spread preventative health messages in campaigns to promote immunisation, better sanitation or safety practices has also been developed, often successfully, by UNICEF and WHO.

One suspects that the problem arises when parents, in particular, feel that by taking on additional activities designed to serve the wider community, the schooling (and especially academic schooling) of their children will suffer.

It is beyond the scope of this chapter to examine the issue further but if a decision is taken to extend the role of the teacher into that of *animateur* then a number of issues need addressing, among them: to what extent is the teacher trained and supported for this role; to what extent is the focus of that activity effectively exploiting existing competencies (rather than developing new ones); and to what extent is one role being developed at the expense of another? Decisions of this kind, as we discussed in Chapter Two, lie at the baseline of any programme to improve the quality of what the teacher does, be it inside or outside the classroom.

A third innovation is the growing interest in schools becoming *self-financing production units*.[24] On 20 July 1975, Kenneth Kaunda of Zambia announced that with immediate effect, all education institutions would become production units. In Somalia, Guinea and Sudan, where, as in other parts of the world, school students board at the school, interest has been shown in raising capital to offset the large costs involved in feeding and lodging students and staff.

There seem to be two types of possibility here: one in which the school produces a commodity, e.g. rice or livestock, and then sells that on the open market; two, the production of services rendered by the school to the community in return for payment, e.g. harvesting, transportation of goods, soil cultivation, etc.

Much will depend on the size of the school, its location, the level of infrastructural development of local community, and the traditions and customs concerning the commissioning of specific community tasks to specific groups. We seem, once again, to be looking to our criteria of quality for guidance.

If we can marry academic study with such productive work, in agriculture for example, by learning the complete process from tilling the soil to negotiating a price, then it would seem both relevant and efficient work, provided that children were mature enough to understand what they were doing. If, on the other hand, such schemes though economically attractive, were simply diverting pupils' attention from study to becoming a pool of cheap labour and from education to simply training, then we would be in danger of losing a sense of balance and distorting the principles that differentiate education from labour.

So far we have examined three strategies for bringing school and community together, hopefully for their mutual benefit. The idea of a 'community school', the nature of the teacher as an *animateur*, and the more recent development of 'self-financing production units' have merit if implemented for the right reasons. These include: making the curriculum more relevant to the world of work; making it more flexible for the different abilities and interests of children; and viewing the school as potentially more than just a place where we teach the young.

However, such innovations also require that both teacher and community member understand and know what is being asked of them; that both are involved in making decisions and in developing and opening channels of communication; that both are supported, particularly in training; and that priorities are constantly kept in mind. These priorities may be traditional (e.g. that all children leave being able to read and write and have had a fair crack at the examinations) or modern (e.g. that all children in their learning have, as far as possible, applied that learning to the much-needed developments around them).

COMMUNITY FINANCING OF EDUCATION[25]

From a government's point of view the attraction of community-oriented education is its cheapness. Kenneth King[26] somewhat cynically uses the syllogism: *expansion + change + cheapness = community* to describe the attraction. As the cost of providing universal primary education has increased, so has the pressure on the community to offer more than just bricks and mortar and parent-teacher associations.

For primary schools to receive government blessing in Nepal (and such a blessing means staffing, salaries and minimum resources), the community are required to raise, by donation, a fixed amount.

In Kenya, parents and students have been asked, through *harambee* (literally 'pull together') committees, to provide funds for building and maintenance, salaries of non-professional staff, and equipment and supplies not adequately provided through government allocation.[27] Ironically these funds, sometimes called 'development fees', have greatly increased since a Presidential decree (1974) relieved parents of paying tuition fees.

It is also interesting to note that parents and local communities in Kenya are required *by law* (in a Presidential directive of 1979) to provide physical facilities such as classrooms, teachers' houses and furniture for primary schools.

Though efforts have been made to curb the excessive collecting of 'activity' fees from parents (through a Presidential statement of 1985), many question the impact upon quality of reliance upon community financing of primary and secondary schooling.

For Lillis, the issue of quality generally is most sharply highlighted in any contrast between the 'quality' of government schools and unaided schools relying heavily upon community financing.[28] He is particularly concerned about the qualitative inferiority of *harambee* education in terms of the provision of teachers and the quality of attainments, particularly at secondary level.

It should be said that *harambee* differs with regard to secondary and primary provision. Whilst, as a whole, less than 23% of Kenya's 2 705 secondary schools are wholly government maintained (22.59% government; 21.44% assisted; 49.5% *harambee*); in the primary sector the 12 493 schools at January 1985 were subject to Ministry control in the form of inspection, curriculum and the provision and payment of teachers. Facilities were to be provided by the communities.

If the issue at secondary level is differentials in teacher quality and attainment levels, at primary level the major problem seems to be what happens in terms of quality when communities fail to produce the funds to build, equip and maintain new classrooms (especially those needed for the eighth 'vocational' year of primary education). For it appears that there is widespread disparity in provision, in spite of government efforts to cajole and coerce communities to become involved. The inability of poor communities to pay for school construction does not necessarily indicate a lack of willingness to assist, rather it highlights the economic divisions within the particular country.

The impact upon the quality of primary education is difficult to assess but signals from the secondary area indicate that whereas community financing has had the beneficial effect of opening up access to schooling to those rural and poor areas, the disparities in quality of provision of education (teachers, resources, buildings, etc) make for the creation of a two-tier education system. As countries poorer than Kenya (Nepal for example) search for radical ways to solve their financial problems, so might they be encouraged to take the same route Kenya has followed.

Once again we return to the idea of *balance* and *partnership*. If the financial burden upon the community becomes too great to bear, one might have a situation where community involvement in other areas: curriculum, management and planning, for example, lessens. To some extent the issue of community financing goes to the heart of the difficult relationship of school to community and community to government.

SCHOOL AND COMMUNITY: A CASE STUDY

We have already referred to Udo Bude's research into the relationship of school and community in the anglophone provinces of the United Republic of Cameroon. We return to it now because it serves to point up the possibilities and limitations in promoting such a relationship.

Bude's investigation showed that though elements of community orientation have become established in the primary schools and are supported by provincial school authorities, schools were not really in a position to solve many of the communities' most urgent problems.

Their major contribution to development was seen as preparing the pupils for examinations. Parents in particular supported this function of the school.

Co-operation between school and community was observed by Bude to operate in the following ways:

1   Parent-teacher associations offer a number of interested community members a limited forum for the expression of opinions on problems of school maintenance and instruction. The parents bear the major part of the cost of equipment and repair work. However, they are not allowed to control the school's local financial transactions.
2   Community members are only seldom invited to instruct the children. Representatives of government or private development institutions are, as a rule, not active at community level. Even in communities where such institutions have their headquarters, there are only isolated contacts between qualified experts working there and the local primary schools.
3   Self-help projects in the sample area have a long tradition and are initiated and implemented primarily without the assistance of the school. In exceptional cases the school may render manual assistance (e.g. transportation of building materials or production of sun-dried building blocks). In contrast, a number of teachers still frequently serve as secretaries to committees or associations which are concerned with the organisation of self-help projects. The level of development reached by a community itself partly determines the community's requirements and possibilities in terms of improving local living conditions. The better an area is developed, the more technically sophisticated and financially expensive are its development projects (e.g. water supply facilities), and these cannot be implemented without external assistance. It follows from this that the primary school becomes increasingly restricted in its scope for promoting community development.
4   The schools assist the communities free of charge by implementing projects which do not require a large volume of technical or financial investment. These goodwill actions relate primarily to the cleaning of public facilities, to hygiene demonstrations and the organisation of leisure-time activities. In ten per cent of the schools the teachers stated that they were holding literacy courses for adults.

    Yet despite the importance of such school activities to rural development, the only communities which reported such activities were those which were poorly or well equipped in infrastructural terms; no such activities were reported in the more disadvantaged communities. Although development projects of the type mentioned above are an integral part of the curriculum, the practical work is in no way linked with the academic subjects of the curriculum.
5   In addition to the work performed free of charge by the school for the community, services are rendered for individual community members or institutions by pupils and teachers in return for payment. In this way the schools acquire funds which may be used for maintenance purposes or

for special events. A school's ability to undertake this type of work depends on the type of community ('development zone') in which the latter is located. As a rule, the work undertaken includes the transportation of agricultural products in remote and isolated communities, harvesting work in well-served rural communities, and auxiliary services for building projects in urban areas. Here again, these non-school activities are not integrated with instruction in academic subjects. Furthermore, such profit-earning activities have often been extended to such a degree that regular teaching was ultimately impaired.

6   Use of school facilities by the community for non-school purposes is very restricted. The existence of classrooms and a sports ground cannot compensate for the lack of facilities which might be of interest to youths and adults. In one quarter of the schools, the classrooms are used for church purposes (services, choir rehearsals, religious instruction). The use of classrooms for non-religious assemblies is even more seldom, since other meeting places, frequently of a traditional nature, are available for these purposes. Teachers use the classrooms during non-school hours primarily for school-oriented purposes such as the provision of additional instruction to examination candidates and, in exceptional cases, for literacy courses or French language courses for adults.

7   Rural science teaching is an integral part of the primary school curriculum, and practical work is performed on the school's own farm. However, rural science is of little relevance to the final school-leaving examination and of no relevance to the secondary school entrance examination.

Rural science instruction in its present form does not contribute much towards community development. Frequently, the school farms simply reflect local conditions and fail to offer an impetus for improvement or innovation in the communities. While schools in remote areas adapt themselves to the local low level of soil cultivation, schools in well-equipped rural communities are adapted community members and have become supernumeraries with only little understanding for and interest in the so-called extended tasks of the school . . .

8   Elements of local culture are incorporated into a variety of school activities. With very few exceptions, these activities are not included into the life of the community. They are frequently undertaken incidentally to or in isolation from cultural events at community level.

Instruction in local culture at school is not used to promote a critical discussion of the traditional modes of behaviour and forms of expression of a variety of cultural groups but to facilitate the initiation of the pupil into the school. Once the first years at school are over, this cultural element is manifest only in the practising of traditional dances and songs and, often for lack of other reasonable sports activities, in sports instruction.[29]

He concludes his study by saying that community orientation of schooling is no substitute for macro-social and-economic reform. He goes on to suggest that national elites pay only lip service to a 'critical and relevant education' for the majority for fear 'of the fundamental social changes which might be brought about by a community/development orientated system'.[30]

Bude's research must be taken for what it is: *one* study in *one* area in *one* country. But the insights it provides may well be widely generalisable. What the research may well imply is that the way forward is for schools to develop closer links with the community rather than attempt to perform a function that properly belongs with regional and national government.

CONCLUSION

It is ironic that in discussing such concepts as the 'community school' we find ourselves describing educational institutions that would have been more familiar to our great-grandparents than to ourselves, schooled in the ways of western-style formal establishments.

Education for a purpose, a blending of theory and practice, learning rooted in the needs and traditions of the community, teaching for wisdom and good sense rather than the acquisition of a certificate – are characteristics of what has been called the 'interface of traditional and non-formal education'. Perhaps in linking quality with the relationship of school to community and vice versa we are calling for, not a return to, but a reaffirmation of older, traditional values.

In this chapter we have examined schools' contribution to community life and the ways in which the locality might enhance their role, in educating their children. We have looked at the idea of 'community schooling' and the current concern with 'community financing' of primary education, epitomised by Kenya's *harambee* movement. The relationship of government to community, important in the issue of finance, seems central to the question of qualitative improvement.

Finally, in discussing the relationship of school and community, we have raised a number of questions, the most important being: to what extent should we expect schools to act as community development agencies? We maintain there is a strong argument for saying that schools should work to improve what they do best, namely the education of the young, and that this is best achieved by involving the community far more in the life of the classroom.

NOTES AND REFERENCES

1 Great Britain Colonial Office, Education Policy in British Tropical Africa, HMSO, 1925, p. 4; quoted in Bray, Clarke & Stephens, *Education and Society in Africa*, Edward Arnold, 1986, p. 116.

2 *Ibid.*, p. 118.

3 UNESCO, *Final Report*: Conference of Ministers of Education of African Member States, Lagos, 1976. Paris, 1976, in Bray M., Clarke P. B. & Stephens D. G., op. cit., p. 118.

4 Ngegba, F. B. S., 'The Bunumbu Experience in Sierra Leone' in UNESCO/UNICEF, *Basic Services for Children: A Continuing Search for Learning Priorities*, International Bureau of Education, Geneva, 1978.
   See also Hawes, H. W. R., *Curriculum and Reality in African Primary Schools*, Longman, Harlow, 1979, p. 60.

5 Bude, U., *Primary Schools, Local Community and Development in Africa*, DSE, 1985.
   For details of attempts to replicate the Impact Project see Cummings, W. K., *Low Cost Primary Education*, International Development Research Centre, Ottawa, 1986.

6 King, K., 'The Community School – Rich World, Poor World' in *Education and Community in Africa*, King, K. (ed.), Centre of African Studies, University of Edinburgh, 1976, p. 1.

7 Thompson, A. R., 'Community Education in the 1980s: What can we learn from experience?', *IJED* vol. 3, no. 1, 1983, p. 3.

8 Bell & Newby, 1972, in King, K., 1976, op. cit.

9 'Community – the exploitation of a concept' by John & Jean Anderson in King, K., 1976, op. cit., p. 161.

10 Bray, M., *New Resources for Education: Community Management and Financing of Schools in less Developed Countries*, Commonwealth Secretariat, London, 1986, p. 11.

11 See Curle, A., *Mystics and Militants: a Study of Awareness: Identity and Social Action*, Tavistock Publications, London, 1972.

12 Bray, M., 1987, op. cit., p. 12.

13 King, K., op. cit.

14 *Ibid*.

15 King, K., op. cit., p. 27.

16 Newmann, F. M., 'Community Education Programs' in *International Encyclopaedia of Education*, Pergamon, Oxford, 1986, p. 847.

17 Bray, M., Clarke P. B. & Stephens D. G., op. cit., p. 118.

18 Thompson, A. R., op. cit., p. 13.

19 Newmann, F. M., op. cit., p. 849.

20 Sinclair, M., 'Education, relevance and the community: a first look at the history of attempts to introduce productive work into the primary school curriculum' in King, K., 1976, op. cit., pp. 45–80.

21 King, K., op. cit., p. 12.

22 Hurst, P., Response to paper by Clifton-Everest – 'School and Community: The Potentials and Constraints of the Private Foundations as a Promoter of Innovation and Change' in *School and Community in Developing Countries*, Proceedings of the 22nd Conference of the ATOE University of Newcastle, 1983, edited by Lillis, K.

23 Thompson, A. R., op. cit., p. 13.

24 See King, K., op. cit., pp. 17–18.

25 Many of ideas for this section have been drawn from the recent writings of Lillis and Ayot, 1986, and Lillis, 1987, respectively: *Community Financing of Education in Kenya*, paper presented at the Commonwealth Secretariat Conference, 'Community financing of education in SADCC countries' held at Gaborone, Botswana; and 'Community financing of education: issues from Kenya' in *Journal of Education Policy*, 1987, vol. 2, no. 2, pp. 99–117.

26 King, K., op. cit.

27 Lillis, K., op. cit., 1987, p. 104.

28 Lillis, K., op. cit., 1987, p. 111.

29 Bude, U., op. cit., pp. 267–276.

30 *Ibid.*, p. 275.

THE ADMINISTRATORS AND MANAGERS

This chapter is in two parts.

In Part I we analyse the task of the third of our five agents of quality. Part II presents a case study from Indonesia representing an exciting and not unsuccessful attempt to provide an integrated support system to teachers, demonstrating the spirit (if not yet the practice) of a co-operative approach to management we believe would substantially improve quality.

PART I ADMINISTRATORS AS AGENTS OF QUALITY

The terms 'administrators', 'supervisors' and 'managers' cover a variety of jobs and roles from the director of education and his planning officer, through the local education officer and inspector to the school manager and the head. Though each has a different role, together they perform a variety of functions crucial to school quality: they plan, provide, manage and administer financial resources; they appoint staff; they set standards and supervise them, seeking to make sure that those who operate the system are accountable for the decisions they make. They also advise and assist users of the education system to do a better and more efficient job.

Of course, as we have stressed in Chapter Three of this book, the decisions they have to take are never as clear-cut as they appear at first. There is no such thing as value free administration, and supervision. It is done by certain people for certain purposes.

TWO SOURCES OF POWER

In Chapter Four we discussed two sources of power in education: on the one hand *access to policy makers* who take main decisions and provide resources, money and materials to enable these decisions to happen; on the other *access to learners* – because the only real measure of success in an educational endeavour is the change in their behaviour. Educational administrators and managers, particularly those at central level, are close to one source of power and far from the other. In order for their efforts to be effective in raising quality there must be a link established between the providers and the users.

Consider some of the essential tasks an administrator does. The administrator:

(i)   *Provides schools* and money for them and helps to ensure that schooling is available for the greatest number of learners in the most effective manner. **BUT** unless those schools are provided, and built in the full understanding of *what* it is that children are going to learn in them and *how* they are going to learn it, then they will not be as effective as they might be.

(ii) *Organises the smooth running of the system* so that decisions can be taken effectively, information communicated and standards monitored and compared. **BUT** unless the particular needs of individual learners and teachers and communities are borne in mind the efficiency of the system may turn out to be apparent and not real, since it will fit the needs of the administrators only, ignoring those of the users.

(iii) *Provides, pays and supervises teachers* to staff the schools efficiently so that the content of education can be effectively taught. **BUT** unless the teachers are made fully aware of the tasks they are expected to perform, and unless these tasks are manageable given the education and training that teachers have actually received, then their output will be low and their morale lower still.

(iv) *Provides, within resources available, suitable equipment and educational materials* to enable teaching to take place as effectively as possible. **BUT** unless this is accompanied by an understanding of how such equipment and materials are actually used by the teachers and children, what the basic priorities are to enable at least a minimum degree of learning to take place, what better local alternatives exist or could be devised to the nationally prescribed, then scarce resources can be misdirected.

Just as the administrators are often remote from the teacher and her classroom, so also are teachers ignorant of the policies and realities which make the administrator take this decision or that. In particular, the amount of financial and material allocation to schools or to individual pupils is seldom, if ever, known. Nor do teachers usually have any voice in the way resources are allocated. Small wonder that they frequently regard allocations, even when they are justly and sensibly apportioned, as arbitrary and unfair.

To any reader with a working knowledge of systems in countries in Asia and Africa, this teacher/administrator divide highlights a number of very serious barriers to quality. For a variety of reasons administrators are not as closely in touch with the 'learner power base' as they should be. The reasons are partly historical: for example in former British systems the distinction between the public school graduate who administered and the white missionaries or black teachers, who actually dealt with children, has been maintained. They are partly to be found in the nature of bureaucracy itself – seeking virtues of uniformity and order among the perverse untidiness, creativity and humanness of those men and women who seek to influence the next generation through their own personalities and ideals. Partly they stem from policies of centralisation bred of a desire to impose a single set of national standards on a diverse and politically fragile state. They are partly, too, a result of sheer overwork, with the administrator so swamped in paper that he finds it impossible to travel out of his office to find out what people are doing. Finally, they are increasingly the result of that dangerous set of double standards in which we seek refuge when the going gets very tough – by pretending that an ideal or at least a manageable situation exists, and resisting opportunities to find out the truth because we are frightened of confronting it and its implications.

As a result of this gap between the administrators and classroom practitioners, efficiency, relevance and ultimately quality frequently suffers. Therefore:

- Buildings are constructed by those who lack knowledge of content and methodology. Additionally, content and methodology is often prescribed by those who choose to ignore the physical limitations of the buildings in which they must operate.
- Inflexibilities appear in regulations both in regard to the organisation of schools and to the presentation of content within them (syllabuses to be covered, timetables to be followed). Perhaps most critical of all, we see a reluctance to devolve any financial responsibility to those best capable of using local initiatives to match local education with local needs. (One reason frequently given for this is that those who might be given .inancial responsibility could misuse it – as if such a state of affa rs were unknown at central level.)
- Too often untrained or undertrained teachers are sent out into the field to do tasks, unaided and unsupervised, which even their trained colleagues could find very difficult.
- Finally, there is great ignorance of what materials are most used and most needed in schools, and consequently therefore inefficient deployment of scant resources.

IMPROVING UNDERSTANDING AND EFFICIENCY

If we seek approaches towards closing the gap we have identified between the *providers* and the *users* we may do well to refer back to the five enabling elements which form part of our 'inner wheel' (p 59). We shall consider them in the following order:

shared goals
information and communication
realism
flexibility
participation at all levels.

Shared goals

Conventionally, the main concerns of administrators have more to do with efficiency than with relevance. They will be far more preoccupied with the smooth administrative and financial management of a school, the effective use of resources and the maintenance of enrolments than what goes on in classes (though all would profess to be interested in goals at a rhetorical level – evidenced by the Principles of Rukunegara in Malaysia or the National Goals of Education in Kenya[1]). After that, concern can easily evaporate – a district education officer or a planning officer proving relatively uninterested in the purposes for teaching different subjects in primary school or even less interested in the principles governing approaches to methodology. Even the inspector may turn out to be more interested in the ledger, the attendance register or the punishment book than the teachers' scheme of work. He may also be satisfied with a schedule of lesson observation which concentrates entirely on the teacher's input to the lesson instead of the pupils' output and which grades the teacher on trivia such as appearance; voice; manner; presentation; use of visual aids; instead of one which gets to grips with the essential elements in the lesson – such as what the objectives were and whether children had achieved them; whether learning skills had been developed and how; whether feedback had been given and to whom; whether content had been related to children's interests and their 'needs now'.

By contrast the classroom teacher, curriculum worker or teacher educator may be indifferent to the political, financial and managerial constraints within which administrators work. As a result of such a mismatch of goals, quality suffers.

In particular, if administrators fail fully to understand the underlying purposes of educating children at primary level or the approaches and methodologies which this invites, they may unwittingly erect a number of barriers to quality through decisions relating to:

        the design of buildings
        the organisation of the timetable
        the arrangement of classrooms
        the provision of furniture
        the supply of learning materials
        the in-service training of teachers
        the assessment criteria for both children and teachers

to name but a few.

The rhetoric of good primary education in all countries emphasises developing abilities to solve daily problems and learning from the environment. Both of these emphasise 'room for manoeuvre' because neither can be nationally predicted and controlled. But once buildings, timetables, furniture, textbooks, teachers and assessment are devised, maintained and programmed on a standardised set course, both these goals are rendered more difficult to attain.

The fundamental importance of understanding goals can be illustrated by the following simple examples:

- A class which wishes to follow through a local survey is inhibited by a restrictive timetable.
- A headteacher who wishes the children to sit together to work out solutions to problems is prevented from doing so by heavy, immovable, sloping desks.
- A school which wishes to focus all its learning round a local event which has absorbed the interest of the community is denied the opportunity of doing so by an inspector who insists that they 'keep up' with the syllabus.
- A teacher who attends an in-service course returns programmed to follow through the textbook and a teachers' guide to the letter, despite her own inclination to vary or depart from it.

None of these checks on quality are inevitable. All can be removed once administrators are more effectively involved in the discussions on goals and purposes and their implications.

Information and communication

The establishment of channels of communication, vital as this is to the process of good administration, is nevertheless peculiarly difficult. For one thing it requires a very fundamental change of attitude towards ownership of information. Instead of being *my* information which I pass down to *you*, it becomes *our* information which we share across the system, with all the changes in authority relationships which this entails. It also entails communication between administrative levels; between different agents of administration, public and private; between the 'administrators' and the 'professionals'; between both of these and the teachers, pupils and parents. Even in a numerically tiny country like Lesotho, the 'map' of communication takes expert reading. For a decision concerning quality to be known and understood by the chief education officer; the inspectorates; the curriculum development centre; the national teachers' college (which trains heads as well as teachers); the three main missionary bodies (which manage schools); the district education officers; and the schools in town, lowlands and highlands: is a considerable feat and one not always achieved.

The difficulty in achieving communication, however, in no way minimises its importance. Two points are worth making. First, the need for information about real conditions in schools and communities on which to base decisions. This point was urged in both Chapters Two and Three. A language of critique is a necessary preliminary to a language of possibility. It is the responsibility of the administrators at all levels to initiate the quest for information, extending from the gathering of current statistical information to information about classroom practices and community wants and needs. The time when such information could

141

be computerised has already been reached in Malaysia and is not too far away in Kenya, though admittedly remote in both Lesotho and Nepal.

The second point relates to the ease and difficulty in achieving such communication. It is far easier to attain it at local than central level – local co-operation and unity of purpose evident in districts such as Nyeri in Kenya and Cianjur (to be described) in Indonesia, underline yet again the importance of devolving power and responsibility as a means of raising quality. For once a joint sense of local ownership is achieved, it is almost inevitable that more and better communication with follow between all those proud to enhance the quality of their local schools and teachers.

Realism

Information and communication should inevitably promote a sense of realism among administrators. Once it is known and accepted that classes are of an unmanageable size (Nepal), that untrained teachers cannot cover the syllabus (Kenya), that literacy in the mother tongue is only attained in a proportion of children by class IV (Lesotho), or that brighter children in classes are ignored and unstimulated (Malaysia), then it is possible to consider realistic and innovative solutions to such problems.

All four cases above do in fact invite attempts at such solutions:

The use of child-to-child approaches
The grouping of teachers, with experienced teachers working alongside inexperienced ones
The use of parents in the teaching of reading
The devising of community and experience-based enrichment material.

None of these solutions would be ruled out either by curriculum workers or administrators; in fact they have all been discussed in the countries concerned. What is needed is the confidence to take a first step towards establishing and monitoring action research in each of these areas. We need to move from talking it over to trying it out.

Flexibility

The fourth of our enabling elements – flexibility – derives naturally from such realism, and is very closely linked to our first principle: the clarification and sharing of goals. For the analogy, 'room to manoeuvre', which we have employed in Chapter Two, implies clearly that we should know where we are going but need freedom to choose paths to get there.

Once administrators are very sure of the outcomes they seek they can afford to be more flexible in their means of attaining them. Let us take two key purposes in primary education: the achievement of permanent functional literacy by the end of Class IV and the achievement of basic knowledge, skills and attitudes in relation to primary health care by the time children complete their basic cycle. In both cases the goals need to be elaborated, explained and clarified:

What *is* literacy?
How do we know whether a child has achieved it?
How can we ensure that it is retained?
What is involved in the concept of primary health care?
What are the particular *local* (as distinct from universal) aspects which need consideration?
What is it appropriate and inappropriate for children (as distinct from adults) to know?

But once these clarifications have been made, many opportunities for administrative room for manoeuvre are apparent. These could include:

Organisation of school time

Literacy
In conditions of great overcrowding it may be expedient to halve the contact time with each class (e.g. two and a half hours with two groups of forty children rather than five hours with one group of eighty). Thus teachers have a chance to interact with individuals and ensure they master basic skills.

This practice is commonly, but unofficially, used in both Lesotho and Indonesia.

Health
Timetables can be interpreted flexibly so that appropriate times can be blocked to enable children to undertake health surveys – to prepare and present health songs and plays – as in Uganda and Zambia.[2]

Materials for learning

Literacy
Rather than relying on the meagre resources distributed by central book distribution schemes, through the release of modest funds to local groups and the encouragement of teacher initiative in collecting and presenting material, a wealth of material can be made available:

- Selections can be made from old newspapers or other printed materials.
- Old books can be cut up and transformed into reading cards
- Teachers, parents, and older children can make reading material for younger ones.
- Children's work can be used as reading material for others.

Health

Local primary health care materials can be introduced and used in schools, e.g. growth monitoring charts. Materials jointly produced by teachers and their pupils (e.g. plays, songs, posters) can be used in the community: once pupils have *used* these materials they will never themselves forget the messages they convey.

Organisation of teaching and learning

Rather than accepting the traditional pattern of class organisation, the traditional distinction between 'teacher and taught', administrators could consider a much freer and more flexible pattern of teaching and learning. For example:

Literacy

- For part of the school programme children can be grouped in 'families' with older children teaching basic skills to younger ones. Such a programme also consolidates skills in older children.
- Literate parents can be invited to help children learn to read.
- By arrangement with secondary schools, older children can be given skills and responsibilities to help younger children in their families and neighbourhood.

Health

- Health workers can be *regularly* invited into schools.
- Older children can be given responsibilities for the health of younger ones in their schools or children of pre-school age. Experience in Botswana suggests that the responsibility for the initiation of such pre-school children will substantially widen and deepen the knowledge and skills of the school-aged children.

These examples are merely illustrative but they demonstrate the many ways in which the exercise of a modest degree of administrative flexibility could substantially affect quality. However, an essential preliminary to local flexibility is a national agreement that such local initiatives will be welcome and supported. This will require to be negotiated and it is encouraging to note that in Asian countries the process is at least being discussed. As long ago as 1980, an important regional seminar in Canberra[3] looked at the different strategies facing those co-ordinating curriculum design and development in its member states. They contrasted centralised with decentralised situations as represented in TABLE XVII. Even at that time there was an anticipation that many countries were moving towards what the seminar described as 'combination situations'. Since then, policy in many of the countries

**TABLE XVI   ROLES OF CURRICULUM CO-ORDINATION IN CENTRALISED AND
DECENTRALISED SYSTEMS (ASIA AND OCEANIA, 1980)**

a Centralised curricula:

National roles (Generally to maintain and reform the curricula)

Plan national standardised curricula to meet national needs
Relate national needs to international demands
Translate these needs into curriculum requirements for the various levels (syllabuses, texts, guides, equipment, micro-testing, etc.)
Design of dissemination
Evaluation of effectiveness on learners
Research and developmental experimentation

Provincial or regional roles

Some participation in the first four roles listed above
Assisting in supervising evaluation of effectiveness of new curricula on learners and feedback of results to national agency

b Decentralised situation with plurality of curricula:

National roles

Assist local bodies to identify local objectives
Transmit to local bodies guidelines *re* the national objectives
Communicate international demands for education for local bodies
Assist local bodies with the curriculum development processes or develop alternative material for them
Act as clearing house
Co-ordinate and prevent duplication and waste of resources
Identify and prepare exemplary material for 'gaps' in curriculum of local bodies
Provide an evaluative function by harnessing *ad hoc* expertise where required
Develop models for, and examples of, training of the curricula expertise required in decentralised curriculum

Provincial or regional or local roles

Indentification of local objectives for curriculum
Detailed curriculum development from national and international guidelines
Identification of alternatives among existing resources
Planning and operation of dissemination of ideas and materials
In-service training of teachers regarding the curriculum
Supervision of implementation of curriculum in schools
Evaluation of effectiveness of new curricula on learner[4]

represented in Canberra has moved perceptibly away from fully centralised strategies in both curriculum, teacher education and the administration of resources, though *not* significantly in the assessment of outcomes. The policy of one important Asian country, Indonesia, is described in slightly greater depth in the latter part of this chapter.

Participation at all levels

The final enabler, 'participation', is implicit in all the previous four. Although never absent from the rhetoric of planners and administrators, particularly in times when they depend upon those at local level to provide money and manpower to keep a hardpressed system going, true participation requires changes of attitudes difficult to achieve in a bureaucratic and hierarchical society. For it involves changing the role of an administrator from making things happen to enabling others to make them happen, a profound and sometimes disturbing change.

In the latter part of this chapter we analyse the long road which the Indonesian inspectors are attempting to travel from *supervision*: 'I tell you what to do,' to *support*: 'I help you help each other.' Those of us working in and with this programme will be far more confident we are succeeding when we see supervisors of in-service courses participating with heads and teachers in making equipment and acting out activities, rather than standing benignly at the edge of an activity group and watching them.

A KEY FIGURE IN ADMINISTRATION – THE HEADTEACHER

While it is hard to single out any level of administrator as more important than any other in the promotion of quality, there is no denying that school heads are second to none in importance and infinitely more numerous than all the rest put together. We have already reminded readers of the vast differences apparent between similar schools with different headteachers. We now consider the even greater potential for the role of headteacher if they were better enabled to effect qualitative improvement in schools.

Roles

A school head, whether in Malaysia, Lesotho, Kenya or anywhere else, performs four relative roles:

an administrative role – he runs the school and manages the staff
a curricular role – he chooses and advises on content and methodology
a research and evaluation role – he collects and interprets information about children and their performance
a community role – relationships with parents, the wider community and the other agencies such as the church or the mosque which jointly provide education for the school child.

Currently the *administrative role* predominates, often fuelled by the demands of bureaucracy. In Indonesia, heads must keep fifteen different types of record for the perusal of the visiting inspector. Moreover, courses for heads (and there are far too few of them) tend to stress this role, relegating the other three to a strictly subordinate status. The *curriculum role*, though recognised, is frequently underemphasised. Chapter Three emphasises the central importance of the head in choosing from alternatives available, making key decisions on the methodology adopted by the school and relating the national plan to local realities; needs later to needs now. The *research and evaluation role* is scarcely stressed. True, headteachers collect statistics which they

---

TABLE XVII RESEARCH AND EVALUATION ACTIVITIES POSSIBLE FOR HEADS AND THEIR TEACHERS TO UNDERTAKE, GIVEN APPROPRIATE TRAINING, ENCOURAGEMENT AND RECOGNITION

---

1 Studies relevant to educational planners

e.g. 1.1 Local case studies of enrolment and dropouts (with reasons).

1.2 Follow-up studies of school leavers.

1.3 Educational provision within an area, e.g. public and private, religious and non-formal opportunities and who makes use of them.

1.4 Educational needs and priorities voiced by local people.

1.5 Financial support available and afforded to school children, e.g. textbooks, exercise books, uniforms, etc.

2 Studies relevant to administration, planning, in-service and support systems for teachers

e.g. 2.1 Information about teachers who actually teach (trained and untrained) and how far they claim that their training has prepared them for the conditions in which they are teaching and the content they are expected to teach.

2.2 Information about content in schools,

e.g. how much is covered?

what is left out and why?

what difficulties are experienced?

what variations are introduced?

what co-curricular activities are undertaken and valued?

2.3 Information about buildings, furniture and equipment in relation to the demands of the syllabus.

3 Inventories of learning resources, as an aid to assist both administrators and curriculum planners

3.1 Physical, human and cultural resources within the environment and the extent to which they could be or were being used by teachers.

3.2 Availability, cost and provision of commercially produced materials, e.g. textbooks, exercise books, chalks, etc.

3.3 Availability and potential use of local alternatives, both natural (e.g. seeds and clay) and manufactured (e.g. bottle tops, old newspapers etc.).

4   Studies of teaching and learning patterns

    4.1   Teaching behaviours – leading to an analysis of good and bad practice as an aid for in-service training.

    4.2   Language comprehension by teachers (of teachers' guide) and learners (of materials).

    4.3   Patterns and approaches to testing, setting and marking of pupils' work, record keeping.

5   Studies of learners, their teachers and their environment as an aid for teacher trainers and curriculum planners

Heads and teachers could assess:

    5.1   Studies of mathematical, scientific and cultural environment of children.

    5.2   Social environment of children and their families, especially in relation to other informal learning which takes place at home.

    5.3   Linguistic environment of children, e.g. languages spoken and understood, reading opportunities available in homes, street, etc.

    5.4   Health and nutrition of children and their communities including patterns of child rearing and children's involvement with their younger brothers and sisters.

    5.5   Interests and aspirations of pupils and their parents.

6   Self-evaluation studies of schools according to certain criteria

    e.g.   organisation and administration

           teaching and learning

           relations with communities.[6]

---

pass on to provincial and national level – but such activities are done with little thought to their educational implications. TABLE XVII indicates the potential of school-based research co-ordinated by headteachers. While it is fully realised that such activities would require a degree of support and recognition not often at present available, it is equally true that there is a considerable willingness to consider the emergence of such a role both on the part of ministries (in all four countries surveyed) and of headteachers, who would welcome the opportunity to become involved, particularly if results could in some way influence their future careers.

Our final role, the *community role*, has always been a headteacher's concern; increasingly, however, it is becoming of even greater importance once community participation of schools and community participation in their programmes becomes a reality.

Support

In order for headteachers adequately to undertake these complicated roles, they need a type and level of support not currently available. Three approaches may be considered:

Extra staff

While the head of a large school in Kuala Lumpur or Nairobi can look forward to having more teachers than classes and would thus be free to plan activities to help teachers or interact with the community, colleagues in smaller schools may be faced with a class to teach (probably the top one) in addition to the usual administrative duties.

While a district administration may wish to post a supernumerary teacher to the school, often funds will not permit it. It is here, therefore, that flexible approaches need to be considered very seriously. Alternatives include:

- easing the timetable
- developing more group- and self-learning strategies
- employing a young teacher's aide
- combining classes for specific areas of content
- enlisting the help of parents

Solutions *may* therefore exist once rigid patterns of management and curriculum are broken down.

Support materials

Though handbooks for heads exist they are often highly unimaginative and totally administrative. Simply produced and attractively presented 'handbooks of suggestions' dealing particularly with how to help assess quality, how to assess and aid teachers, how to promote better children's work, how to make best use of physical and human community resources – are badly needed. It is ironical that in the United States and Britain, countries with well trained teachers and heads, such books abound; yet with few exceptions[7] they are lacking in Asian and African countries.

Support from colleagues

Experience is gained through sharing. The promotion of frequent opportunities for headteachers to meet and compare approaches is valuable, particularly so if such occasions are built round specific tasks such as the joint preparation of material for in-servicing untrained teachers or the discussion of criteria for assessment of quality in pupils, teachers or schools. The creation and operation of successful groups for heads has been one of the most successful features of the Indonesian support systems described in the second half of this chapter.

Training

The importance of training and the current shortcomings have been discussed. Considerable thought is now being given to this issue in all our five countries, with specific institutions such as the Kenya Education Staff Institute being specifically charged with this purpose.

Here, much thought needs to be given towards the preparation of programmes and materials which tackle problems as they *are* (few funds, overcrowded classrooms, overloaded curricula, undertrained teachers) rather than as they should be.

The whole issue of training is taken up in some greater depth in our next section.

Administrators' and managers' recruitment and training

Good recruitment and adequate training of educational managers is fundamental to the quality of education. But, although this has been recognised by almost every international educational conference in the past decade, the resultant action has everywhere been disappointing. For, because of quantitative pressures within and upon systems, education officers, supervisors and inspectors are still appointed to undertake these crucial roles with no training at the outset and little if any training on the job. Even when action *is* taken to mount courses or establish institutions to provide training, content still tends to address management as a set of skills and techniques in themselves, divorced from their most important goal, that of achieving desired *changes in the behaviour of learners*.

The root cause lies in the structure and staffing of the institutions that train the managers. Until these can be persuaded to take a wider view of management and of quality, the gap between the ledger and the learner will remain unbridged.

PART II FROM SUPERVISION TO SUPPORT: A CASE STUDY FROM INDONESIA

The second part of this chapter contains a case study examining in some depth a qualitative improvement programme in primary education in Indonesia. There are two reasons for its inclusion in this book: first, because both authors have been closely involved in the programme and have no doubt of its importance internationally; and second, because we believe that its planning, its achievements and its difficulties all help to illuminate not only the principles discussed in the first half of this chapter but also those examined throughout this book.

The programme described was initiated in 1979 through a five year action project with the rather cumbersome title 'Qualitative Improvement Through Professional Support For Teachers In Primary School'. As the name implies, it aims to achieve two goals – improving the quality of the content in primary schools and providing a support system to make this happen. Both are necessary, both are ambitious and both are exceptionally difficult to achieve.

THE CONTEXT: INDONESIA

To attempt a comprehensive description of the Indonesian education system would be foolish, but certain facts need to be established as a basis for the description which follows. The system, like the country itself, is enormous in size. There are 25.5 million children currently enrolled in the six grades of primary school and over 879 000 teachers.[8] It is also, for historical and political reasons, remarkably centralised in comparison with other great systems like USA, Nigeria, Brazil or India. While the need to further devolve control is accepted and local initiatives often encouraged, there seems no undue haste to do so. Discussions, of forthcoming changes in the national syllabus and nationally produced textbooks to be realised in the next few years, are still based on the premise of one single national product.

Like many large centralised systems, Indonesian education is bureaucratic. There is a strongly defined hierarchy of educational decision-making and a considerable degree of compartmentalisation within the system. Responsibility is divided between three Ministries, Education, Home Affairs and Religious Affairs and, within these, separate agencies are often responsible for activities which should be closely related: one agency for the production of textbooks, another for the design of syllabuses; one for pre-service training of teachers, another for most in-service training; one for the employment and conditions of teachers, another for those of inspectors.

One reason for the centralised nature of Indonesian education lies in the commitment to the planned development of education in five year planning periods within the framework of national development goals, and a strongly stressed national code of moral and personal development, 'Pancesilla', which every Indonesian is expected to know and follow. Here the record over the years has been impressive (though achieved in the teeth of rapid population growth): a steady rise of enrolments towards universal primary education; a parallel drop in illiteracy rates and, now beginning to emerge, a growing concern to improve quality in line with quantitative improvements. Schemes for qualitative improvement tend to be very large and very centralised. At primary level in the decade 1970–80 they included the issue (in 1975) of a new curriculum plan based on the behavioural objectives model, the writing and supply to all schools in Indonesia (a gigantic undertaking) of textbooks in four key subjects throughout the primary level, together with an equally vast scheme to provide courses in their use on a subject basis for all teachers in rotation. These courses were planned on a nationally devised content and almost inevitably on the 'cascade' system, with master-trainers instructing trainers at local level who, in turn, instruct teachers. The word 'instruct' adequately describes the approach used. It was generally didactic, lectures being delivered to large groups of teachers whose participation was very slight.

By the end of the decade, however, concern was being expressed, particularly from the Ministry's Office of Educational Research and Development,[9] that despite vast inputs into primary education neither the relevance nor the efficiency of the system were achieving the improvements which had been expected by its planners. Approaches remained formal and didactic despite calls for more active approaches, and student achievement, measured in a major study in 1976, did not seem to be greatly affected by the costly inputs of textbooks and in-service training. However, in examining what the study called 'classroom climate variables', a very interesting finding emerged. The report of the study published in 1978 describes this:

> Early in the analysis it was discovered that some schools produced consistently high achievement while others were consistently low. Yet the home background and school policies examined could explain less than 20% of the pupils' variability, thus leaving largely unexplained the large differences between schools. One possible explanation was the influence of the classroom climate brought about by the interaction of teacher and pupils.[10]

Further examination of the correlations between different variables and children's performance underlined these findings. The correlation between performance and classmates' achievement mean far outweighed all other variables. This led the authors of the survey to hypothesise that:

> Certain teachers are better able to bring about high achievement in their classes, not because they are better qualified, or more experienced, or more modern or have better facilities, or textbooks or smaller classes, but because they have better teaching skills and interpersonal relationships with their pupils. Such teachers may be able to perceive children's needs, adapt their teaching to the children's levels, interest and motivate them, and maintain an industrious classroom climate.[11]

As a result of such concerns and after a high level planning seminar where alternatives were weighed and discussed, the Office of Educational Research and Development resolved to plan, conduct and monitor a five year action project in a district, Cianjur, in the province of West Java. Although the whole district was identified as an area for innovation, training and monitoring were initially confined to three sub-districts (together containing about 200 primary schools). Sub-districts were chosen because of their different characteristics, one urban, a second rural but accessible, a third remote. The project plan spelt out a series of general objectives to guide both planning and management as follows:

General objectives
Following a survey of present practices:
to construct working models in contrasting educational contexts in Indonesia in order to explore means of improving the quality of instruction through improving the quality of support to teachers at local level;
to monitor progress and modify the models during the course of the project as a result of periodic evaluation.
As a result of experience gained from the project; *to produce* a national

plan for modification and improvement of support systems to teachers which:

(i)   can substantially improve quality of primary education;
(ii) is feasible to introduce within the financial, administrative and human resources likely to be available to the government of Indonesia;
(iii) is flexible enough to be effective in contrasting educational contexts in Indonesia.[12]

Although the original objectives did not make such distinctions, those of us who have worked with the project and the national programmes which have subsequently derived from it, now realise that the tasks to be faced could, in fact, be divided into four:

(i)   The setting up of a support and communication system which operated both vertically from ministry right down to school and teacher, and horizontally, so as to bring together all the agencies which support the teacher and which should (but usually don't) support each other. This involves changing the attitudes and practice of current supervisors.

(ii) Defining the task of qualitative improvement in terms of a set of 'teacher behaviours' to be improved, linked with a content which is both relevant to children's needs and possible for ordinary teachers to handle. The phrase 'student active learning' is used by Indonesian policy-makers to describe the new approaches they seek to introduce. But to promote such active learning involves not only defining it but also observing its practicall application in schools so as to differentiate dreams from reality.

(iii) Developing and refining a pattern of in-service training which can enable those within the support system to improve their content and approaches and to link them to the context in which the system operates. Such training depends in turn on the generation of good materials for teachers, heads and inspectors and their improvement as a result of experience gained in using them.

(iv) Developing a national resource for continued professional assistance to primary education so that both the system and its content can gradually grow, evolve and improve.

Let us consider this in rather more detail.

THE SUPPORT SYSTEM
At central and provincial level

Structures were planned to ensure a better flow of information and participation in decision-making between different ministries and directorates within ministries who shared interests in the project and responsibilities for participating teachers. In theory such co-operation was badly needed.

A head of a school in Indonesia, we should reflect:

> is employed and deployed by the Ministry of Home Affairs who also supply his equipment and mend his buildings (though if he is wise he may also seek help from the parents and community).
> His school may possess a room for prayer and employ a religious teacher controlled by the Ministry of Religious Affairs.
> The rest of his professional activities are supervised by the Ministry of Education but not less than five different bureaucracies have responsibility for:
> > his curriculum
> > his inspection
> > his in-service education
> > his pre-service education
> > his further studies.

In practice, as we shall discuss later, such co-ordination proved exceptionally difficult to achieve.

At district, sub-district and school level

The core of the new support system is the *school cluster* and the teachers' groups working from it. Schools are organised into groups of five to ten depending on ease of communication between them. Each cluster of schools has a system of *teachers' groups* working within it. The composition of such groups varies. Occasionally they are organised around subject interests but more often by class level. Lower, middle or upper primary teachers within the cluster meet for half a day every three or four weeks to discuss their problems and successes, compare and devise materials or watch and criticise one of their number teaching. *Parents' representatives* frequently attend group meetings. Within each cluster of schools certain teachers become identified as *subject resource teachers* because of their interest and expertise as they are encouraged to help their fellows. At *school level* there are regular *professional meetings* called and chaired by the head who is encouraged to take a greater interest and initiative in professional leadership. This interest is supported by regular meetings of *heads' groups*.

At sub-district level (50–80 schools) small *teacher-resource centres* are built and equipped. They are used, where possible, as venues for *teachers' groups, heads' groups* and *regular meetings of local inspectors* who themselves are trained and encouraged to take a more actively professional role, particularly in identifying good schools, good heads and good teachers capable of helping each other. Thus inspectors are increasingly seen as organisers of facilities for teacher support.

Above them, at district level there is a *co-ordinating committee* together with identified *subject organisers*, who help give professional leadership and advice to their colleagues at local level.

The initial plan also envisaged a close integration between the support system, which provides opportunities for school-based qualitative improvement, with the *local teachers' colleges* which prepare new teachers for the schools. The failure to achieve such an effective integration however remains one of the greatest weaknesses in the system. Figure 4 indicates how the various agencies of support were expected to complement each other.

New approaches to teaching and learning at primary level

The initial project identified four subject areas at primary level (language, mathematics, social studies and science) and eight key teacher behaviours which it hoped could be improved. They were:

1 Awareness of objectives
2 Proper use of time available for learning
3 Proper organisation of the classroom to facilitate and encourage good learning
4 Effective class management so that maximum use is made of class, group and individual activities
5 Development of thought and creativity in learners (rather than concentration on the recall of factual information)
6 Effective use of the environment and children's direct experience as a source for learning
7 Awareness and management of individual differences in learners
8 Use of feedback to promote and reinforce learning[13]

More generally, the Ministry of Education, particularly the curriculum division of the Office of Educational Research and Development, have been encouraging efforts at all levels to promote student active learning.

In one of its recent publications *'active learning'* is described in the following terms:

Its aim is to produce children who can:
• Think and reason actively, ask questions, examine evidence, solve problems.
• Take responsibility for their own learning so they can learn effectively from a teacher, from educational materials, from each other, from the environment.

But the concept is frequently misunderstood. Not only do some schools still confuse physical and mental activity, but even the concept of mental activity is sometimes misapplied. We found one group who had been writing poetry the evening before, itself a wonderful innovation, 'actively' combining in a group to make all their poems into one single poem. Those organising the project are, therefore, keenly aware of the need for schools to process along a continuum, from active children through active methods in the classroom to active thinking and problem-solving, based on a real understanding of the nature of different areas of experience.

But there can be no doubt of the generally beneficial effects of the call for activity in school classrooms or its incorporation into new trial syllabuses (1984) and new teaching/learning materials.

Training

In order to match the improved content with the new support system, training and materials for training were necessary. Through association with the Institute of Education, London University, a group of core trainers was built up and is being extended. Though the first team of core trainers came largely from the Office of Educational Research and Development and from colleges of education (IKIPS), subsequent trainers have been drawn mainly from field staff. These core trainers, along with their colleagues from the London Institute, organised training in the project areas from 1980 onwards. Subject advisers, inspectors, and selected heads and teachers worked intensively for three weeks every year, not only to gain new skills but also to review the work of the teachers' groups during the past year and plan for the next. Prototype materials were generated, together with notes for guidance of teachers and heads. All training demonstrates rather than preaches 'student active learning'. The teachers, and even the inspectors, practise doing everything that they will ask their children to do. Later the participants attending these courses hold their own programme of training with the teachers in their area and continue to interact with them during the next year in schools.

Material for supervisors and teachers (though not nearly enough of it) has been generated by the project team. An essential principle in both training and materials production is the sharing of goals and materials. The goals and principles of the project are invariably displayed on posters in teachers' centres. Everyone involved knows, or should know, what kind of teaching behaviours have been identified and what improvements are to be aimed for; what a well organised class should look like; what is expected from children's work; what ought to be evaluated and how. These centrally produced handbooks are available not just for supervisors but also to heads and teachers. They also form the basis for other materials written by the teachers themselves in their groups and during their training. In this way the dangerous situation where knowledge is restricted and becomes used as an instrument of power wielded by those 'higher' in the system over those 'lower' down is averted.

Centres for assistance in raising primary school quality

From the outset of the programme it was realised that to ensure the

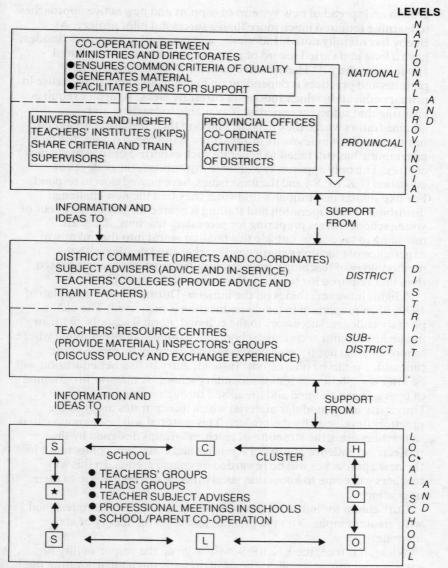

Figure 4 Indonesian Project: '(ALPS) Active learning through professional support' — levels of co-operation.

growth and spread of new systems of support and new active approaches to learning required much more than a successful pilot project. As Beeby has ruefully noted, Indonesia, and many other countries besides, have a long and varied record of pilot projects which never piloted anyone anywhere.[14] The effective national dissemination of new patterns and practices is dependent on building up a core of expertise in primary education which Indonesia currently lacks. It further requires ensuring that sufficient expertise is available to teachers and administrators where they need it, that is in their own local areas and not thousands of miles away in Jakarta or Bandung. To date, the new programme has still failed to generate such expertise or to activate new centres. The only apparently available institutions, the colleges of education (I.K.I.P.S.) and the universities, have proved slow to respond. For like similar institutions worldwide, they find the new challenge disturbing. Their operation and staffing is geared largely to the needs of young school leavers preparing for secondary teaching. They are unwilling to take steps outside this familiar world into the unknown experience of teaching experienced teachers and dealing with the methodology of teaching young children (so much more complicated than that required for teaching classes in a high school).

A light, however, shines on the horizon. During the five year plan of 1990–95, a revolution in teacher education is projected. The old primary colleges, successors to the colonial 'normal schools', with an intake after junior secondary school and a three year programme where school and teacher training content strive uneasily for space in the timetable, are to be phased out. Instead, entry to teacher education will be after completion of senior secondary school. A massive programme of upgrading is planned and organised through Indonesia's Open University using modular material which incorporates many of the practices developed by the project. This material will be communicated to teachers using the structure of teachers' groups designed by the project. Attendance at project seminars and classroom competence in the new approaches will be rewarded by course credits. In this way teachers will come to know that good practice will contribute to their upgrading.

Curriculum for initial training will, at the same time, be redesigned with greater emphasis on the practice as well as the theory of active learning.

While, it is true, the I.K.I.P.S. will be given the responsibility for carrying out this new policy, they will do so through incorporating the best of the current training colleges and their staff. From such a partnership, institutions could emerge capable of providing the expertise and assistance which is so vitally needed.

The extension of the 'Cianjur Project'

By 1984, there was little doubt of the apparent success of the five year supervision project. The schools and school clusters in Cianjur seemed for the first time to be giving a practical example of the catchphrase 'student active learning'. An official evaluation was mounted and turned up with a favourable report. Much less thorough, but infinitely more influential, was the report by a group of parliamentarians who toured the area in 1984 and presented a very encouraging impression to the Assembly. Cianjur became a focus of interest, both lay and professional. During the years 1984–86, an average of 6 000 official visitors a year toured the schools from all over Indonesia, as well as outside it. In the years 1987–89 the numbers swelled to nearly one thousand a month. Most of them came prepared to be convinced and though the district administration showed them a wide variety of schools, they naturally avoided the bad ones, so impressions were almost universally favourable and the practices began to spread both officially and unofficially.

Six new areas have officially been permitted to start similar projects and more have been identified, through a number of unofficial systems are in operation all over Indonesia, some in government and some in private schools – how many are really effective is unknown. In the years 1988–89, the rapid proliferation of new systems, a trend resisted by the Office of Educational Research and Development who lacked staff to monitor and advise new areas, slowed down somewhat in the light of the very savage financial cuts which have been made, since 1986, in the recurrent budgets. This has given planners a breathing space to undertake some monitoring and development, in areas already operating support systems, to plan and produce more materials and to build up a little more expertise with the help of British aid. Already very interesting variations, both in quality and approach of support systems, are becoming apparent and it is not at all surprising to discover that where local sense of ownership is strongest and where active participation in decision-making by inspectors, heads and teachers is most encouraged, there the best results are observed.[15] As this book goes to press in 1990, the system is posed for another rapid expansion of support systems. Within the next seven years all provinces in Indonesia will have at least one district developed as a 'centre for better practice'.

Long term futures

Those of us involved in the new primary school improvement programme in Indonesia have been immensely heartened by what has happened in the schools and, moreover, hopeful that with nearly ten years' modelling behind them some areas will have reached a point where no one will readily accept a return to the old, dull and monotonous pattern of learning from which they changed. Schools do feel different. There is ample evidence that teachers recognise this.

When asked why they continue to make the considerable effort to prepare and supervise active approaches to learning, a common response from better teachers is 'we like teaching this way' or 'the children like it'. This response we find entirely credible. It is not meretricious and it is demonstrably backed up by practices in the classroom – not show lessons but evidence of interesting work over a long period by individuals and groups of children. One very heartening feature is the way in which the spirit of self-help groups among teachers and children extends outside the classroom. In at least one urban area (Cianjur town) groups of children are encouraged regularly to prepare assignments together, often based on investigations within the community. Equally heartening is the way in which parents and teachers appear prepared to invest their own resources of time and even money into providing additional resources in classrooms and additional training for teachers.

But nobody pretends that the new approaches in Indonesia are anything more than a start upon a long journey. For they require fundamental changes in attitudes by decision-makers inviting them to devolve power and responsibility, to progress from an autocratic to a more democratic style of management, and to loosen bureaucratic constraints so that those at local level can exercise a greater degree of decision-making. In short, 'room for manoeuvre' is being widened. Moreover, the current rapid and uneven spread of the model has brought Indonesian policy makers face to face with the realities of the process of change. It is slow, erratic, and often promotes rather than diminishes inequalities. In the traditional pattern these realities could be ignored. The intention could be separated from its execution; implementation of a programme from its real assimilation in schools. But once the 'cascade' system of training is abandoned, support replaces supervision, and implementation is revealed as dependent on the will, the manpower and the resources available within a community, then some very disturbing truths emerge:

- Some areas may achieve qualitative improvement faster than others. The time span for the new approaches to work their way through the system is likely to be a very long one.
- Some parts of Indonesia, which have stronger traditions of participatory democracy at local level, may improve more quickly than others; and most disturbing of all:
- Those areas better able to mobilise money and manpower will almost inevitably take initiatives before those less able to do so.

Consequently, gaps may open up between regions and districts and between towns and rural areas.

These truths become even more stark when they are set against the current financial climate. For since the national budget is so constrained, there is no longer any prospect of a tightly controlled national campaign to improve quality. Hence, realistically, the government appears to accept that those areas and communities that wish improve their schools should be encouraged to do so.

Currently, therefore, political commitment behind the ideas is considerable. The new approach styled 'Active Learning through Professional Support' is now accepted as a long-term goal running parallel to a ministerial commitment to increasing both local responsibility for decision-making and the introduction of locally relevant content into the curriculum.

In the face of lack of central funding, local investment is welcome and with it a considerable measure of local autonomy to plan and manage programmes of dissemination. In the longer term, the need for very considerable investment to develop local institutions capable of training leaders in Indonesia is now accepted.

Thus, despite the long road that lies ahead, those of us who have been involved in the Indonesian programme and who have watched the impact which its ideas and its achievements have made in the nation, the region and worldwide, have been very heartened by the response it has provoked. It appears to show how our five elements: shared goals; information and communication; realism; flexibility and participation can be applied at all levels from the planner to the pupils and how as a result of this, quality appears to be improving, not only if it is measured as we would wish it to be, but as it is measured now, through conventional attainment tests and statistics of enrolment and retention.

QUALITY, ADMINISTRATION AND THE PURSUIT OF POWER

The two parts of this chapter complement each other. In the first we have discussed how those key agents of quality, the administrators, supervisors and managers, could be brought closer to those other agents, the teachers, parents and children. In the second part we have briefly described one attempt to do so.

Yet though at one level the suggestions made and the model provided offer us a way forward towards improving quality, there are very deep currents eddying beneath the surface. For 'administration', 'management' and 'supervision' denote power; whereas 'support' and 'consultation' do not. Many years ago, one of us remembers meeting an ex-student in the street. We enquired after his career and found him in jubilant mood. He had been promoted out of the classroom. 'I have become a more-than-teacher,' he announced proudly. How can we make such more-than-teachers accept a role as facilitators rather than arbiters of quality?

NOTES AND REFERENCES

1 Government of Kenya, *Report of the National Commission on Educational Objectives and Priorities*, Government Printer, Nairobi, 1977.

2 Described in Tony Somerset, *Child-to-Child: A Survey*, London Institutes of Education and Child Health, Child-to-Child Programme, 1988, pp. 69–71.

3 Asian Programme of Educational Innovation in Development (APEID), *National Strategies for Curriculum Design and Development*, Report of a Regional Seminar, UNESCO, Bangkok, 1980.

4 *Ibid.*, p. 46.

5 In Kenya official criteria for upgrading status of primary teachers do give authorities discretion to take locally-based research and curriculum development into consideration.

6 A fuller listing is given in the occasional paper by H. W. R. Hawes, *Locally Based Educational Research and Curriculum Development in Developing Countries: The Teacher's Role*, Occasional Paper 40, UNESCO/I.I.E.P., Paris, 1976.

7 Attempts to produce such publications in Indonesia are described later in the chapter. In Nigeria useful and informative *Inpectors' Handbooks* were published in various editions between 1969 and 1975.

8 Source: Government of Indonesia, Ministry of Education and Culture with United States Agency for International Development, Education and Human Resources Sector Review 1986, *Improving the Efficiency of Education Systems*, Vol. 2, Florida State University, 1987, pp. 3–6.

9 Its Indonesian acronym is now BALITBANG DIKBUD, formerly BP3K. All its publications (mostly in Indonesian) are listed under these headings.

10 BP3K (Office of Educational and Cultural Research and Development), *Grade VI Survey of Student Achievement*, Ministry of Education and Culture, Jakarta, 1978, p. 66.

11 *Ibid.*

12 BP3K (Office of Educational and Cultural Research and Development), *Qualitative Improvement Through Professional Support for Teachers in Primary Schools*, An Action Project 1979–1984, Ministry of Education and Culture, Jakarta, 1984, pp. 1–2.

13 The competencies are described more fully in a monograph: Agus Tangyong *et al, Quality Through Support for Teachers: A Case Study from Indonesia*, Department of International and Comparative Education, University of London, 1989, p. 50.

14 Beeby, C. E., *Assessment of Indonesian Education: A Guide to Planning*, Oxford University Press, Wellington, 1979, p. 302.

15 Tangyong *et al* (1989), op. cit., pp. 73–91.

EVALUATION AND ASSESSMENT

To devote a separate chapter to evaluation is perhaps to suggest it is in some way a discrete activity, apart from everything else we have focused upon so far. In fact, in broad terms, most, if not all of this book is concerned with *evaluation*, in that we have: *identified* areas of concern; critically *assessed* strengths and weaknesses (of teacher training and the teaching-learning process for example); made *judgements* about changes we would like to see made.

In making these judgements we have been involved in prioritising our areas of concern, ascribing more *value* to that and less to this, in *weighing up* strengths and weaknesses, in *deciding* what *we* consider to be worthwhile, good, of quality, etc.

Evaluation is, therefore, very much concerned with value judgements and decision-making:

- decisions about curricula: materials and methods, content and change;
- decisions about individuals: the needs of pupils now and needs later, the training and retraining of teachers, and so on;
- decisions about administration: judgements of schools, projects, innovation and, occasionally, the system as a whole;
- decisions in the area of values and their application to education.

All these decisions are taken within two contexts. Firstly, the narrower context of the child and his programme of learning in a particular school. Secondly, the broader context of the educational system.

In this chapter we shall try and relate these two contexts by addressing ourselves both to the assessment of learners (through tests, examinations, etc.) and, in broader terms, how data from these assessments can be used to decide issues concerned with wider educational issues. We shall pay particular attention to the most common form of pupil assessment, the examination, and ourselves evaluate efforts being made in places like Kenya, to improve the quality of these instruments of assessment. Finally, we will look at one important function of evaluation: the collection and dissemination of information essential to educational decision-makers.

In this introduction we have used both the terms 'assessment' and 'evaluation' and it may be useful now to clarify our position and establish working definitions.

What is the difference between 'evaluation' and 'assessment'?

In educational literature these terms are often used interchangeably and therefore confusingly. For the purposes of our discussion we shall view 'evaluation' in broad terms, our focus not upon an individual pupil but upon the efficacy and quality of the education system and its component parts and processes.

'Assessment' seems to imply something more focused and more related to the individual pupil's progress through the learning process. It might relate to various ways of monitoring that progress and so, in this sense, would comprise one component of a larger evaluation process.[1] Another way of looking at the relationship of evaluation and assessment is to see them both in terms of what they intend to *measure*.

Eliot Eisner in *The Art of Educational Evaluation*[2] describes evaluation as a 'normatic enterprise' which measures the attainment or not of educational aims and objectives. He, like us, stresses the subjective and 'value-loaded' nature of that enterprise, invoking the vocabulary of 'priorities', 'standards' and 'preference'.

For him evaluation consists of four interrelated factors: context, input, process and product, meaning that any 'measurement' ought to be concerned

> with the context in which teaching and learning take place, with the quality of the input or curriculum to which students have access, and with the pedagogical processes employed by the teacher as students and teacher interact. Finally it is interested in the product, or more aptly the outcomes of the foregoing.

We can thus take these four interrelated factors and apply to them our criteria of quality. We are then able to *evaluate* our 'inputs', e.g. resources or 'pedagogical processes', e.g. teaching of science to Class in terms of relevance, efficiency, etc., and answer such questions as, 'are schools using their resources in the best way?' or 'is science taught in a relevant manner?'

What we have in mind therefore are two related levels of measurement: one, 'assessment', focused on the individual child, and the other, 'evaluation', concerned with the broader scenario of class, school, etc. And it seems that we are concerned, in the long run, with two interrelated goals:

(a) to improve the assessment procedures so that they measure the things that matter, are fairer, more efficient and give us greater knowledge of how individual pupils fare in the education system; and

(b) to employ that information in the broader landscape of educational evaluation, i.e. in the overall improvement of the educational system.

Assessment procedures have, therefore, not only a 'backwash' effect on the curriculum and teaching-learning process but also on the ways we evaluate the system of which they are a part.

165

THE ASSESSMENT OF LEARNING AND LEARNERS

Though some weight is given to school reports and teacher recommendations in the assessment of children, much more use is made, the world over, of tests or examinations, usually at the end of a prescribed course of study.

There seems nothing intrinsically wrong with testing anybody or anything; rather that it is an essential part of the learning and educational decision-making process.

After being instructed in driving a motor car, and after sufficient practice, it seems perfectly reasonable to test the proficiency of the drivers before they are let loose upon the roads. Such a test may well tell us something about the process of instruction leading up to the test, something of the curriculum employed by the driving school, and maybe something of the learner's background. However, what is primarily being assessed is the *skill* of the novice driver coupled perhaps with some knowledge of traffic rules and regulations. Perhaps aptitude for and general attitude to the business of driving are also being assessed.

Given that the test was relevant to current and likely future road conditions, that the examiners treated all candidates in a similar fashion, and that entry was open to all, regardless of race, gender or wealth, there seems to be a strong argument for welcoming its role in producing drivers of skill. But are they necessarily drivers of quality?

The value of this kind of test lies in its focus: driving skills and their application to real-life circumstances. However, it may be that the focus of the test needs to be widened to embrace more than just the safe manipulation of a car or a knowledge of traffic regulations. Should we test for courtesy to other drivers? or for basic motor mechanics? or the ability to take responsibility in a crisis? Given the increasing number of road accidents, is there a strong case for testing more than just skills? Should knowledge and attitudes be equally assessed? Perhaps what is wrong is the examination itself rather than the preparation for it. To answer such questions it is necessary to examine what it is we *should* be testing, whether driving skills, knowledge of economics, agriculture or civic consciousness.

Knowledge and skills

In terms of knowledge we would wish to come to a decision about the range of knowledge we wished to assess: for example, that which is useful for further study (mathematical concepts for example) as opposed to that of immediate use in daily life, given that a large proportion of school pupils will need to leave school equipped with knowledge for 'now' as well as knowledge for 'later', i.e. needed for expected life in the years ahead or should needs and wishes change.

We would also wish to judge our learners at various stages in the acquisition of their knowledge, perhaps to assess *retention* and *memory* and the internalisation of information over time, assuming of course that we value these attributes over others.

In the area of skills we might match our learners' abilities against local and national standards of attainment, asking ourselves such questions as: can they write? can they manipulate numbers for particular purposes? can they analyse and present information to a particular standard? Such attainment levels would relate directly to the overall goals of the education system. If a large majority of pupils were assessed to be failing to meet predicted levels of attainment we might use that information to evaluate the broader context of the children's education.

A quality assessment would review knowledge and skills regularly for relevance to contemporary demands, future needs and to bring them into line with current views of 'minimum standards' of literacy, etc.

The examination would need to assess a child's *process* of learning – how the learner moved from one cognitive stage to another – and for that reason might assess individual's *qua* individuals or as members of one learning cohort.

Attitudes and dispositions

Deciding which attitudes and dispositions are to be developed and rewarded lies at the heart of the normative nature of assessment and evaluation. Questions such as: is our learner respectful to his leaders? proud of his country? capable of showing individual initiative? prepared to sacrifice individual initiative for community well-being? reveal as much about the questioner as they do the answerer.

We might also focus upon particular personal qualities: co-operation and toleration of others; the desire to continue learning independently of school and tutor. Importantly we would also wish to assess the capability of the learner to handle *change* and to be ready and willing to participate in the decision-making processes at local and national level. An inherent paradox of current examinations is that whereas, on the one hand, they seek to assess a learner's ability to handle change, on the other, because of their need to maintain standards over time, they often seek to test outmoded attitudes and dispositions.

Ironically, too, it seems that the attitude of students *to* examinations and vice versa: deference and fear on the one side, authoritarianism and condescension on the other, contrast markedly with overt attitudes and dispositions which examinations in particular and teaching generally seek to foster. It seems, for example, difficult to promote the attitude of co-operation and social unity through the teaching – learning process and then to test that attitude by means of an assessment exercise that is covertly competitive and socially divisive.

There are many who would argue too that to change the attitudes and dispositions of pupils first requires an improvement in the attitudes and dispositions of teachers and heads.

Extending the repertoire of assessment procedures to include both internal and external modes of assessment will mean teachers having to make choices, take decisions and ultimately *assess* the methods of assessment employed. Such an activity, supported by training and research, can only lead to an improvement in the attitude of teachers (and ultimately pupils) towards examinations, but may be distrusted by the administrator keen to remove the human element, and with it the possibility of corruption or favouritism from the examination equation.

The Quality of Examinations

The 'hidden curriculum' of assessment brings us on to an analysis of examinations and how much they may fall short of our previously described ideal.

We seem to be concerned with two issues:

(a) the role and impact of examinations upon the curriculum;
(b) the internal quality of examinations, e.g. the way questions are set, papers moderated, examinations developed, etc.

(a) The impact of examinations upon the curriculum

A major problem with modern examinations seems to be their disproportionate power over the curriculum, to such an extent that 'we teach what is tested rather than test what is taught'.[3]

The Jobs and Skills Programme for Africa study (J.A.S.P.A. 1981)[4] of formal qualifications and school-leaver unemployment in Africa analysed selection examinations in eight countries. It concluded, amongst other things, that though many of the examinations were of good quality in a technical sense, i.e. much skill and care had gone into their construction and presentation, the range of content over which knowledge and skills were tested was narrowly limited, e.g. in Sierra Leone, The Gambia and Ghana, it was confined to English and mathematics, with competence in areas of the curriculum such as health, nutrition and agriculture not tested at all. The range of intellectual skills tested was also limited, with most items testing only the ability to recall memorised knowledge.

If examinations of this kind are the sole means of assessment (and they often are), they easily become the tail that wags the educational dog, producing a backwash effect upon content and methodology in the curriculum.

This 'backwash effect' not only has a detrimental effect on the quality of the curriculum, but can rob other agencies, notably teachers, in our quality wheel, of the power to influence the very results produced by the examination. The power of examinations, irrespective of how intrinsically good or bad they are, seems to have dwarfed other equally legitimate influences upon directions of learning and teaching.

What seems to have happened though is that examinations have, for many complex reasons, taken on *economic* and *social* roles as well as educational.

The Government of Ceylon in 1972 recognised this when a report stated that national examinations 'served one main purpose . . . that of screening the candidates for further education or for middle grade jobs'.[6]

Examinations *of this kind*, therefore, have little to do with assessment of learning and a lot to do with allocating 'life chances'.[7] We are all aware of what happens to the learning-teaching relationship: better teachers tend to be channelled to exam classes who are also given the best accommodation and equipment; teachers within those classes focus on examination areas of the curriculum, the institution of 'repeater classes' is established and legitimised (at great expense in terms of time, money and emotion); in richer urban areas private 'tutors' appear, often schoolteachers whose private work can interfere with their regular employment; public and private producers of educational resources concentrate their attention upon 'pass notes', 'key facts' and all the rigmarole of the examination business.

Somerset suggests that the heavy reliance by developing countries upon external examinations is 'not the result of conservatism or lack of knowledge of the alternatives. Rather it is the consequence of the economic and social context in which third-world education systems must operate.'[8]

He identifies four aspects that determines this reliance:

1   *Limited educational resources* leading to restricted opportunities for children to pursue their education beyond the primary stage (he cites 13% of Kenya's primary schools progressing to the secondary cycle with 20–25% of those moving from secondary to higher).
2   *Intense competition* by school-leavers for a limited number of modern sector employment opportunities (he cites the years 1975–79 in Kenya when 650 000 primary school leavers and 230 000 'O' level graduates competed for 150 000 new jobs).
3   *Increased employment opportunities* relating to the length of education experienced and examination passes possessed.
4   *Starting wage* or salary of a school-leaver in a job geared closely to examination success.

These factors indicate that the screening function of examinations is an extremely important one. Because the rewards of success in the examination are high, e.g. a modern sector job, a place at secondary school, many, quite rightly, desire the examination mode of assessment to be as objective and as fair as possible, hence the wariness with which proposals for continuous assessment or pupil profiling are received.

If, however, we wish to make changes in the assessment procedures, we need to do two things: make very sure that any substitution for any external form of assessment is well introduced (and by 'well' we might mean professionally trialled and implemented) and secondly, that we continue to make efforts to raise the 'internal' quality of external examinations.

(b) The internal quality of examinations

There is considerable evidence from Kenya to suggest that improvements in the 'internal' quality of examinations have a 'backwash effect' on quality elsewhere.[9] Examinations for the Certificate of Primary Education (C.P.E.) have been changed to assess educational outcomes promoted by new curricula in English, mathematics and science.[10] By changing the type of questions asked of candidates, i.e. to assess intellectual skills rather than solely test recall of information and by closely monitoring school performance in relation to these examination reforms, evidence is now available to show that, with a good system of feedback and support to schools, examination reform can lead rather than obstruct curriculum change.[11] However, the whole success of such an operation in Kenya, as elsewhere, depends on building up the *skills* not only of those who devise the items but also ultimately of the children who read them, since a 'thinking type' question almost invariably employs more difficult language structures than a 'recall type'.

The Jobs and Skills Programme for Africa survey of examinations provided us with a useful *critique* of current practice in selected national contexts. Reforms in Kenya indicate well the 'language of *possibility*', the room for manoeuvre.

It appears that we are being asked to do three things:

- first to develop assessment instruments that serve the traditional social and economic functions, the 'screening function', and yet *also* support successful curriculum reform
- second to involve the 'examination world' in the quality debate: to recognise the effect the former has on the latter and to push for greater *control* of examinations and other forms of assessment by teachers, curriculum developers, parents, etc.
- thirdly to improve the communication (the 'feedback issue') between teachers and examiners.

It is easy for examinations to be seen as solely indicators of pupil ability rather than to be used diagnostically, i.e. communicating to the teacher weaknesses and strengths in teaching method, particular language problems, areas where greater concentration needs to be given to study skills, etc.

This calls initially for a better relationship between school and examination board. At the moment the climate seems one of secrecy and distance, resulting perhaps from problems of logistics and the power examinations have traditionally had in 'judging' not only pupils but schools, teachers and learning styles.

Improved assessment, therefore, comes with better or more varied instruments of assessment; a widening of involvement in the control of examinations; and an overall acceptance of the practice of feedback – from examination to school and from teacher to pupil.

Let us look a little more closely at these three factors and the part they play in improving the quality of assessment. The conclusions we reach may well assist us in our later evaluation of the broader educational scenarios.

(i) Improved methods of assessment

One relatively effective way to improve pedagogy would be to give teachers more information about techniques of assessment. Without going into too much detail, the following would seem useful 'content' for an in-service course on assessment procedures:

- strategies to *balance* assessment relying not only on summative but continuous modes; thereby effecting the means to assess the product as well as the process of learning;
- an understanding of normative and criterion-referenced tests: the former to assist in the comparison of one learner's performance against another; the latter to help with measuring how well an individual can do something measured against an 'external' standard;
- skills and knowledge related to the application of technology to assessment. Problems of teacher bias and 'subjectivity' can often be reduced by balancing one form of assessment, e.g. the multiple-choice test against another, e.g. the extended essay. The quantitative style of examination can be assisted by the use of computerised marking sheets and tabulation of results. Such procedures, it must be stressed, are only of value when assessing appropriate and suitable competencies, e.g. recall of factual information, items that require right or wrong answers. Computer-assisted learning is part and parcel of the application of technology to assessment. As teachers in countries such as Malaysia and Indonesia become more familiar with the use of such technology in their teaching and assessment procedures, so will pupils benefit when given opportunities to use technology in their own self-assessment.
  Equally, teachers will be able to monitor their own subjectivity or bias when balancing the composition of assessment procedures used. For example, in assessing language, teachers might use a multiple-choice test to assess correct use of grammar, and balance this with a 'subjective' essay form of assessment for the assessment of pupils' creative use of language;
- discussion of the value of profiling[12] as a supplement to end-of-course examinations. This would involve teachers in systematically compiling cumulative records of pupils' progress and achievements.[13] As with continuous assessment, profiling has the advantage in offering a more balanced view of the learner, recording a variety of aspects of his or her progress and attainments, both cognitive and non-cognitive.

171

Critics of continuous assessment and pupil profiling point to the problems of teacher bias and verification. Surely, they say, teachers would write glowing profiles of all their pupils and so we would have a lowering, if not an abandonment, of standards? The assumption behind this criticism is that teachers are unable to operate in a professional manner, whereas examiners are. Given that a large number of teachers work for periods of the year as examiners, coupled with an effective system of moderation to maintain equity and avoid corruption, plus improved in-service training in assessment procedures, there seems no reason why teachers could not handle such innovations in a professional and effective manner.

Those worried about teachers operating in this way would no doubt raise the four factors we discussed earlier in explaining why many countries rely heavily on external examinations. The question seems to be: can we move forward and involve teachers much more in the assessment process and at the same time maintain the standards and practices we have come to value from our examination officers?

If we look not only at the examination at the end of schooling but at the whole range of assessment activities presently used in schools: the setting and marking of homework; end-of-term tests; school reports and record keeping, and endeavour to draw on some of these procedures, along with external examinations, we are much more likely to produce a balanced, relevant and fair assessment of a child's progress and performance.

We would do well to remember that even more educational carnage (including dropouts and repeating) often results from the 'backwash effect' of poorly set teacher tests and assignments than it does from the rather better set external examinations.

(ii) Democratisation of the control of assessment

In the hands of teachers, tests and examinations are important tools in the move to raise standards in schools.[14]

For too long, assessment has been seen as an 'outsider' activity and as a result teachers have had little experience in the design and implementation of new forms of assessment.

In Britain, the new General Certificate of Secondary Education (G.C.S.E.) (replacing the old G.C.E. 'O' level) calls for teachers to play a much greater role in the administration of the examination system. Though training for this role has been inadequate, teachers working in local groups have been able to decide such issues as how much of the curriculum will be assessed by coursework and how much by end-of-year examination.[15]

Control of assessment and decision-making about it are both sides of the same educational coin. At the beginning of this chapter we equated evaluation with decision-making and it seems never more important in the area of assessment. More teacher control over assessment procedures means, of course, a greater say in formal evaluation of the whole system. And with such responsibility comes a greater degree of teacher accountability.[16]

We will return to this issue when we broaden the discussion and look at formal evaluation and the major decisions involved.

(iii) Better communication between school and examination council

As part of an overall package of reforms (some mentioned earlier) the Kenyan National Examinations Council, in the mid-1970s, introduced the *C.P.E. Newsletter*, aiming to keep teachers informed about the philosophy, style and approaches used in the new examination.[17] The newsletter had a practical orientation which 'advised teachers on how to teach particular topics better. It explained test items where even teachers appeared to have missed the point and in later issues gave statistical data on national performance in the examination.'[18]

By talking openly about examinations, by opening up channels of communication like this, examinations became much more part and parcel of school life and therefore less threatening to both teachers and pupils. If teachers are to assume more control over assessment procedures there seems to be a strong case for extending that control to pupils and, as with decision-making, to involve them more in assessing their own progress.

Self-assessment

There would seem to be no reason why a balanced assessment system: some through continuous assessment, some by final examination and some through a pupil profile, might not include pupils' assessment of their own progress.

As teachers, we are all guilty of spending vast amounts of time coaxing pupils to *answer* questions either from ourselves, the textbook or written down in an examination; whereas, we correspondingly devote little time to encouraging children to construct and *ask questions* about what they have learnt and are learning. An example of a simple, yet effective, method of assessment is to set learners the task of reviewing, say, a term's work and then constructing sets of questions or tasks to be performed related to areas chosen. The questions could be evaluated by the class and then 'answered' either informally as a quiz or formally as a test, with all the rigour and status of a 'proper' examination. Such an exercise will:

- give the teacher a product she can assess in terms of knowledge covered, presentation of information, etc.
- give the pupils an insight into assessment procedures and, importantly, an experience of controlling those procedures
- give both teachers and pupils the satisfaction of devising an examination free of the problems of 'question leaking', fear of the unknown and the other negative aspects associated with external examinations.

173

As we said in our earlier chapter on decision-making, control over one's learning is a sure way to improve motivation. It also develops skills and abilities, e.g. using questioning language, writing in a concise manner, and reduces anxieties so often associated with assessment.

Many primary teachers, the world over, have found value in asking pupils to select pieces of work they consider worthwhile and then to exhibit or present that work either on the walls or as part of a class/school magazine.

Self-assessment of this kind enhances the idea that assessment is not solely about testing and grading; but is also concerned with the development of critical skills, awareness of one's own progress, and pride in displaying work to public gaze (albeit one's classroom peers!).

The pupils' exercise books: a simple tool for assessment and self-evaluation

One of the simplest ways of improving assessment is through systematically monitoring children's exercise books. These books represent a cumulative record of pupils' work and also indicate to a third party, such as the school head, the volume, style and progression of work set by the teacher.

At their best they can demonstrate a range of creative work, from simple environmental enquiries such as surveys of a pond or stream, to creative writing. At their worst they reveal all the dreary misunderstandings conveyed in pages of uncorrected sums or ill-copied notes.

Once pupils, teachers and hopefully even outside assessors, such as teachers from other schools, know what kind of products, standards and range of work are desirable in a pupil's book, they have something to aim for, a standard to reach, a basis for criticism or congratulation . . . and quality is enhanced.

FROM ASSESSMENT TO EVALUATION[19]

Evaluation is ubiquitous in our lives and is a critical part of any responsible educational enterprise.

Elliot Eisner[2]

How can we use the mass of information generated by pupil assessment (both informal and formal) to assist us in evaluation of broader educational scenarios?

We mentioned earlier Elliot Eisner's four interrelated factors that he would say constitute the components of our 'broader educational scenario': the *context* in which learning-teaching occurs; the *inputs* or *curriculum* to which students have access; the *process* by which they learn through interaction and involvement with fellow-pupils, teachers and community; and the *product* or *outcomes* which we have identified in terms of knowledge, skills, attitudes and dispositions.

If we look at two of these factors: process and product, we might raise the following questions:

(a) *process of learning*

- are the relationships between teacher and pupil conducive to the building of trust and the spirit of enquiry?
- is the school guiding the children well (i.e. efficiently, relevantly, etc.) through a series of activities that provide for both depth and breadth of learning?
- are the children learning from their mistakes and equally initiating learning from their successes?

(b) *product of learning*

- are there clear differences between standards of social or linguistic groups or between sexes, e.g. are girls achieving less in terms of science and mathematics than boys? If so, why?
- are pupils at a given stage reaching minimum standards in literacy and numeracy?[21]
- are pupils throughout the school producing and displaying work relevant to community issues?

We might wish to research these questions by focusing upon a particular subject area and age level (or perhaps look at one gender,[22] pupils from rural or urban environments or those exposed to a particularly new method of teaching, etc.) and then develop the enquiry by examining the progress of a selected group of pupils. Their individual assessments would form a useful basic for judgements to be made about the overall strengths and weaknesses of a particular educational factor. It might be revealed, for example, that one of the reasons why pupils generally produce better work in one subject area is *not* because of the gender or training of a particular teacher but because the syllabus of that subject is more relevant and is therefore of more interest to pupils at a particular stage in their learning.

Studies of this kind can range from those undertaken by the class teacher to large scale meta-evaluations undertaken by a team of evaluators.

What we see as important is that teachers not only acquire competencies in undertaking evaluations, large or small, but integrate this activity into their professional life.

A response of some will be, 'We haven't time to do this when we are teaching and marking!' An answer is for teachers to discover that effective evaluation can actually save time by making the teaching more efficient and relevant, i.e. focusing it where it has most effect; and by seeing that pupil assessment, e.g. marking and testing, can be put to useful diagnostic purposes. The challenge to help them discover these truths is, as ever, with 'the people trainers'.

175

Decisions to be taken in evaluation

The content or 'what' of evaluation is perhaps easier to identify than the 'how'. Evaluation, like schooling, is very much a process and one involving decisions at each stage in the operation. These seem to involve the following:[23]

1   Decisions about the *aims* of evaluation. What is it for (e.g. information for the District Education Office, parents, heads, teacher development, community development, etc)?
2   Decisions about the *focus* of evaluation. What aspects of school life are to be evaluated (e.g. pupil performance, teacher performance, curriculum goals and content, teaching methods, resources, processes, outcomes)?
3   Decisions about the *criteria* of evaluation. What will be the nature of the criteria for judging the worth and/or effectiveness of the aspects of school life to be studied? (In terms of 'quality' how will teacher '*x*' be deemed 'efficient'? Or lesson '*y*' be judged 'relevant'?)
4   Decisions about the *methods*[24] of evaluation to be used. Will the approach be quantitative, i.e. of the more 'objective' kind utilising a mass of data, or qualitative, i.e. of the more subjective/ethnographic type utilising case studies and small-scale collections of data?
    Whatever approach is used, judgements will have to be made concerning the character and source of the evidence (e.g. children's written work, behaviour, attitudes; teachers' co-operation, classroom display, etc)? Who will make the judgement (e.g. teacher, head, advisor, child)?
5   Decisions about *organisation*. How will the evaluation be conducted (e.g. through tests, checklists, appraisal interviews, profiles; yearly, monthly, weekly; individually, collectively, etc)?
6   Decisions about *dissemination*. What means for recording and reporting evaluation judgements will be used? To whom will they be available? What will be the extent of confidentiality?
7   Decisions about *application*. To what uses will evaluation be put, and how will they be enabled to inform decision-making (e.g. through newsletters, discussion papers, in-service group activities, etc)?
8   Decisions about *control* and *accountability*. This is the overriding decision because it determines the direction of the answers to all other questions. Who, then, decides? Heads, individual teachers, teachers collectively, advisors?

Importantly, these questions establish the sort of framework within a school in which *discussion* and *communication* are prerequisites of decision-making.

Because evaluation is about *values* and *valuing*, it is important to delineate which areas of evaluation are the province of the 'expert', e.g. teachers, heads and administration; and which are legitimately the concern of all, e.g. parents, community leaders, advisors. And we must remember that values and valuing do not exist in a vacuum: they are prescribed by cultural, economic, social and political variables which equally inform our definitions of quality and terms like 'efficiency', 'relevance' and 'balance'.

FROM EVALUATION TO QUALITY

So far we have been largely concerned with a language of critique: an examination of relationships such as: assessment and evaluation; evaluation and decision-making.

Qualitative improvement lies in the realm of the possible; and so it is worthwhile now to look at what can be done, in Nepal, Lesotho, Kenya, Indonesia, Malaysia and elsewhere, to enhance the quality of assessment and in turn that of the broader educational concerns. Though we stand in danger of repetition, we shall try and pull together some of the conclusions made so far in this chapter.

We believe there are *four* basic areas where action will be most possible and most effective:

(a) More information better shared

The quality of decision-making concerning assessment and evaluation rests upon the quality of information available at all levels of the education system.

Such information comes from a number of sources: bodies specifically established to research the field (university departments of education, curriculum development centres, international conferences, etc.); data generated by personnel involved in improving the quality of education at school, district, and national level (the reports of subject boards, school staff meetings, recommendations of inspectors and advisors) and, most importantly, those at the 'chalk face' who can provide us with a wealth of information about *what is actually happening in primary school classrooms*.

Such information is only valuable if it is communicable and communicated. Its dissemination has usually been conceived as being dispensed from on high in the manner of prophets expounding the law, with ministerial working parties issuing reports and circulars that often remain unread and unused in dusty staff rooms.

It is our contention that good practice in one school can serve to inform good practice elsewhere and that for this to happen communication networks need to be established and consolidated top-down, down-top and side-to-side. How often have teachers from one school invited teachers from a neighbouring school to come and experience models of good practice or to share ideas about an issue of common concern?

The Kenya examination newsletter stands as a lonely example of what *can* be done to establish channels of communication between teachers and parents and examination boards. Such information-sharing, we believe, needs to go further and be communicated from teacher to pupil and from school to school.

Decisions, as we have said, can only be taken properly if supported by as much information as possible. A summary of common examination errors of the previous year could form the basis of an effective in-school in-service workshop. An examiner might be invited to attend to lead the discussion, and teachers be invited to prepare papers dealing with common problems as they perceive them. Such information-gathering might well involve a cluster of schools in one locality: giving teachers the opportunity of demonstrating new methods of assessment currently 'under trial'. The 'teachers' groups' in Indonesia are one example which may prove effective as a means for disseminating new ideas and discussing common problems.

But for these approaches to work, there has to exist or be fostered the attitude that teachers (and pupils) have a right to know more about how learning and teaching in schools is assessed. It seems that since examination boards and schools struggle to prevent 'leaking' of papers and marks before time, what results is a siege mentality in which *everything* remotely concerned with assessment is kept under wraps. Such an attitude does little to solve the real problems of security and hinders the desire of professional teachers to learn from the results of formal examination procedures.

Given the time and initiative required to open up these channels of communication, it seems reasonable to expect head teachers and advisors to lead the way and set up improved facilities for exchange of information and ideas.

(b) A wider view of the assessment process

We have established the idea that assessment is not only about examinations; but that if it is predominantly concerned with examinations we need to widen our view of what constitutes an effective, terminal form of assessment.

We can, it seems, do two things:

1   improve the *product* of assessment, i.e. look to see if the traditional end-of-course examination can be supplemented or balanced by the inclusion of continually-assessed work, pupil profiles and the results of self-assessment exercises. The examination can also be reformed, as has been achieved in Kenya, to include better questions, a greater emphasis upon testing of skills, and so on. Perhaps what we are working *towards* here is a situation where pupils leave school with a full, balanced, progressive *record of achievement*;

2   improve the *process* of assessment, i.e. to take some of the sting out of traditional examinations by teaching 'assessment' and the

principles of evaluation as part of curriculum content, by inviting children routinely to ask and answer the question 'how do we know what we have learnt?' Such a move would tie up with our earlier suggestion to involve children more in day-to-day classroom decision-making procedures.

Equally, teachers need much more exposure to the mechanics of formal assessment, ways in which they can integrate these into their teaching, and in so doing *assist* examiners in their task of assessing pupils.

Lastly, the assessment process needs to be widened to include such things as assessment of schemes of work, the marking of students' work, the difficulties of assessing group work and advantages and disadvantages of streaming, grouping and so on. Once again, the challenge seems to fall to both pre- and in-service training, the reformed roles of school head and advisor and the collective actions of the teachers themselves.

(c) Devolution of power

The question: 'who controls assessment?' is part of the larger question: 'who decides the priorities in education?' For to have a say in assessment, particularly at the end of the primary cycle, is to exert an important influence over the whole educational system. To call for greater teacher *and* pupil participation in examinations is to call for a greater democratisation of educational decision-making practices.

It is also a call for closer links with teacher-classroom behaviour, in terms of assessment, and the activities of universities and examination councils (often one and the same) who set the direction of assessment patterns.

Increased devolved power to the locality will have to be matched with parallel changes in models of assessment utilised by schools. In other words, the phasing in of some form of continuous assessment will automatically mean more decision-making power is accorded to teachers. Such power will not, of course, come without the associated responsibility and accountability. Equally, if children are to become more involved in self-assessment exercises, they will need guidance in what naturally follows from such a change, i.e. skills in deciding which work to select for assessment, knowledge of criteria for making that assessment, attitudes of equity to manage and feel committed to the exercise.

(d) Improvement in the training of teachers

In the last analysis, measures of attainment and effectiveness are matters of judgement and judgement has to be made by people. These 'people', we have argued, should include not only examiners but teachers, heads, advisors and, in terms of self-assessment, the pupils themselves. Such individuals cannot be expected to make decisions without support from *training* and the provisions of resource *materials*.

179

In terms of training, a first step may be for teachers, under the guidance of a head or advisor, to meet together in-school to critically assess current procedures (Freire's 'language of critique' stage). The next is to examine the possibilities for reform – the available 'room for manoeuvre'. A great deal of improvement can be had from collecting together and focusing upon one or two issues of concern, e.g. security during and after examinations, effective marking of pupils' work, strategies for assessing group, practical work. By *taking control* of the situation (perhaps by inviting an examiner or acknowledged expert from the ministry or university department of education) teachers will discover their potential for active involvement in the decision-making process. Such action need not threaten existing political and educational hierarchies, if planned and carried out with co-operation from interested parties, from ministry of education through to parent-teacher association.

Other forms of training have been discussed elsewhere; what can be mentioned here are the possibilities of assessment-training for pupils – the selection and display of work, training in criteria of what is considered 'well done', self-evaluation or the discussion of likes and dislikes.

The paucity of resource material to support teachers in coming to decisions about assessment is lamentable. Handbooks for teachers dealing with the following questions might go a long way to remedying the situation:

- are we measuring the right thing?
- are we measuring the whole thing?
- are our measurements effective?
- are our measurement techniques out of step with our changed classroom procedures?
- are our measurements of one subject area suitable for another area?
- are we varied enough in our assessment procedures?
- are we involving the learners enough in measurement of their progress?
- are we utilising the data from our assessment exercises for an effective evaluation of broader educational concerns?

Questions of this kind are only useful when placed within a matrix of 'process and product' on the one hand and criteria of quality, i.e. relevance, efficiency and 'something more' on the other. By framing our questions in this way we provide our evaluation with focus and therefore the likelihood that it might be of good use.

It will also be important for such materials to be regularly revised, preferably by the teachers themselves, to incorporate insights generated from use and changing circumstances.

EVALUATION, ASSESSMENT AND QUALITY: A CHANGE OF EMPHASIS

In this chapter we have argued for a number of improvements in the way we assess the progress of children at primary level. We have suggested that a more co-operative approach be taken to the management and control of assessment procedures. And we have put forward the case for assessment data to be utilised in evaluation of broader educational scenarios.

Throughout, we have stressed the centrality of the teacher (rather than the examiner) within the decision-making machineries. Support for the teacher, we argue, must come from training, resources and the dissemination of information gathered by those bodies such as examination councils, university researchers and curriculum development centres which are involved in evaluative exercises.

But perhaps, what is most important, is a change in basic attitudes towards both assessment and evaluation. There are two fundamental aspects of such a change. Traditionally, evaluation is seen as something 'they' do to 'us'. Increasingly, we need to emphasise what 'we' do for ourselves. Traditionally, when called upon to assess a particular child's work or evaluate the implementation of such and such an educational innovation, we tend to focus our attention on the *negative*: 'Mohamed should try harder'; '. . . the following corrections need attention . . . ;' or 'this project won't work because . . .' Perhaps if our initial priority was the *positive*, i.e. 'What has been achieved by pupil, school and system?' we could then build on that success and instil and develop a greater sense of pride in achievement.

Assessment, in the end, is surely knowing as much about how well one has done, how much one has progressed, as it is about what needs to be done.

NOTES AND REFERENCES

1 Gibby, W. in Lawton, D., *Theory and Practice of Curriculum Studies*, Routledge, 1978.

2 Eisner, E., *The Art of Educational Evaluation: a Personal View*, Falmer, 1985, p. 7.

3 Dore, R., *The Diploma Disease: Education, Qualifications and Development*, Allen and Unwin, London, 1976, p. 182.

4 See Somerset, H. C. A., *Examination Reform: The Kenya Experience*, World Bank, 1982, p. 13.

5 Fetterman, D. M., Pitman, M. A. (eds.), *Educational Evaluation: Ethnography in Theory, Practice and Politics*, Sage, 1986, p. 219.

6 Govt. of Ceylon, 1972, 'Selection and Curriculum Reform' in Lewin, K., in Oxenham J. (ed.), *Education Versus Qualifications*, Allen and Unwin, 1984.

7 Dore, R., op. cit., p. 64.

8 Somerset, H. C. A., op. cit., p. 4.

9 Somerset, H. C. A., op. cit; Somerset, H. C. A., 'Who goes to secondary school? Relevance, Reliability and Equity in Secondary School Selection', in Court, D. and Ghai, D. (eds.), *Education, Society and Development*, OUP, Nairobi, 1974, pp. 149–86.

10 Lewin, K., op. cit., p. 144.

11 *Ibid.*

12 For a discussion of profiling see Broadfoot, P., *Introducing Profiling – A Practical Manual*, Macmillan, 1987.

13 Dove, L., *Teachers and Teacher Education in Developing Countries: Issues in Planning, Management and Training*, Croom Helm, Beckenham, 1986, p. 70.

14 Dove, L., op. cit., pp. 68–9.

15 *The Observer*, 29.11.87., reports that one school, Churchill Comprehensive in Avon, 'has opted to do a pilot course in which only 68% of the marks (in maths) are awarded for the written paper . . . and in which English is examined entirely by coursework', p. 29.

16 Lacey, C. and Lawton, D. (eds.), *Issues in Evaluation and Accountability*, Methuen, 1981.

17 Dove, L., op. cit., p. 73.

18 *Ibid.*

19 See Torrance, H., 'What can examinations contribute to school evaluation?' in Murphy, R. and Torrance, H., *Evaluating Education: Issues and Methods*, Harper, London, 1987, pp. 184–97.

20 Eisner, E., op. cit., p. 5.

21 In a consultative report to the Government of Lesotho, 1977, one of the authors argued strongly for a functional literary test at the end of the fourth year to ensure that the large number of children who left midway through the school cycle were taught minimum skills before that time.

22 See for example Walden, R. and Walkerdine, V., 1985, 'Girls and Mathematics', *Bedford Way Papers*, Univ. of London Institute of Education, London.

23 List adapted from Alexander, R., *Primary Teaching*, Holt, 1984, adapted from Adelman and Alexander, 1982.

24 See the very useful Section I 'Methodological Debates: The Politics and Process of Educational Evaluation' in Murphy, R. and Torrance, H. (eds), op. cit.

CONCLUSION

First, the good news. Ngingyang Primary School, several miles beyond the tarmac road that takes tourists to Kenya's plush Lake Baringo Club, has a new teacher. His name is Yusuf Losute, he is about nineteen, has just completed his secondary education (not quite enough G.C.E. 'O' level passes to get into the sixth form), is a member of the Pokot ethnic group who live around Baringo, and he's doing very well indeed.

On a recent visit we found both the teacher and his class (just a handful of boys, as the elder Pokot are yet to be convinced of Western-style schooling, besides, the lack of rains has driven them further and further in search of good land) working through an elementary mathematics problem on an easel propped up against a tree in the school compound.

With three classes and two classrooms it seemed the best arrangement. Yusuf likes teaching, though he still has a yearning for college and a career in forestry. He, like many others, is learning by experience. As a Pokot it comes naturally.

The bad news: more than one child in every ten born in Yusuf's village will die before they reach school age ('. . . one death in every three in the world is the death of a child under five . . .'[1]).

Many of those who start his school will never finish and many who finish will enter a world where they can find little security of mind; where paid work will be difficult to find yet where traditional farming and herding duties will no longer satisfy; where the culture of the old and young will be increasingly at variance; where traditional values are questioned yet where new values prove hard to define: a wide, restless exciting world where it is easy to lose one's Pokot identity.

But are things getting 'better' or 'worse' for Yusuf's children? In terms of their survival rate, certainly better. The director of UNICEF can report, '. . . despite the difficult economic climate, the limited promotion of new low-cost means of protecting children's lives and growth is already resulting in the saving of nearly 40 000 young lives each week.'[2]

So is Yusuf's school a 'new low-cost means of protecting children's lives' and promoting their growth? Will it improve the quality of its children's lives by helping them, now and in the future, to fit into a changing world? Will what is good and just and productive and happy in Pokot society be threatened or enhanced by it? Finally, will it have the minimum resources in money, manpower and time to do an honest job for the children who attend it?

In order to understand the challenges facing it and us in this task of improving quality, it is necessary to be aware of economic realities.

ECONOMIC REALITIES

These exist on both a grand and a small scale. Worldwide, the language is one of falling commodity prices, high interest rates, fluctuating oil prices, the debt crisis. The latter means that when we take into account investment, official aid and private lending, and subtract repayments of interest and capital, the net flow of resources is now *from* the developing world to the industrialised world. On a small scale, our teacher, Yusuf writes to one of us recently to tell of

> . . . shortage of pasture for the animals, water problems and some other problems . . . My Mum has to follow up the few goats we have since no one else could assist her, that is why I have to keep on visiting her and taking some water for her.

Yusuf's father died in the big drought of 1982. There is no running water or provision of wells in Pokot country. The nearest post office is in Nakuru, a day's lorry journey away.

Kenya's population is estimated to expand at 4.1% per annum. Life expectancy has increased from 42 years in 1960 to 55 years in 1986. For children under 5 years of age, mortality rate has plummeted from 208 per 1 000 born alive in 1960 to 118 in 1986. The good news is also the bad news.

And let us not forget that Kenya's per capita GNP is currently around $330 (US), with the United States, itself, standing at approximately $18 530 (US)[3]. Likewise, of course, we must remember that there are many driving to work in Nairobi whose lives are very different from the average Pokot. Gaps in life styles and life chances continue to grow between countries and within them.

Yet, if economic life is becoming more difficult for the world's poor, it seems that in the social, health and education spheres, in numerical terms at least, progress is being made. Furthermore, far more children are going to school. As we said in Chapter Three, while it is dangerous to think of increases in percentage enrolments as synonymous with educational improvement, there is no doubt that more young children achieve minimum literacy and numeracy than in the past.

A major economic and educational reality is therefore the relationship between demographic change and schooling. Nations heavily involved in the economic recession are the very nations with high percentages of their populations under the age of five. Indonesia, suffering from a fall in oil prices, has a population of 169 million. A third of them are under the age of 16. In Nepal, just under half the population are of school age. Lesotho is in a similar position, though distorted by the huge number of young men and boys leaving for work in South Africa's gold mines.

Progress in health and efforts to re-prioritise scarce economic resources mean that the pressures upon the primary school sector will increase. In spite of the problems of school-leaver unemployment and the poor quality of education provided in many schools, parents in the less developed world still view schooling as a worthwhile economic investment, as indeed it is for some, and 'some' in the eyes of every parent quite naturally includes 'my child'. Such economic expectations are reinforced by social pressures. Gone are the days when 'my child' can be illiterate and unstigmatised. In our opinion such days will never return.

However, today educationists, no matter how well they understand individual hopes and aspirations of parents, are far less convinced of the general economic investment potential of schooling. This view is in sharp contrast to that held at the start of the 1960s and the optimism and enthusiasm for making schools the engine of development.

Earlier we referred to such terms as 'debt crisis' as reflecting the language of the late 1980s. The economic language of post-Independence was very different: then we read of Rostow's optimistic 'stages' of economic development. Economies were expected eventually to take off like jet liners and modernisation theorists led the day. In the intervening quarter century we seem to have thought more deeply about the concept of development and realised the inappropriacy of working around simplistic notions developed in industrialised nations and cheerfully exported, like some consumer good, to developing ones.

It is now questioned whether industrialisation and incorporation into the international capitalist system are necessarily desirable goals for the majority of those living in less developed countries.[4] Industrialisation may provide high incomes for some but seems also to increase the gap between the rich and poor; between those in the urban areas and those in the subsistence, rural sector. In many ways, industrialisation can lead to a process of underdevelopment and problems of competition with Northern, established industrial states, who keep control of commodity prices and tariff barriers.

If development economics has changed, so have perspectives on schooling. Whereas the '60s saw the flourishing of human capital theories, with economists looking to education to provide a profitable 'rate of return', it is now recognised not only that the link between more schooling and improved economic production is unproved but also that the process and institutionalisation of schooling is itself an expensive business.[5] Thus concerned politicians and educationists, convinced of the demand for education yet appalled by its costs and sceptical of its output, now seek to take a look at the *process* of schooling and to see, frankly, whether more can be done with less.

As nations have struggled to come to terms with political instability, large-scale unemployment, the rural-urban population drift, high drop-out rates from the education system and reinforced social stratification; the focus has imperceptibly shifted from the quantity of schooling provided to the quality of that provision. Even the definition of schooling is beginning to be examined, as are the rigid distinctions between formal and non-formal education[6], though a great gap still exists between talking about these issues and resultant action.

THE MANAGEMENT OF PLANNED CHANGE

Dynamic change is now a way of life for all of us. When we talk of change now we need to discard the somewhat naive notions of 'take off' and 'modernisation' and look instead to adjusting to economic realities so that, '. . . maximum protection for the most vulnerable (can) be squeezed from every dollar available for health care, education or social welfare.'[7]

Management in these circumstances is concerned with two fundamentals: realignment of priorities within the development programmes and more effective control over the management of those programmes.

If change is no longer seen as linear or simple, equally many are questioning the old *mechanistic* view of development: the input/output systems approach to change which seemed to imply that development was really only measured by end-product achievement of behavioural objectives. More students were leaving school with higher examination passes; therefore schooling was working. The flaw in the reasoning is that, first, greater weight is given to that which is easily *measured*, i.e. examination grades; and, secondly, that little regard is accorded the time spent between changing from an input to an output.

Given that for many the years of schooling can account for almost a third of their life span, it seems reasonable to assess the quality of that experience; and in particular the management of that time. This leads towards a view of education as:

- meeting individual and community needs 'now' and 'later'
- laying a foundation for lifelong learning and building within the process of schooling 'learning for change'
- providing breadth of educational experience that is rooted in direct experience
- providing depth of learning that carries learners forward into a future where new competencies and abilities will be called for
- taking into account children in school's right to exercise choice, enjoy respect and enjoy their work in exactly the same way as any other citizens.

We are asking, therefore, for education to be managed and changed at the same time (no easy task!). We are calling for one eye to be fixed, of course, upon adult life at the end of schooling and for education to inculcate skills and abilities related to the changing economic realities; but equally, for one eye to be kept firmly focused upon the condition of schools, the quality of society in those schools, the quality of the curriculum and concomitant strategies of improvement as we go along.

187

Hence our analogy of a wheel with a centre hub of basic elements of quality we consider common in any system: the goals and basic principles of practice; and two concentric outer rings which relate to conditions necessary for successful implementation of change, and the agents of implementation who are to take action if the wheel is to roll forward smoothly.

THE QUALITY WHEEL

We have stressed throughout this book that the achievement of educational goals is ultimately measured not by the quantity of educational participation but by the quality of educational experience.

We have defined quality as consisting of three interdependent and mutually reinforcing strands:

- quality as efficiency in meeting set goals (and here we have identified reaching, maintaining and improving standards)
- quality as relevance to human and environmental conditions and needs (to needs 'now' and needs 'later') (both 'now' and 'later')
- quality as 'something more' in relation to the pursuit of excellence and human betterment (as we write we watch athletes from around the world strive to break barriers and set new targets. We ask for teachers and pupils to do likewise and to remember that education originally meant 'to lead').

To attain these dimensions of quality requires intellectual, economic and moral resourcing.

On an *intellectual* level, a need has emerged for a broadening and deepening of research into primary quality. In writing this book, and in compiling bibliographic material, we have found a marked lack of useful data on such issues as: impact of language policies at primary school level including such vital issues as whether children in primary school can actually comprehend their textbooks; the training of primary teachers in relation to their needs in the field; analyses examining the use and non-use of syllabuses and textbooks. Much more classroom-based research needs to be done by university researchers; and equally much more of the research that is done needs to be taken up by publishers. We have very little evidence, even now, of what really goes on in classrooms as distinct from what is intended.

Equally, there needs to be a deepening in the type of research done. As we said in our first chapter, international research seems to have been dominated by an input/output paradigm which is useful in measuring what it itself considers important but omits crucial aspects of process by focusing too narrowly.

Finally, we must be concerned at the ways in which such research is presented and communicated. At present what is available, almost all of it from universities, tends to be presented mainly for consumption by other academics with dense prose and full of excessive statistical jargon. Thus even if hard-pressed administrators comprehend it they are hardly motivated to read it. Strangely, too, in an age when we receive most of our day to day information from the spoken word or the visual image, research findings are almost invariably confined to print.

Hence another turnaround in thinking may be necessary. We may need to ask whether a new approach to the presentation of research is necessary; an approach which places far more emphasis on the purpose of research in relation to the *audience* for whom it is intended.

On the *economic* level, we have throughout this book stressed the need for a re-examination of priorities.

A recent study of primary education in Cameroon revealed that, whereas higher education in that country was enjoyed by 0.6% of the school-attending population; it receives 22.5% of the resources allocated to education generally. These figures could be paralleled in many countries. The fact is that we resource higher education at the expense of primary and lower-secondary levels. Such a situation, in practice, means that we deprive higher education of the very people we would like to see there: they having fallen by the wayside way back down the line because of *economic* underfunding of primary education.

However, to change the percentage in favour of primary education would do little to improve its quality unless deep thought is given to *where* new resources, necessarily spread thinly because of the size of the primary sector, should be deployed.

Here again, a sense of realism must determine resource allocation:

- there is *no* prospect of avoiding large teacher/pupil ratios:
  there *is* an opportunity for ensuring that children have suitable books to use and materials to write on.
- there is *no* prospect of abolishing selection procedures at the end of primary school:
  there *are* opportunities to invest in the creation of a selection system whose 'backwash' effect on primary education is largely positive.
- there is *no* prospect in most countries of achieving a fully qualified and trained teacher force in primary school:
  there *are* opportunities to ensure that all teachers receive effective professional help and support on the job while they are doing it.

Given real thought and commitment, a modest increase in investment in primary education could yield large gains in its quality.

Lastly, there is a need for *moral* commitment from those who are in powerful positions to decide priorities to remember their own early years at school. They might to remember that all are not so fortunate as to be able to send their children to a private school in the city, and that it is a moral duty of those who plan education to be aware of the realities in which those plans can be implemented, so that change for education will be based upon democratic principles.

What we are saying, therefore, is that what pushes our quality wheel forward is the actions of people involved: the main agents of change.

PEOPLE AS MAIN AGENTS OF CHANGE

While watching our friend, Yusuf Losute, teach outside in the compound of his school, we were taken with one thing: his sense of the worth of what he was doing and his realisation of the *power* he had, there and then, to influence the pupils lined up on the ground before him.

He had taken a number of important decisions that day, among them to continue teaching in spite of being a room short; to make the best use of resources, i.e. pupils' knowledge, easel, chalk, tree; and to communicate the intricacies of number work in the best ways he knew how (in this case some Pokot, some Swahili, lots of miming and laughing).

This particular teacher, though lacking in any training, shows us the realities of *empowerment* and how intertwined this concept is with support for initiative and encouragement to make decisions without waiting to be told what to do.

Empowerment is related to four necessary conditions:

- that teachers and those supporting them possess more *knowledge* of what they are supposed to teach and of the professional competencies that come from pre- and in-service education
- that education workers capitalise on the strength they possess collectively by *communicating* good practice and by co-operating much more, particularly at school level
- that *trust* be seen as a professional characteristic to be called for openly and demonstrated in the way we deal with such issues as examination reform or decentralisation of decision-making
- that if we encourage trust we equally put centre-stage the notion of *accountability*. Being held to what we agree to do might, in the short term anyway, reduce the rhetoric and force us all to look to areas of 'room for manoeuvre' where we can, at the next PTA, or teachers' club meeting, 'stand up and be a accounted'!

These four characteristics: knowledge, trust, co-operation and accountability are necessary conditions for empowering people like Yusuf and for guiding them in the process of qualitative change.

UNDERSTANDING THE PROCESS OF QUALITATIVE CHANGE

As we said, in Chapter Two, we view the process of change as consisting of three basic ingredients: *choice, decision-making*, and *power* to implement decisions taken. They operate in two distinct, though interrelated stages.

First, the stage of critique in which reflection, understanding and consideration provide the 'vocabulary' of the 'language' of that initial part of the change process.

Secondly, the stage of possibility, in which Paulo Freire interprets change in terms of hope, involvement and responsibility.

In sum, quality decision-making is about two stages of a process: a critical understanding of the present situation followed by effective action for change.

Let us apply this paradigm to the existing decision-making process, particularly with regard to aid to education, and look *critically* at what currently happens and what we might *possibly* be able to do about it.

THE LANGUAGE OF CRITIQUE

At each level of the decision-making process: local, regional, national and international, we need to ask: who makes the decisions? And what are the influences that affect those contexts in which decisions are taken?

Because levels of economic resources so critically affect all public policies, it is hardly surprising that, beneath nearly every educational decision-maker of importance lies an economist struggling to assert himself. It is no coincidence that one of the largest donor agencies calls itself a 'Bank' (that, in fact, is what it is) and equally unsurprising that the language of economics, e.g. rates of return, investment, human capital, has so long dominated the educational policy frames of reference.

The result of this – and it is noticeable in the 'closed worldness' of World Bank reports – is that change is seen in a somewhat mechanistic light where input is measured against output, where 'success' is related to certain universally accepted objectives which are rarely questioned. (Success rates in examinations are important evidence but we must also be well aware of what such an examination is and is not measuring!)

A problem for economists, particularly, and those who want a neat and tidy accounts sheet, is that quality of education is difficult to measure by an objective rule of thumb (unlike the large quantities of US dollars numbered, balanced and juggled at the end of each fiscal year). What is inherent in our analysis of quality is that it is defined and negotiated and achieved differently in different contexts and furthermore, that the process of understanding, achieving and monitoring it is as important as the outcome. The achievement of quality is an *internal* struggle by the curriculum worker, the supervisor, the teacher and the pupil. External aid can only facilitate their success by making it easier for them to come to decisions and act upon them.

Consequently, we may consider certain strategies appropriate to those who provide aid to enhance quality at primary level. Four lines of thought and action appear possible.

1 *Investment in clarifying purpose and priorities at local as well as central level* – Let us offer an example of such a process in action.

In 1988 a working seminar was convened in Uganda, sponsored by the Harold Macmillan Trust, to launch a programme for production of locally produced and locally relevant materials for teacher education[8].

The seminar, whose composition included all those nationally responsible for teacher education and curriculum design, recommended that following an appraisal of present conditions in schools and colleges there should be a comprehensive and considered analysis of purpose:

- what development needs should schools serve?
- in what areas of experience should primary schools develop capacities to meet such needs?
- consequently, what knowledge, skills and attitudes would teachers need to possess and how should training materials be devised to develop these?

The clarification of such purposes will require considerable investment in money and time. It can only come as a result of a considerable period of structured discussion, not by a 'project appraisal team' but exclusively by Ugandans themselves.

2 *A widening rather than narrowing of the parameters of aid and assistance* – that is, by supporting and building upon activities that are working rather than concentrating solely on large projects and attempts to generalise policy at international conferences. This inevitably means aid funding for smaller initiatives, sometimes non-governmental ones, and it is significant to note that even the World Bank now contemplates such a change of emphasis.

3 *A focus on short-term rather than long-term improvements* – The language of debate needs to be less grand and tied closer to the achievement of objectives, perhaps within the lifetime of one primary school cohort.

4 *Maintenance of tighter control over what is actually happening on the ground during the process of change* – with increased flexibility built into the management process to modify approaches in the light of experience.

192

Much time and effort is spent upon summative evaluation of aid projects, with scant regard paid to what happens from the day of signed agreements to design and implementation.

Raising the status of primary education

One critical focus for action both for international aid and within countries themselves is to combat the lack of *status* accorded primary education. This seems manifest in a number of ways:

- decision-makers in all aspects of primary policies usually lack any experience of working in the sector: we can have the bizarre situation where lecturers in education to primary trainees are actually people promoted to the tertiary sector from the secondary
- the attitudes and expectations of those charged with deciding issues pertinent to the primary sector are influenced not by client concerns but by the institutional ethos of the centre, institute or university in which they were trained and now work
- the air surrounding the decision-making process becomes rarified – wrapped up in pseudo-academic jargon which in turn breeds a discipline devoted to the deciphering and discussing of terminology, rather than ensuring that concepts have been communicated or evaluated *in situ*.

We can see this happening at universities where studies of educational foundations eclipse practice; in curriculum centres where doctrinaire adherence to principles of curriculum development drives out common sense; in colleges and planning units of ministries. What is urgent and vital is to invest in a form of training which on the one hand elevates the status of those well grounded in primary practice, and on the other makes such practice and the analysis of it as academically respectable as the studies of philosophy and sociology. Evidence from attempts to achieve these goals in Indonesia (Chapter Seven), Lesotho (Chapter Five) and Kenya (Chapter One) indicate that universities may well resist such attempts to bring them closer to reality.

THE LANGUAGE OF POSSIBILITY

Throughout this book we have taken the view that to enhance quality in education the agents of change on the outer rim of our wheel must work together to secure the inner goals and principles and to lay down the necessary conditions which will transform principles into practice.

In this conclusion we have identified five strategies, that for us, speak the language of possibility:

1 Towards realism

Here we look to the reappraisal of our critical knowledge of *what is happening* in our primary schools. We look to research institutions to focus their intellectual energies and resources upon illuminating realities. This need not have connotations with 'finding out the worst' but should strive to provide teachers like Yusuf with models of good practice, possibilities for making more of what little he has and opportunities for initiative and personal decision-making. If a teachers' centre is to be established, could its resources be taken out to a number of schools on a regular basis? Perhaps 'school clusters' and identified 'resource persons', as operational in Nepal, will work elsewhere? Perhaps, the idea of 'teachers' groups' from Indonesia might work amongst schools in the Lake Baringo region?

Equally, we require opportunities for teachers to meet to talk through issues and clarify goals and practices. School-focused curriculum development is slowly being recognised as a very effective and realistic way to in-service teachers and as an effective means of helping those responsible for running training workshops further relate their theories to practice.

2 Identifying, training, supporting enablers

At every level of support to the primary school teacher we identify, train and support those called upon to manage the change processes. In particular we look to enhancing the leadership capabilities of a key figure in administration: the school head; for by improving and differentiating the roles a headteacher is called upon to perform, we can increase the potential for him to effect qualitative improvement in schools.

We have identified, in Chapter Seven, the roles of administrator, curriculum developer, researcher and evaluator, and community leader the headteacher is called to perform, and we placed such a call in one national context – Indonesia – in which a particular innovation is working to enhance leadership roles and provide a support system to sustain it.

The success of the innovation illustrates the way in which our five elements: shared goals; information and communication; realism; flexibility and participation can be applied at all levels from the planner to the pupils and how as a result of this, quality appears to be improving not only if it is measured as we would wish it to be but as it really is measured now – through conventional attainment tests and data on enrolment and retention.

3 Helping to create 'room for manoeuvre'

Recently, one of the authors of this book watched a raw recruit to the teaching profession (it was her first day of a one-year teacher training course, so she was excused!) demonstrate how she would write an instruction on the blackboard. Picking up the chalk, she leant precariously across a small table and, by stretching on tiptoe, managed to scrawl the instruction on the board.

When a colleague suggested at the end of the activity she move the table, she said she thought she 'wasn't supposed to'.

Creating room for manoeuvre, in this case literally, is working not from the position that *is* but adapting surroundings to what *might be*. How often have we continued to teach a topic that is patently taking us nowhere? Or have thrown away half a textbook for being out-of-date and irrelevant?

In Chapter Two we referred to a small school in Northern Nepal. One of the first things a teacher in that school had done on entering the room was to throw out half the furniture and bring in bush mats for the pupils to sit on. As he said, they were cheap, easier to maintain and clean, and were much more versatile when he wanted to rearrange the seating. 'Room for manoeuvre' starts by taking a long, hard and critical look at the way things are; and by asking, often, the most obvious and sensible questions.

It may not only be concerned with over- or under-crowded rooms: it may relate to syllabuses; the curriculum (both usually cluttered with too much mental furniture); the role of the community; or ways in which we test what is taught. Sometimes it is just a change of attitude (how often do we see teachers writing a list of answers on the board and asking students to read 'the passage' for the 'right question'?); sometimes a matter of adapting resources for new uses; sometimes knowledge of and exposure to models of good practice.

A way forward is to avoid immediately assuming that the solution to a particular problem must always come from outside the school (and probably from the ministry in the form of a local purchasing order). By encouraging initiative from *all* those living within the school community we are invoking the double-sided coin of responsibility and accountability.

Equally, we are not suggesting that this ability to expand 'room for manoeuvre', like teachers of old, is 'God given'. As professionals, we can take a leaf out of the business community and see that opportunities to open up 'the market' (in this case the learning market) can be acquired through pre- and in-service training and support.

Lastly, we are assuming that those in positions of responsibility in the bureaucracy will support those at local level who create such room for manoeuvre (accepting mistakes and misjudgements as an inevitable part of the process!). Unfortunately, such support is often withheld. One of the authors works with a school improvement project in Bombay[9]. In poorer schools there is no prospect of children from slum backgrounds covering the official syllabus. Those responsible for their improvement well recognise this fact and have devised an alternative programme which, by ensuring that children master the fundamentals of reading, enables them to catch up with the official syllabus by the end of Class III. They asked for such 'room for manoeuvre'. They were denied. Children in Class I now proceed down the sloping bottom of the swimming pool and disappear under the surface. We would consider such an attitude on the part of the bureaucracy merely misjudged and uninformed. The decision-makers were almost certainly innocent of any knowledge of the primary syllabus. However, those angrier and more cynical than ourselves might easily note that these slum children came from communities without power or influence . . . so who cared about them!

4 'Moving the goalposts'

Finally, and throughout this book, we have emphasised the importance of taking a long hard look at established educational practice in the light of current needs and realities.

In ministries, in colleges, in universities, in schools, as well as among those who finance and aid education, is it not time that we sat together to examine some of the goalposts we aim at? It could well be that we may find them ill-sited.

So much of our education is a result of received mythology that does not stand up to scrutiny. Let us consider some of it under certain convenient categories.

4.1 The planning and management of education
Received wisdom
There are planners, administrators, advisors, headteachers. Their roles are different, some are administrative, some professional.

Common sense
But the roles aren't different. There is a massive degree of overlap. Every administrator needs to be aware of professional priorities; every professional of administrative constraints. Training and job descriptions should reflect this. Otherwise quality suffers.

4.2 The organisation and management of the teaching force
Received wisdom (1)
Teachers must be well educated and well trained first. Those who are suitably qualified may need a little 'refreshment' during their career but generally in-service provision needs to be given only to the unqualified.

Common sense
The training that teachers received 10 or 15 years ago isn't much good to them now. The context and content of what they teach has changed out of all recognition. Besides, much of the theory they learnt in college made little sense with no experience to hang it on. Perhaps shorter initial training and greater investment in training on the job would make more sense. If teachers are out of date and disillusioned, quality suffers.

Received wisdom (2)
Teaching is a profession. A profession is a collection of qualified persons. Anyone who isn't qualified isn't a professional.

Common sense

Half of those teaching in schools, like Yusuf, are not trained. Are they therefore not real teachers, or not as good as real teachers? And what about those other potential teachers we have identified in the course of this book: parents, community members, older children – are they of secondary importance to the man or woman with a framed certificate? Unless we can redefine teacher as 'one who teaches' and accept that quality is best served by a partnership of those who teach, each contributing what they can to the process, then many opportunities to improve quality will be missed.

4.3 *The process of training and monitoring teachers*

Received wisdom (1)

The basis of all good teaching is good lesson preparation. All lessons should be carefully prepared with objectives and stepwise content followed by an activity.

Common sense

Good serving teachers seldom prepare this way. They can't. There isn't time. Besides they have no idea how much the children will be able to grasp. Often their introduction involves merely taking off from 'where we got to' last time. To serve quality better, work surely needs to be planned as units of teaching and learning and not as individual lessons.

Received wisdom (2)

Progress through the syllabus is measured by what a teacher has taught. (And, for that reason, record books are often mandatory.)

Common sense

If a Nobel prize winner teaches us physics, it doesn't follow that we will learn anything, and it seems relatively certain that we will learn different amounts. Quality is only measured by what learners learn and understand, and what they learn is as much controlled by motivation as it is by ability. That is why classroom interaction and classroom decision-making are so vital to quality and why records of progress are probably more important than records of ground covered.

4.4 *The curriculum*

Received wisdom (1)

The national curriculum is planned centrally and contains content which needs to be covered by all primary schools so that all will get a fair chance.

Common sense

Whilst every child in a nation needs to attain certain minimum skills and

197

competencies in primary school, it is unrealistic to imagine that they can or should master the same content. Content *must* be linked with individual interests and abilities and with social and cultural contexts. That is why room to manoeuvre at the level of school curriculum planning is so important. If a single detailed content is planned, inevitably it will reflect the needs of the sons and daughters of those who drafted it . . . almost invariably middle-class town dwellers. Their children may well receive content of quality. Others will 'drown'.

Received wisdom (2)
The curriculum needs to be divided into subjects. It is easier to plan and teach it that way – according to a school timetable.

Common sense
Nobody expects schools in developing countries to practise an integrated curriculum in the way some well-staffed and -equipped English schools do. Nevertheless, one teacher usually teaches all subjects in a primary class. Frequently, her work is made harder and not easier by the fact that subjects overlap and duplicate each other. If greater co-ordination could be achieved; if content were organised around areas of experience rather than strictly around subjects; if teachers could be helped and encouraged to be more flexible in the way they interpreted time and integrated learning experiences at classroom level then quality would benefit.

4.5 *Methods of teaching*

Received wisdom
In large classes and with poorly trained teachers, teacher-centred class teaching is the only effective option. We need to concentrate on making such teaching effective.

Common sense
Such teaching is probably easier on the teacher's nerves and possibly cheaper, but it is certainly not the only effective option. Poorly trained teachers in adult education don't teach that way, neither do parents. Traditionally, in most cultures, there are many examples both of learning by doing and of peer groups helping each other. If children can read and materials are available, they can teach themselves and each other. Many do so already. Quality will vastly benefit from more thought and action towards such alternative methods of teaching and learning.

4.6 *Assessment and evaluation*

Received wisdom
These are separate activities and both are done by specialists in the field.

Common sense
The two activities are closely linked. We need to start to use the results of assessment to illustrate issues of evaluation of policies, practices and possibilities and to train and support teachers both to take part in evaluation and, by improving their own expertise in assessment, to recapture some of the ground lost to distant examination bodies.

4.7 *Supervision and authority*

Received wisdom
Supervision, expert, kindly but firm, must be provided for schools and teachers so that quality may be monitored and improved.

Common sense
Supervisors, however kindly and informed, don't know as much as good teachers about local conditions and besides they don't come round very often. We need to re-examine the concept of supervision and the place of authority in our education system, perhaps through discussing new ways of support and co-ordination where change can be managed rather than bossed, and where leadership doesn't always have to come from top-down.

4.8 *The relationship between formal and non-formal education*

Received wisdom
Formal, non-formal and informal education are separate enterprises. All are important.

Common sense
In fact, even the teacher uses all three modes at different times and to the *children* what is important is what they learn and not how they learn it. If we can work harder to capitalise on the complementary contexts in which children learn, so that, for instance, Islamic, community, and family education complement one other, then quality is increased. Once room for manoeuvre is established, once schools and their communities are empowered to make decisions about content, such action becomes not only possible but even natural.

5 Risking 'something more'

Just as quality involves efficiency, relevance and 'something more', so a strategy can exist which relies upon agents of change on the outer rim of our wheel doing that 'something more' (as many unsung heroes already do) for no extra financial reward but because it is rewarding in terms of satisfaction and the enjoyment it brings.

One wonders sometimes whether some, albeit hard-pressed, educationists, actually *like* teaching or have even stopped to consider whether they enjoy the company of children? But empathy and a love of what one does can only come when teachers believe that they, in turn, are loved, valued and respected members of the community.

We began this book with a heading: 'cause for concern', in which we wrote of the concern we felt for the future development of less developed countries and for the children of them growing up in a world changing at a pace faster than at any time in its history.

Perhaps we can end by raising a final heading: our *cause for hope*. Throughout this book, we have spoken the 'language of critique' and have looked long and hard at what really happens in schools. We have done so in the belief that we also speak the 'language of possibility' and that the improvement of quality remains firmly within our capability, provided we set our minds very seriously to the issue.

NOTES TO CONCLUSION

1 UNICEF, *The State of the World's Children*, UNICEF, New York, and Oxford University Press, 1988, p. 5.

2 *Ibid*.

3 World Bank, World Development Report, 1989.

4 Bray, M., Clarke, P. and Stephens, D., *Education and Society in Africa*, Edward Arnold, 1986.

5 *Ibid*, p. 170.

6 As in the vast yet still diffuse literature on Lifelong Education beginning with the report *Learning to Be*, UNESCO, Paris, 1972.

7 UNICEF, op. cit., p. 35.

8 Report of a seminar on Teacher Education and Materials Development in Uganda, Harold Macmillan Trust, London, September 1988.

9 Parisar Asha: a private foundation based on St Xavier's Institute of Education and aided both by UNICEF and the Aga Khan Foundation.

APPENDIX

COUNTRY COMPARATIVE DATA

		NEPAL	LESOTHO	KENYA	MALAYSIA	INDONESIA
Area (square kilometres)		145 504	30 350	582 646	336 700	1 904 569
GNP (US$)	1987	160	370	330	1 810	450
Population (millions)	1988	18.2	1.7	23.1	16.6	175.0
Population increase (%)	1980–87	2.6	2.8	4.1	2.3	1.8
Life expectancy at birth (years)	1988	51	56	59	70	56
Under-five mortality	1960 (%)	297	208	208	106	235
(of 1 000)	1988 (%)	197	136	113	32	119
Literacy (%) 1985	male	39	62	70	81	83
	female	12	84	49	66	65
Primary enrolment (%) gross	male	104	102	98	102	120
1986–1988	female	47	127	93	102	115
Primary completers (%)	1985–87	28	52	62	97	80
Secondary enrolment (%)	male	35	18	27	59	45
1986–88	female	11	26	19	59	34
Budget (%) of expenditure	1986–87	12	16	23	—	9

Source: *The State of the World's Children Unicef, 1990*

BIBLIOGRAPHY

Our bibliography has been arranged very simply in alphabetical order. It includes only those works which are available to readers and which are of direct relevance to the issue of quality in primary education.

Statistics

Two sources for statistics have been used. The World Bank's *World Development Report* and UNICEF's *State of the World's Children* both published in association with Oxford University Press. We have used volumes from 1987 and 1988. Readers will be advised to refer to current volumes.

GENERAL REFERENCES

AHMED, S. B. A., 'Implementing a new curriculum for primary schools: a case study from Malaysia', Ph.D thesis, University of London, 1986.

ALKIN, M. C., 'Quality of Education Indicators', special section in *Studies in Educational Evaluation*, Vol. 14, 1988.

ASIAN PROGRAMME OF EDUCATIONAL INNOVATION IN DEVELOPMENT (A.P.E.I.D), *National Strategies for Curriculum Design and Development*, Report of a Regional Seminar, Bangkok, UNESCO, 1980.

AVALOS, B. and HADDAD, W., *A Review of Teacher Effectiveness Research in Africa, India etc.*, IDRC, Ottawa, 1979.

AZIZ, A. A. and AHMAD, H., 'Malaysia: System of Education' in *International Encyclopaedia of Education*, pp. 3165–70, Oxford, Pergamon Press, 1985.

BEEBY, C. E., 'Improving the Quality of Education' in *Papua New Guinea Journal of Education*, Vol. 5, No. 1, May 1967.

BEEBY, C. E., *The Qualitative Aspects of Educational Planning*, Paris: UNESCO/I.I.E.P., 1969.

BEEBY, C. E., *The Quality of Education in Developing Countries*, Harvard University Press, 1966.

BEEBY, C. E., *Assessment of Indonesian Education: A Guide to Planning,* Wellington, Oxford University Press, 1979.

BLOOM, B. S. et al. (ed.), *Taxonomy of Educational Objectives: the Classification of Education Goals. Handbook I – The Cognitive Domain*, Harlow, Longman, 1956.

BOTKIN, J. W. et al., *No Limits to Learning. A Report to the Club of Rome*, New York, Pergamon Press, 1979.

BOULDING, K., *Human Betterment,* Beverly Hills, California, Sage Publications, 1985.

BOWMAN, M. J., 'Links between general and vocational education: does the one enhance the other?' in *International Review of Education*, Vol. 34, No. 2, 1988.

BRAY, M., CLARKE, P. and STEPHENS, D., *Education and Society in Africa*, Sevenoaks, Edward Arnold, 1986

BRAY, M. with LILLIS, K. M., *Community Financing of Education: Issues and Policy Implications in Less Developed Countries*, Oxford, Pergamon Press, 1988.

BRAY, M., *New Resources for Education: Community Management and Financing of Schools in Less Developed Countries*, London, Commonwealth Secretariat, 1986.

BRUNER, J., *Towards a Theory of Instruction*, Harvard University Press, 1966.

BRUNER, J., *The Process of Education*, Harvard University Press, 1960.

BUDE, U., *Primary Schools, Local Community and Development in Africa*, Bonn, D.S.E., 1985.

CERID, *Primary Education in Nepal: a status report*, CERID, Kathmandu, 1983.

COOMBS, P. H., *The World Crisis in Education: The View from the Eighties,* Oxford University Press, 1985.

COOMBS, P. H. with PROSSER, R. C. and AHMED, M., *New Paths To Learning*, New York, International Council for Educational Development for UNICEF, 1973.

COURT, D., 'The Education System as a Response to Inequality in Kenya and Tanzania' in *Journal of Modern African Studies*, Vol. 14, No. 4, 1976.

CUMMINGS, W. L., *Low Cost Primary Education – Implementing an Innovation in Six Nations*, Ottawa, International Development Research Centre, 1986.

CURLE, A., *Mystics and Militants: a Study of Awareness, Identity and Social Action*, London, Tavistock Publications, 1972.

CURRICULUM DEVELOPMENT CENTRE, CANBERRA, 'Core Curriculum for Australian Primary Schools' in Horton, T. and Raggat, P. (1982), *Challenge and Change in the Curriculum*; Sevenoaks, Hodder and Stoughton, pp. 104–17, 1980.

DEPARTMENT OF EDUCATION AND SCIENCE, *Teaching Quality*, London, HMSO, 1983.

DEPARTMENT OF EDUCATION AND SCIENCE (WELSH OFFICE), *The School Curriculum*, London, HMSO, 1980.

DEPARTMENT OF EDUCATION AND SCIENCE, *Curriculum Matters – The Curriculum from 5 to 16*, London, HMSO, 1985.

DORE, R., *The Diploma Disease: Education, Qualifications and Development,* London, George Allen and Unwin, 1976.

DOVE, L., *Teachers and Teacher Education in Developing Countries: Issues in Planning, Management and Training*, Beckenham, Croom Helm, 1985.

203

EISEMON, T. O., *Benefiting from Basic Education, School Quality and Functional Literacy in Kenya*, Oxford, Pergamon Press, 1988.

EISNER, E., *The Art of Educational Evaluation: a Personal View*, Lewes, Falmer.

ERAUT, M., 'Strategies for promoting Teacher Development' in *British Journal of In-Service Education*, Vol. 4, Nos. 1–2, 1977.

ESHIWANI, G. S., 'Kenya: System of Education' in *International Encyclopaedia of Education*, Oxford, Pergamon Press, pp. 2803–10, 1985.

FLORES, P. V., *Educational Innovation in the Philippines. A Case Study of Project Impact*, Ottawa, International Development Research Centre, 1981.

FREIRE, P., *Pedagogy of the Oppressed*, Harmondsworth, Penguin Books, 1972.

FREIRE, P., *Education: The Practice of Freedom*, London Writers' and Readers' Publishing Co-operative, 1976.

FREIRE, P., *The Politics of Education. Culture, Power and Liberation*, Basingstoke, Macmillan, 1985.

FULLER, B., 'Is Primary School Quality Eroding in the Third World?' in *Comparative Education Review*, Vol. 30, No. 4, 1980.

FULLER, B. and KAPAKASA, A., 'What Factors Shape Teacher Quality? Evidence from Malawi' in *I.J.E.D.*, Vol. 9, No. 2, 1988.

FULLER, B., 'What School Factors Raise Achievement in the Third World' in *Review of Educational Research*, Vol. 57, No. 3, 1987.

FULLER B., *Raising School Quality in Developing Countries: What Investments Boost Learning?*, Discussion Paper No.ED17, Washington, World Bank, 1985.

GARDNER, R. et al., *Quality Through Support for Teachers: A Case Study From Indonesia*, University of London Institute of Education, Department of International and Comparative Education, 1989.

GOVERNMENT OF KENYA, (The Gacathi Committee), *Report of the National Commission on Educational Objectives and Practices*, Nairobi, Government Printer, 1977.

GREENLAND, J. (ed.), *In-service Training of Primary Teachers in Africa*, Basingstoke, Macmillan, 1983.

GRIFFITHS, V. L., *Teacher Centred: Quality in Sudan Primary Education 1930–1970*, Harlow, Longman, 1975.

GUTHRIE, G., 'Stages of Education Development? Beeby Revisited' in *International Review of Education*, Vol. 26, No. 4, 1980.

HARGREAVES, A., 'Teaching Quality: a Sociological Analysis' in *Journal of Curriculum Studies*, Vol. 20, No. 3, 1988.

HAVELOCK, R. and HUBERMAN, M., *Solving Educational Problems*, Paris, UNESCO, 1977.

HAWES, H. W. R., *Locally Based Education Research and Curriculum Development in Developing Countries: The Teacher's Role*, I.I.E.P. Occasional Paper No. 40, Paris, UNESCO I.I.E.P., 1976.

HAWES, H. W. R., *Curriculum and Reality in African Primary Schools*, Harlow, Longman, 1979.

HAWES, H. W. R., *Child-to-Child: Another Path to Learning*, Hamburg, UNESCO Institute for Education, 1988.

HAWES, H. W. R., and COOMBE, T. (eds.), *'Education Practices and Aid Responses in Sub-Saharan Africa'*, London, HMSO, 1986.

HEYNEMAN, S., 'Improving the Quality of Education in Developing Countries' in *Education and Development: Views from the World Bank*, Habte, A. et al (eds.), Washington, World Bank, 1983.

HEYNEMAN, S. and LOXLEY, W., 'The Effect of Primary School Quality on Academic Achievement Across 29 High- and Low-Income Countries' in *American Journal of Sociology*, Vol. 88, No. 6, 1983.

HEYNEMAN, S. and LOXLEY, W., 'Distribution of Primary School Quality' in *Comparative Education Review*, Vol. 27, No. 1, 1983.

HIRST, P. H., *Knowledge and the Curriculum*, London, Routledge & Kegan Paul, 1974.

HURST, P., *Implementing Educational Change: A Critical Review of the Literature*, Occasional Paper No.5, University of London Institute of Education, Department of Education in Developing Countries, 1983.

HURST, P., 'Some Issues in Improving the Quality of Education' in *Comparative Education*, Vol. 17, No. 2, 1981.

HURST, P. and RODWELL, S., *Training Third World Educational Administrators – Methods and Materials: Final Report*, University of London Institute of Education, 1986.

HUSEN, T., SAHA, L. J. and NOONAN, R., *Teacher Training and Student Achievement in Less Developed Countries*, Working Paper No. 310, World Bank, Washington, 1978.

JOYCE, B. R., HERSH, R. M. and McKIBBIN, M., *The Structure of School Improvement*, New York, Longman, 1983.

KASAJVI, P. K. et al., 'Nepal: System of Education' in *International Encyclopaedia of Education*, Oxford, Pergamon Press, pp. 3498–501, 1985.

KELLY, G. and LASSA, P., 'The Quality of Learning in Nigerian Primary Education' in *International Review of Education*, Vol. 29, No. 2, 1983.

KING, K., 'The Community School: Rich World, Poor World' in King, K. (ed.), *Education and Community in Africa*, University of Edinburgh, Centre for African Studies, 1976.

KINGDOM OF LESOTHO (MINISTRY OF EDUCATION), *Report on the Views and Recommendations of the Basotho Nation Regarding the Future of Education in Lesotho*, Maseru, Government Printer, 1978.

KRATHWOHL, D., *Taxonomy of Educational Objectives: the Classification of Education Goals. Handbook II The Affective Domain*, Harlow, Longman, 1964.

LACEY, C. and LAWTON, D., *Issues in Evaluation and Accountability*, London, Methuen, 1981.

LAUGLO, J. and McLEAN, M. (eds.), *Patterns of Control*, Heinemann/University of London Institute of Education, 1985.

LAWTON, D., *Curriculum Studies and Educational Planning*, Sevenoaks, Hodder and Stoughton, 1983.

LEWIN, K. M., 'Quality in Question: a New Agenda for Reform in Developing Countries' in *Comparative Education*, Vol. 21, No. 2, 1985.

LEWIN, K. M., 'Perspectives on Planning: Initiatives for the 'Nineties' in *Educational Review*, Vol. 40, No. 2, 1988.

LILLIS, K. and AYOT, H., 'Community Financing of Education in Kenya'. Paper presented at the Commonwealth Secretariat Conference on 'Community Financing of Education in SADCC Countries' held at Gabearone, Botswana, 1986.

MACKIE, R. (ed.), *Literacy and Revolution, the Pedagogy of Paulo Freire*, London, Pluto, 1980.

MASLOW, A. H., *Motivation and Personality*, New York, Harper and Row, 1970.

MOSHA, J. H., 'A Reassessment of the Indicators of Primary Education Quality in Developing Countries: Emerging evidence from Tanzania' in *International Review of Education*, Vol. 34, No. 1, 1988.

MURERIA, M. and OKATCHA, F. M., 'Conservation of Concept of Length, Area and Volume among Kikuyu Primary School Pupils' in Okatcha, F. M. (ed.), *Modern Psychology and Cultural Adaptation*, Nairobi, Swahili Language Consultants and Publishers, 1977.

MURPHY, R. and TORRANCE, H., *Evaluating Education: Issues and Methods*, London, Harper and Row, 1987.

OHUCHE, R. O. and OTAALA, B. (eds.), *The African Child and His Environment*, Oxford, Pergamon Press, 1981.

OTAALA, B. and LETSIE, M. A. (eds.), *National Teacher Training College Curriculum: A Review and Reappraisal*. Report of a Workshop June 9–13, 1986. Maseru, National Teacher Training College, Instructional Materials Resource Centre, 1987.

OXENHAM, J., *Education versus Qualifications? A Study of Relationships between Education, Selection for Employment and the Productivity of Labour*, London, Allen and Unwin, 1984.

PHENIX, P., 'Realms of Meaning' in Golby, M. et al., *Curriculum Design*, London, Croom Helm, pp.165–73, 1979.

PSACHAROPOULOS, G. and WOODALL, M., *Education in Development. An Analysis of Investment Choices*, Oxford University Press for the World Bank, 1985.

SCANLON, D., *Traditions of African Education*, Columbia University Press, 1964.

SCHOOLS COUNCIL, *Primary Practice*, Working Paper No. 75, London, Methuen Educational, 1983.

SCHWAB, J. J., 'Structure of the Disciplines' in Golby, M. et al. (eds.), *Curriculum Design*, London, Croom Helm, 1979.

SHRESTHA, G. M. et al, 'Determinants of Educational Participation in Rural Nepal' in *Comparative Education Review*, Vol. 30, 4, 1982.

SIFUNA, D. N., *Revolution in Primary Education, New Approach in Kenya*, East African Literature Bureau, Nairobi, 1975.

SINYANGWE-MAIMBOLWA, I. and LEIMU, K., 'Lesotho: System of Education' in *International Encyclopaedia of Education*, Oxford, Pergamon Press, 1985, pp.2998–3002.

SINCLAIR, M. E. with LILLIS, K., *School and Community in the Third World*, London, Croom Helm, 1980.

SKILBECK, M., *School-Based Curriculum Development*. London, Harper and Row, 1984.

SMITH, D. L. and FRASER, B. J., 'Towards a Confluence of Quantitative and Qualitative Approaches to Curriculum Evaluation' in *Journal of Curriculum Studies*, Vol. 12, No. 4, 1980.

SOMERSET, H. C. A., *Examination Reform: the Kenya Experience*, Washington, World Bank, 1982.

STEPHENS, D. G., 'A Study of Teacher Education and Attitudes over Two Generations in the Kano Metropolitan Area of Northern Nigeria', Unpublished Ph.D. Thesis, University of Exeter, 1982.

STEPHENS, D. G., 'Decentralisation of Education in Northern Nigeria: A Case of Continuing 'In-Direct Rule'?' in Lauglo, J. and McLean, M. (eds.), *Control versus Decentralised Control in Education. Comparative and International Perspectives*, London, U.L.I.E./Heinemann, 1985.

TANGYONG, A. et al, *Quality through Support to Teachers*, Office of Educational Research and Culture, Indonesia and Department of International and Comparative Education, University of London, Jakarta and London, 1989.

TURNER, J., 'Educational Policy in Teacher Education' in *International Journal of Educational Development*, Vol. 4, No. 2, 1984.

UNESCO, *Quality of Life: Problems of Assessment and Measurement*, Paris, UNESCO, 1983.

UNESCO-UNICEF CO-OPERATIVE PROGRAMME, *Basic Services for Children – a Continuing Search for Learning Priorities*, Vols. 1 and 2, Paris, UNESCO, 1978.

UNICEF, *Within Human Reach – A Future for Africa's Children*, New York, UNICEF and Oxford University Press, 1985.

UNICEF, *The State of the World's Children,* New York, UNICEF and Oxford University Press, 1988 and 1990

VITTACHI, V., 'The People Factor' in *The State of the World's Children*, New York, UNICEF, 1987.

INDEX